Economic Interests
and Institutions

For my mother, and my wife Joyce,
with love and appreciation

Economic Interests and Institutions

THE CONCEPTUAL FOUNDATIONS OF PUBLIC POLICY

Daniel W. Bromley

Basil Blackwell

First published 1989

Basil Blackwell Inc.
432 Park Avenue South, Suite 1503
New York, NY 10016, USA

Basil Blackwell Ltd
108 Cowley Road, Oxford OX4 1JF, UK

Library of Congress Cataloging in Publication Data
Bromley, Daniel W., 1940–
  Economic interests and institutions.
  Bibliography: p.
  Includes index.
  1. Institutional economics.   2. Policy sciences.
I. Title.
HB99.5.B76   1989   361.6′ 1   88–63974
ISBN 1–55786–014–9

British Library Cataloguing in Publication Data
Bromley, Daniel W.
  Economic interests and institutions: the conceptual
  foundations of public policy.
  1. Institutional economics
I. Title
330.155
ISBN 1–55786–014–9

Typeset in 10½ on 12 point Sabon
by Dobbie Typesetting Limited
Printed in Great Britain by
Bookcraft (Bath) Ltd.

Contents

Acknowledgments

Places often inspire as much, if not more, than individuals. In this particular instance I was fortunate to have had the quite extraordinary inspiration of a year's tenure as a Visiting Fellow of Wolfson College, Cambridge, and as a visiting scholar in the Department of Land Economy at the University of Cambridge. Few other sinecures could provide comparable motivation to ponder the meaning of economic interests and institutions. To walk and write where Bacon, Newton, Russell, Whitehead, Wittgenstein, Marshall, Pigou, Keynes, Robinson, Sraffa, Dobb, and Kaldor – just to name a few of the more illustrious – created so much was reason enough to concentrate the mind. And concentration was indeed difficult when confronted with the unrivaled ambience and beauty of that most stunning of university settings. To President David Williams of Wolfson College, and Professor Gordon Cameron of Land Economy, I shall be forever grateful. My gratitude runs, as well, to the University of Wisconsin. Dean Leo Walsh offered time off, and the Wisconsin Alumni Research Foundation and the Graduate School provided additional financial support to make my pilgrimage to Cambridge possible.

But ideas are the real grist of inspiration, and here too I have not suffered for lack of colleagues to teach me, and to improve what I wrote. I have learned much from my friend Allan Schmid, whose insights into the economic process are legendary. I have been constantly inspired by the commitment to scholarship of my early mentor Emery N. Castle. And I benefited greatly from a more recent mentor R. C. O. Matthews, Master of Clare College, Cambridge, whose seminar in institutional economics provided much-needed motivation when I became mired in self-doubt.

Several individuals spent much time with earlier versions of the book, and here I am particularly indebted to Christoph Badelt, Paul Barkley, John Braden, Douglass North, Robert Rowthorn, Vernon Ruttan, and

Gunter Schmitt. Particular sections benefited from comments by Richard Bishop, Bruce Caldwell, Michael Carter, Bonnie Colby, Alexander Field, Delworth Gardner, Henry Hansmann, Ian Hodge, Chris Nunn, Kathleen Segerson, and Harald von Witzke.

Finally, as in all of my endeavors, there are two who stand out for their abundant and selfless support. My secretary Mary J. Johnson creates order out of chaos, and allows me to keep focused on the main task. Her assistance, and her commitment, are simply beyond comparison. My wife, Joyce, is a constant source of inspiration, humor, wise counsel, and nurturing. Her devotion to me – and to good scholarship – keeps me going when I hit the rough patches. Without her I would be nothing.

Daniel W. Bromley
Madison

1
Economic Interests
and Institutions

Most economists are prepared, even eager, to make prescriptions and recommendations about economic matters based on their specialized knowledge . . . It is a source of concern to many people that economists who are so eager to prescribe policies often disagree among themselves as to which policies should be followed, and even advocate conflicting policies. This is a legitimate concern, especially since the basis for their differing views is often obscure, not only to the interested listener, but even to the economists themselves.

Boadway and Bruce, *Welfare Economics*

I THE INTELLECTUAL PROBLEM

The study of public policy offers the economist both challenge and frustration. Few other disciplines are as well suited to a serious inquiry concerning individual and collective decision making. And yet the economist faces several annoying frustrations. Neither the processes nor the outcomes of public policy seem to conform to the expectation that such serious business should be driven – indeed dominated – by the quest for efficiency in actions to be pursued. Too often, or so it seems, the obvious course of action is forsaken for one that promises to entail excessive costs, or to interfere with volitional exchange among responsible and well-meaning agents, or to cater to the wishes of the "special interests."

To many economists the correct policy course is straightforward; one does what is in the interest of economic efficiency unless there are overriding reasons why one should do otherwise. The reasons for doing otherwise are usually lumped together under the heading of *distributional considerations*. If one follows other than the efficient course, it is to distribute income (or a benefit stream) either to particular regions of the country, or to particular groups of citizens.

The economist will ordinarily feel confident that the efficient course of action can be identified. It is, in general, the one that will leave the largest surplus of net benefits – regardless of how those benefits might be distributed across the polity. If a separate decision is made that the resulting distribution is not desired, then lump-sum redistribution should be undertaken for political reasons.

But rarely does collective action follow the insights that economics seems to offer. Tariffs and import policies distort principles of comparative advantage; regulations cause industry to do things in a more expensive way than otherwise; agricultural support prices distort economic incentives and bring forth scandalous abuse and surpluses. The economist will often look in vain for public policy that accords with rather general notions of rationality and efficiency.

A second source of frustration arises for quite different reasons. This is a frustration born of methodological, as opposed to political, origins. I have in mind the concern that welfare economics offers only limited guidance for deciding what is best to do. Efficiency is appealing to economists because it seems to require the fewest value judgments. The first of these is the primacy of individual preferences. The second value judgment is the *Pareto principle* that if social state I is ranked higher than social state II by one person, while all others rank I at least as high as II, then a *social* ordering would regard I preferred to II.

But this advantage for efficiency is purchased with several strong and tenuous assumptions. There are a large number of Pareto-optimal allocations of resources, each associated with a different distribution of satisfaction across members of society. Additionally, for every possible distribution of income among the citizenry there is a Pareto-optimal allocation. This leads to serious problems for the economist intent on a definitive role in policy science:

> The many Pareto optimal outcomes themselves are Pareto non-comparable. Furthermore, even a particular Pareto optimal allocation does not dominate all non-Pareto optimal allocations on Pareto grounds; that is, certain non-Pareto allocations will be Pareto non-comparable with respect to Pareto optimal ones. This reflects the fact that rankings based solely upon the Pareto principle are incomplete. (Boadway and Bruce 1984, p. 4)

As suggested by Boadway and Bruce, an effort might then be extended to go beyond concepts of economic efficiency based on the Pareto principle. This would entail a search for means to determine the utilities of different members of society – a process that requires yet stronger value judgments. Such value judgments are reflected in the particular form of the social welfare function being invoked. The social welfare function is an aggregating mechanism that presumes to convey a complete ordering of possible social states. It is here that the economist becomes increasingly nervous. For to presume a particular social ordering is to make explicit value judgments across members of society. It is also to make assumptions regarding the quality of information concerning the measurability of individual levels of satisfaction (Boadway and Bruce 1984).

The ultimate frustration comes when the economist realizes the full nature of the dilemma. To adhere to the precepts of scientific objectivity is to run the risk of having to stand on the sidelines, as it were, while public policy proceeds unabated. Few committed social scientists relish the thought of being irrelevant to the formulation of public policy. And yet to become engaged in policy is to require that the many caveats of welfare economics be temporarily disregarded. We teach our graduate students one thing, and then we practice something quite different.[1]

There is a middle ground however. That is the quite common course of simply analyzing the "efficiency implications" of various policy proposals on the grounds that scientific objectivity will safely allow that – but nothing more. The comfort in "sticking to one's last", as Sir Dennis Robertson has put it, is then reinforced by the view that if the politicians wish to do otherwise, that is their job – and their problem. The economist has at least stayed true to the norms of science.

Indeed the prevailing ethic among economists seems precisely captured in this view. Preferences are presumed to be given, institutional considerations are exogenous, and income is presumed to be acceptably distributed.[2] The economist may then indicate – within these constraints – which course of action is efficient. Beyond that, if the politicians wish to do otherwise, then it is, obviously, for other reasons. The economist can indicate the "efficiency costs" of a distributional policy choice, but to say more than that is beyond the pale. This view of the proper stance of the economist, despite its general acceptance, causes some discomfort for several reasons.

For each possible distribution of both income and utility across members of society there is an efficient allocation of resources. Therefore, doing what is efficient requires the strong assumption that income is *optimally* distributed, not just acceptably distributed.[3]

Hence, the common belief that by advocating efficiency the economist is avoiding value judgments is clearly false. Secondly, public policy is about changes in resource endowments and utilities across individuals and groups. Therefore, to compare alternative possible efficient outcomes is to confront the problem of Pareto non-comparability.

Thirdly, efficiency calculations rest upon the current structure of institutional arrangements that determine what is a cost – and for whom. If chemical companies currently have the ability to discharge toxins into rivers, then an efficiency-driven policy debate on banning those emissions will lead to a different level of pollution than if the status quo institutional setup did not allow dumping. Under this alternative possible institutional arrangement, the policy debate would be concerned with a possible relaxation of such restrictions.

Finally, there is a problem of concepts and language. To identify the *efficient* policy choice against which others are to be compared is to load the debate. There is *no single efficient policy choice* but rather an efficient policy choice for every possible presumed institutional setup. To select one efficient outcome is also to select one particular structure of institutional arrangements and its corresponding distribution of income. What matters is not efficiency, but *efficiency for whom*? This is the conceptual side that is reasonably well understood among economists. I am also, however, concerned here with language. To tell the decision maker(s) that policy A is efficient, while policies B, C, and D are not, is to run the risk of influencing policy choices on false grounds.

No politician is anxious to undertake actions that are inefficient, in spite of our best caricature of them. Since all policies have distributional implications – and politicians know this more clearly than anyone else – they will be inclined to select the "efficient" policy on the belief that this is the most cost-effective way to carry out the pending redistribution. The economist, on the other hand, will advocate the "efficient policy" on the belief that this is the only policy that does not hold distributional implications.

However, from the fundamental theorems of welfare economics, there is a distribution of endowments (income and entitlements) for which policies B, C, and D *are also efficient*. Policy A is efficient in this case because of the underlying institutional setup. When the economist says that to do B, or C, or D is to cater to distributional considerations, this is only half true. If the status quo were different, *or if our assumptions about the status quo were different*, then policy B, or C, or D would be efficient.

A book about economic interests and institutions must deal precisely with this problem. It must address the fundamental circularity between the institutional structure of an economy and the efficiency judgments that can be inferred therefrom. If notions of efficiency and distribution are at the core of welfare economics and public policy, then economic institutions are at the core as well. The concern here will be to explore contemporary welfare theory – and the theory of institutional change – to determine whether or not the economist has an adequate conceptual basis upon which to engage in the policy process. I will be particularly concerned with the belief among economists that efficiency recommendations provide a value-free basis upon which to pronounce on public policy. To quote T. W. Hutchison:

> In its Paretian form welfare analysis may have inhibiting effects in favour of the *status quo*. In any case, excessive claims for welfare economics have fostered the illusion of policies without politics, or that significant policy recommendations can be made without controversial value-judgments (i.e. other than that it is better to have more wants satisfied rather than less). In its fuller-blooded "Utilitarian" form, the effects of welfare analysis may tend not so much to paralyse policy recommendations as to obscure policy choices by leaving essential value-judgments latent and policy objectives not sufficiently, fully and precisely stated. (1964, p. 165)

II THE PLAN OF THE BOOK

The book is divided into three parts. In part I the concern will be to address the matter of economic *interests* and *institutions* as those concepts are commonly understood. To become concerned with economic interests and institutions requires a careful consideration of the prevailing views regarding institutions and institutional change. Chapter 2 is concerned with reviewing several contemporary views of institutional change, primarily those associated with the work of Demsetz, Coase, Posner, North, Binswanger, Hayami, and Ruttan. I will argue here that these conventional views misspecify the sources of institutional change, and that they also fail to reflect the fact that a model of institutional change driven by efficiency considerations is largely tautological.

In chapter 3 I turn to a treatment of the concept of institutions as conventions and entitlements. It is institutions that determine the nature and scope of individual choice sets from within which maximizing decisions will be selected. The task here will be to show that efficiency is an artifact of the presumed institutional arrangements. I will also be concerned with the common belief that institutional change represents coercion of the individual by the state – or those able to use the state in their behalf – while market-based outcomes are free from coercion.

Chapter 4 is concerned with preferences, choices, and institutions. I will here explore the matter of preferences for institutional arrangements as logically prior to preferences for outcomes within those institutional arrangements. It is the standard practice to take existing institutions (and preferences for those institutions) as given and then to explore maximizing behavior from within that constrained environment. But individuals have preferences with respect to their choice domain, just as they have preferences over choices made within that domain. A clear understanding of this important distinction is critical to an improved understanding of institutions, collective action, and public policy.

In part II the emphasis turns to the matter of institutional change as I prefer to model that process. In chapter 5 I will introduce the concept of *institutional transactions* to denote a class of economic behavior concerning the institutional arrangements – and so the choice sets – that define the arena of choice for individual utility-maximizing agents. Public policy is about institutional transactions that redefine the domain of volitional choice. I will argue that there are four kinds of institutional transactions. The first concerns those instances in which institutional change will improve the economy's productive efficiency. The second institutional change concerns those instances in which the distribution of income is purposefully altered for whatever reason. These two kinds of institutional transactions are well understood within welfare economics.

But there are two other kinds of institutional transactions that have not as yet been given conceptual content. I call the first of these institutional transactions that reallocate economic opportunity. The second of these I call institutional transactions that redistribute economic advantage. These two kinds of institutional transactions represent the dominant aspect of public policy. They have previously been regarded as "merely" redistributive of income and not generally in the interest of economic efficiency. Indeed, with recent interest in rent-seeking behavior, these two classes of institutional change have been lumped together as examples of the pernicious behaviors of special interests. The critical distinction between institutional change that reallocates economic opportunity, and institutional change that redistributes economic advantage, will be seen to promise a more robust role for the economist in public policy debates.

In chapter 6 I will be concerned with several illustrations of how this new perspective on institutional change allows a more complete specification of the efficiency implications of collective action and public policy.

Property rights are central to any clear understanding of economic interests and institutions. In chapter 7 I will devote attention to the concept and practice of property, to the essence of ownership, and to the philosophical case for particular forms of property rights – but especially that of private property. I will also describe and explain the structure of legal entitlements that give meaning to different forms of property.

The final part of the book will concern the public policy process. Specifically, I will suggest that the institutional perspective offered here holds important implications for the conduct of policy analysis. In chapter 8 I will be particularly concerned with methodological issues pertinent to the study of institutional change and public policy. That is, the positivist era in economics arose approximately two decades after philosophers of science had abandoned logical positivism and logical empiricism. The persistent belief in positivism among economists is thus seen to be on a questionable philosophical foundation. I will argue, however, that the loss of legitimacy for positivism does not threaten the goal of scientific objectivity. Objectivity is a property of how the economist does science and not a property of the science. The economist can engage in policy science across a rather wide range of activity and still retain the necessary objectivity that a science demands. This conclusion offers support for the economist frustrated by the limited role in public policy dictated by the conventional preoccupation with economic efficiency.

Finally, in chapter 9, I summarize the argument by presenting, in brief form, the general approach suggested here. It is a model of institutional change that emphasizes institutional arrangements, policy objectives, policy instruments, patterns of interaction among atomistic agents, policy outcomes, and then continuing assessment against socially articulated expectations. It is a model that holds for the economist a richer role than heretofore imagined – or permitted – by the false connection between economic efficiency and scientific objectivity.

NOTES

1   As Mark Blaug puts it: "I hold that there is nothing much wrong with standard economic methodology as laid down in the first chapter of almost every textbook in economic theory; what is wrong is that economists do not practice what they preach." (1980, p. xiii)

2   Actually, income must be presumed to be *optimally distributed*, not just "acceptably" distributed. It is impossible to specify an efficiency implication that permits one to ignore the distribution of income, without presuming that the marginal utility of increments to income are everywhere equal across the populace. The only way in which one can presume that income is *optimally* distributed is to presume equality of marginal utilities of income over all those affected, either on the financing side, or on the benefit side. In the absence of this assumption, "efficiency" implications are inseparable from "distributional" implications (Azzi and Cox 1973). See also Graaff (1967) and Little (1950).

3   See note 2 above.

Part I

Interests and Institutions

2
On Institutional Change: the Conventional Views

> If the illusion is propagated that political decisions and choices between conflicting norms can somehow be conjured away by welfare-economic expertise, the only result sooner or later is likely to be public confusion and disillusion regarding the application and applicability of economic knowledge to public policy.
>
> Hutchison, *"Positive" Economics and Policy Objectives*

The social and economic conditions in a given society are under constant flux as new things become scarce, as tastes and preferences change, as population increases, and as technology opens up new promises – and new problems. The usual practice is to treat these changes as exogenous and then to attempt to explain or predict the probable response of economic actors. An interesting development within economic thought concerns a renewed interest in attempts to understand, to explain, and to predict the nature and scope of changes in the economic conditions. Because economic conditions are determined by the institutional arrangements in society, this interest finds itself concerned with institutional change (Field 1979).

It is to be expected that economists, upon becoming interested in institutional change, would focus on economic manifestations (costs, prices, profits) of new circumstances as the logical engine of institutional change. In this regard, three generally accepted views of institutional change seem to have emerged over the past decade, all of them giving some prominence to changes in income streams as engines of institutional change. Once institutional change has occurred, these new opportunities (or challenges) will have been responded to and the economy will move closer to a restored equilibrium – at least until the next exogenous change appears to stimulate its own institutional response.

In this introductory material I will start with the basic and most widely believed notion of institutional change – that of the "property-rights school" usually associated with the writings of Ronald Coase, Harold Demsetz, and Richard Posner. From there I will turn to a recent variant of the property-rights approach which is referred to as "induced institutional innovation." This work is associated with the writings of Hans Binswanger, Vernon Ruttan, and Yujiro Hayami. The third view is that associated with the economic historian Douglass North.[1] Although North has, in one instance at least, adopted the property-rights model of institutional change, his approach will be given separate treatment here. I will then offer a critique of each approach, and attempt to show that the engine of institutional change in each of these models – new economic opportunities – is itself only defined by the very institutions under transition. Put somewhat differently, it is the institutional structure of an economy that defines what is considered to be efficient. Models of institutional change driven by a rationale of efficiency are tautological at best because the very meaning of efficiency derives from the institutional setup that defines the arena within which gains from exchange can occur.

I   THE PROPERTY-RIGHTS VIEW

A   The Model

It is generally recognized that Harold Demsetz gave the property-rights school of institutional change its conceptual foundations with an article entitled "Toward a theory of property rights" in which he argues that:

> Changes in knowledge result in changes in production functions, market values, and aspirations. New techniques, new ways of doing the same things, and doing new things – all invoke harmful and beneficial effects to which society has not been accustomed . . . the emergence of new property rights takes place in response to the desires of the interacting persons for adjustment to new benefit–cost possibilities . . . property rights develop to internalize externalities when the gains of internalization become larger than the cost of internalization. (Demsetz 1967, p. 350)

This institutional adjustment in the structure of property rights was not to be left to chance, however, for Demsetz was quite clear that only private property rights would accomplish the necessary task of furthering markets and economic efficiency. In the Demsetz view:

> If a single person owns land, he will attempt to maximize its present value by taking into account alternative future time streams of benefits and costs and selecting that one which he believes will maximize the present value of his privately owned land rights . . . In effect, an owner of a private right to use land acts as a broker whose wealth depends on how well he takes into account the competing claims of the present and the future. But with communal rights there is no broker, and the claims of the present generation will be given an uneconomically large weight in determining the intensity with which the land is worked. (p. 335)

Richard Posner has expressed similar views regarding the ultimate wisdom of institutional change in the direction of atomistic property arrangements over resources:

> The proper incentives [for economic efficiency] are created by the parceling out among the members of society of mutually exclusive rights to the exclusive use of particular resources. If every piece of land is owned by someone, in the sense that there is always an individual who can exclude all others from access to any given area, then individuals will endeavor by cultivation or other improvements to maximize the value of land . . . The foregoing discussion suggests three criteria of an efficient system of property rights. The first is *universality*. Ideally, all resources should be owned or ownable, by someone, except resources so plentiful that everybody can consume as much of them as he wants without reducing consumption by anyone else . . . The second criterion . . . is *exclusivity* . . . The third criterion of an efficient system of property rights is *transferability*. If a property right cannot be transferred, there is no way of shifting a resource from a less productive to a more productive use through voluntary exchange. (Posner 1977, pp. 10–13)

The Demsetz-Posner position on the superiority of private property rights is consistent with prevailing economic thought. That is, contemporary economics is built upon, indeed requires, several assumptions that assure the Demsetz-Posner view of the inevitable wisdom of this form of institutional progression toward thoroughgoing private property. First, the role of the individual as an atomistic wealth-maximizing agent demands that all resources be partible and controllable at this same level; the scope of entitlements must match the scope of the relevant decision unit. Therefore, it is tautological that atomistic decision makers have control over atomistic pieces of resources. Secondly, well-functioning markets require that all resources be infinitely mobile and complete privatization enhances mobility.

Finally, because the property-rights approach seeks to minimize transaction costs, institutional change in the direction of complete atomization of decision-making authority reduces the need for coordination and consultation among co-owners.

As intimated earlier, Douglass North, although not regarded as adhering to the property-rights thesis, has argued that it provides the only possible construct with which to understand the "first economic revolution." In his work with Thomas he argues that prior to the development of this approach to institutional change:

> There simply was no applicable theory that could be used to explain the Neolithic Revolution. This situation has changed with the recent development of theory to deal with common property resources and the evolution of property rights . . . The key to our explanation is that the development of exclusive property rights over the resource base provided a change in incentives sufficient to encourage the development of cultivation and domestication. (North and Thomas 1977, p. 230)

They continue by suggesting that:

> When common property rights over resources exist, there is little incentive for the acquisition of superior technology and learning. In contrast, exclusive property rights which reward the owners provide a direct incentive to improve efficiency and productivity, or, in more fundamental terms, to acquire more knowledge and new techniques. It is this change in incentive that explains the rapid progress made by mankind in the last 10,000 years in contrast to his slow development during the era as a primitive hunter/gatherer. (p. 241)

The property-rights view of institutional change is one that is primarily concerned with the level of transaction costs that arise from jointly held assets. The model suggests that the market can only work efficiently if individual wealth-maximizing agents are free to respond to private incentives to manage valuable assets in their own private interest. Hence, in this view, atomization of property arrangements leads to economic efficiency.

B   A Critique

The property-rights approach to institutional change obscures the difference between institutional arrangements that give rise to a situation of open access, and those that define common property. As will be developed in chapter 7, open access (what Demsetz calls communal property) is not property at all but a free-for-all. By failing to understand the concept of property and therefore being unable to comprehend the notion of common property as a constellation of rights for the co-owners – including the most fundamental right to exclude non-owners – Demsetz is led to elevate private property to the status of a major institutional defense against resource destruction. By positing a false polarity between the free-for-all of open access and the presumed wisdom of private property, Demsetz and others distort institutional arrangements and, more importantly, elevate one particular institutional structure (complete private property) as the only efficient institutional form. Dahlman, in his analysis of the open-field system in medieval England, comments on the prevailing wisdom of the property-rights view:

> For historians and economists alike, there is one formidable "psychological" obstacle to construing models of the past: it is almost universally believed that past economic institutions were "inefficient", and that this is the ultimate reason for their disappearance. As a theory of institutions and institutional change, this leaves much to be desired. It is a truism that not only present day technology of production, but also modern institutions, represent developments of ideas and traditions inherited from the past, and it is perhaps also true that institutions, as well as technology, have seen a period of advance that stretches back over a considerable period of time. But to make out of this a theory that states that the past was inefficient because it did not organize production or exchange in a way that we have learnt is superior is to render any theoretical explanation for past events pointless and empty. (Dahlman 1980, p. 94)

In discussing the presumed optimality of private property rights, Dahlman suggests that the Demsetz-Posner-North analysis overlooks the very real costs of establishing private rights, and of protecting those rights once established. The logic of the property-rights school can be captured in an expression such as the following:

$$\text{economic yield} = f(\text{property rights}) \qquad (2.1)$$

That is, as property rights evolve toward exclusive private rights, the economic yield attainable from a piece of land will increase. An alternative model of institutional change in land might be formulated as:

$$\text{property rights} = g(\text{economic yield}) \qquad (2.2)$$

This captures the idea that the appropriate structure of property rights in productive assets is a dependent variable, as opposed to an explanatory variable as suggested by the property-rights school. One should understand "economic yield" to be long-run expected value such that uncertainty is accounted for; this permits the recognition that atomistic choice in asset management may result in immoderate social losses to the group. The idea in equation (2.2) is simply that different forms of property rights (institutions) will require different levels of supporting infrastructure to define rights and duties, to demarcate boundaries, and to enforce that structure of rights; and that therefore the economically appropriate structure, whether private property, state property, or common property, is a function of the economic surplus available to support those differential costs.

Moreover, the particular property structure chosen will recognize the social costs of a mistake and will reflect the group's efforts to moderate the costs of being wrong. Under current technology, the economic surplus available from the summer pastures of Switzerland is insufficient to make it economically feasible to divide those pastures into privately held parcels. To do so would require extensive fencing and water development so that each small parcel would be self-contained. As it stands the several farmers who jointly own a summer pasture are able to share the cost of a single herder to move the animals around to water, and to select those areas for grazing where the vegetation is particularly lush. If the summer pastures were owned in severalty, it might then be possible for one strategically located owner to prevent all others from gaining access to water – a potentially serious issue for the welfare of the group. The current level of economic surplus from the summer pastures makes common property the most efficient property arrangement, while private property is the efficient institutional structure in the more productive arable land.

These considerations would seem to suggest that the property-rights view of institutional change is both too simplistic, and too unidirectional. It seems more plausible to argue that rather than private property giving rise to wealth, new wealth possibilities provide the economic surplus necessary to further articulate institutional arrangements. The central role of technology must be clearly understood in this process. For if there were cows that did not need to drink water, and that could also recognize and obey property boundaries without the necessity of expensive fences, then perhaps the division and privatization of the Swiss commons would be economically feasible. Until that time however, common property is the most efficient institutional form. Dahlman reaches similar conclusions regarding the ancient open-field system:

The conclusion is therefore unambiguous: if there are private property rights in the arable, if outside non-owners can be kept out, and if each farmer practices mixed husbandry, collective rights in the grazing areas can unambiguously be shown to save on transaction costs as compared with private ownership if there are increasing returns to scale in grazing. This conclusion can only be strengthened if the waste has additional uses which every farmer would want a share in, such as digging peat, gathering firewood, cutting timber, excavating minerals, irrigating meadows, as long as there are some returns to scale in the production of these services. (Dahlman 1980, p. 121)

There has also been the suggestion among economic historians that the scattering of strips in the open fields was the essence of inefficiency. On the contrary, Dahlman argues that scattering constituted the least costly way

to ensure the collective decision making necessary to realize the returns to scale in livestock. Scattering achieves a change in constraints and incentives, rather than creating negative rewards in terms of punishment for keeping out of the collective. (p. 129)

Dahlman concludes his assessment by suggesting that the key to the choice of property (and other) institutions is found in the nature of transaction costs and the particular objectives of the decision group:

It is necessary to show the exact relationship between productive technology on the one hand, and transaction costs on the other. Institutions serve to decrease transaction costs; that is well known. But the transaction costs themselves are related to the nature of the production process under consideration. Both must be accounted for. (p. 138)

In summary, the property-rights view of institutional change posits two polar extremes: open access, which is doomed to overuse; and private property, which is said to represent the wise and efficient property regime. On this view, the only efficient form of institutional change is in the direction of private property rights. The abundant evidence of misuse of private lands seems not to matter to those who advocate complete privatization as the essence of social wisdom. More seriously, when private rights are absent and resource degradation is observed, adherence to the property-rights model would suggest that it is the institutional arrangement (non-private property) that is to blame. On the contrary, when resource degradation is observed on private lands – agricultural soil erosion, the excessive logging of private forest lands – the property-rights model would not allow one to focus on property institutions (private rights in land) but finds the blame to lie elsewhere – imperfect markets, excessive private rates of time preference, and the like. The property-rights model thus yields the curious asymmetry that institutional arrangements (non-private property) are the direct cause of land degradation in one instance, yet in the counterfactual institutional setting (private rights) it is not the property institutions at all but rather market imperfections or myopia that are to blame.

There is a need, it would seem, for a more careful consideration of institutions and of institutional change than a model that regards one particular institutional form (private rights) as universally responsible for economic efficiency, stewardship, and higher civilization. There are, to be sure, numerous settings in which the private control of valuable assets is both efficient in the broadest sense of that term, and socially beneficial. But it does not follow from the arguments advanced by the property-rights school that this is universally so.

II INDUCED INSTITUTIONAL CHANGE

The second model of institutional change is described as induced institutional innovation, an approach that derives from the Hicksian model of induced technical change.

A   The Model

In an article entitled "Toward a theory of induced institutional innovation" Ruttan and Hayami offer perhaps the most complete explanation of their model of the process of institutional change – or of induced institutional innovation as they prefer to put it.[2] This model is based upon a concept of institutions that appears to be consistent with the approach to be taken here (see chapter 3). Ruttan and Hayami state that:

> Institutions are the rules of a society or of organisations that facilitate coordination among people by helping them form expectations which each person can reasonably hold in dealings with others. They reflect the conventions that have evolved in different societies regarding the behaviour of individuals and groups relative to their own behaviour and the behaviour of others. In the area of economic relations they have a crucial role in establishing expectations about the rights to use resources in economic activities and about the partitioning of income streams resulting from economic activity – institutions provide *assurance*

respecting the actions of others, and give order and stability to expectations in the complex and uncertain world of economic relations. (Ruttan and Hayami 1984, p. 204)[3]

The Ruttan-Hayami model of institutional change has a familiar neoclassical hue in that they posit a "demand for institutional innovation" and a "supply of institutional innovation." The demand for institutional change is, as in Marx, primarily driven by technical change; but it goes beyond that. They add that it is more complex by considering that "changes in factor endowments and product demand are equally important sources of institutional change." (pp. 204–5) They depart from Marx by suggesting that institutional change is not necessarily dramatic or revolutionary, but is instead a process in which the

basic institutions such as property rights and markets are more typically altered through cumulation of "secondary" or incremental institutional changes such as modifications in contractual relations or shifts in the boundaries between market and non-market activities. (p. 205)

The supply dimension of institutional change is reflected in the fact that collective action leading to changes in the supply of institutional innovations involves struggles among various vested interest groups, a process that is more complex than the classic Marxian dichotomy.

In our view, the supply of institutional innovations is strongly influenced by the cost of achieving social consensus (or of suppressing opposition). How costly a form of institutional change is to be accepted in a society depends on the power structure among vested interest groups. It also depends critically on cultural tradition and ideology, such as nationalism, that make certain institutional arrangements more easily accepted than others . . . Advances in knowledge in the social sciences (and in related professions such as law, administration, planning, and social service) can reduce the cost of institutional change in a somewhat similar manner as advances in the natural sciences reduce the cost of technical change. Education, both general and technical, that facilitates a better understanding among people of their common interests can also reduce the cost of institutional innovation. (p. 205)

The induced institutional innovation model is offered by its proponents in the hope that it will permit institutional innovation to be reckoned as endogenous to the economic system. This desire for a model that is consistent with conventional analytical economics leads Ruttan and Hayami to suggest an approach that is familiar to any economist:

It is useful to think in terms of a supply schedule of institutional innovation that is determined by the marginal cost schedule facing political entrepreneurs as they attempt to design new institutions and resolve conflicts among vested interest groups (or suppression of opposition when necessary). We hypothesise that institutional innovations will be supplied if the expected return from the innovation that accrues to the political entrepreneurs exceeds the marginal cost of mobilising the resources necessary to introduce the innovation. To the extent that the private return to the political entrepreneurs is different from the social return, the institutional innovation will not be supplied at a socially optimum level. (p. 213)

Ruttan and Hayami test their model of induced institutional innovation with data on land tenancy relations in a rice-growing village of the Philippines for the period 1956–76. In the study area, rice production per hectare increased by a factor of almost 2.7 due to (1) the availability of irrigation water and (2) the availability of new high yielding varieties of rice, accompanied by the increased use of fertilizer and pesticides, and by the adoption of new cultural practices such as straight-row planting and better weeding. Over the twenty-year period population growth in the area was pronounced while the cultivated area remained rather constant, the number of landless laborer households more than doubled, and the average farm size fell from 2.3 hectares to 2.0. The vast majority of the land had been farmed by tenants, with the predominant institutional form being one of share tenancy. In 1963 a new land reform code was implemented with the purpose of breaking the power of the landlords and providing better incentives to peasant producers of food crops. This would be an example of equation (2.2) where new economic returns drove a change in institutional arrangements.

A major feature of the new legislation was an arrangement that permitted tenants to initiate a shift from share tenant to leasehold, with rent under the leasehold set at 25 percent of the average yield for the previous three years. Implementation of the code between the mid-1960s and the mid-1970s resulted in a decline in the percentage of land farmed under share tenure to 30 percent . . . There was a sharp increase in the number of plots farmed under subtenancy arrangements . . . Subtenancy is illegal under the land reform code. The subtenancy arrangements are usually made without the formal consent of the landowner. All cases of subtenancy were on land farmed under a leasehold arrangement. (p. 207)

The authors hypothesize from their model of institutional innovation that there was an incentive for the development of the subtenancy institution since the rent paid to the landlords under the leasehold arrangement was below the equilibrium rent, the level which would reflect both the higher yields of rice obtained with the new technology and the lower wage rates implied by the increase in population pressure against the land . . . To test this hypothesis, market prices were used to compute the value of the unpaid factor inputs (family labour and capital) for different tenure arrangements during the 1976 wet season. The results indicate that the share-to-land was the lowest and the operators' surplus was highest for the land under leasehold tenancy. In contrast, the share-to-land was highest and no surplus was left for the operator who cultivated the land under the subtenancy arrangement . . . Indeed, the share-to-land when the land was farmed under subtenancy was very close to the sum of the share-to-land plus the operators' surplus under the other tenure arrangement. The results are consistent with the hypothesis. A substantial portion of the economic rent was captured by the leasehold tenants in the form of operators' surplus. On the land farmed under a subtenancy arrangement, the rent was shared between the leaseholder and the landlord. (pp. 207–8)

Yet another institutional change was observed in this rice village, and that was the change in the relations between farm operators and landless workers. Traditionally, farm workers had received a one-sixth share in the harvest for their contribution to that process; the new wage structure was one in which laborers could not participate in the harvest unless they had donated unpaid labor to the weeding process. Ruttan and Hayami state that this was an institutional change to reduce the wage rate for harvesting to the marginal value product of labor. It is claimed that in the 1950s,

when the rice yield per hectare was low and labour was less abundant, the one-sixth share may have approximated an equilibrium wage level. With the higher yields and the more abundant supply of labour, the one-sixth share became larger than the marginal product of labour in the harvesting operation. To test the hypothesis that the [new labour payment] system was adopted primarily because it represented an institutional innovation that permitted farm operators to equate the harvesters' share of output to the marginal productivity of labour, imputed wage costs were compared with the actual harvesters' shares . . . The results indicate that a substantial gap existed between the imputed wage for the harvesters' labour alone and the actual harvesters' shares. This gap was eliminated if the imputed wages for harvesting and weeding were added. (1984, pp. 208–9)[4]

The authors claim that the results are consistent with the hypothesis that the changes in institutional arrangements governing the use of productive factors were induced when

disequilibria between the marginal returns and the marginal costs of factor inputs occurred as a result of changes of factor endowments and technical change. Institutional change, therefore, was directed toward the establishment of a new equilibrium in factor markets. (p. 209)

In essence, the induced institutional innovation model seems to suggest that new institutions will evolve when the benefits of some new structure exceed the costs of the change; if institutions do not change then the costs of change exceed the benefits.

B   A Critique

I will address the adequacy of the induced institutional innovation model from two general perspectives: (1) its internal logic; and (2) its relationship to the process of institutional change. The first critique evaluates the induced institutional innovation model on its own terms, while the second evaluates it as a reasonable representation of reality.

The Internal Logic of the Model

Two issues in the induced institutional innovation paradigm merit concern. The first is the notion of an institution as defined by Ruttan and Hayami. The second is their use of that term as the core of their model of institutional change.

1   *The meaning of institutions*   There is reason to be wary of a model of institutional innovation that starts with a definition of institutions in which there is no way to differentiate between institutions as the "rules and conventions of society that facilitate coordination among people regarding their behaviour", and institutions as organizations such as a city council, a university, a church, an agricultural research station, or other governmental agencies. But there is a more compelling argument. If one wishes to model observable phenomena so as to predict when they will and will not change, it seems necessary to have clearly in mind precisely what is being predicted. If one is interested in predicting when, and under what conditions, the boundary between market and non-market processes will shift, then that is entirely consistent with a definition that sees institutions as the "rules and conventions that define individual behaviour" since shifts in the boundaries of market and non-market processes are a change in the ways in which individuals interact – no more and no less. That is, if I no longer must bribe my neighbor to keep her shade trees pruned low, but can instead rely on a zoning rule that protects my interest in solar rays, then our behaviors have been shifted from a "market" to a "non-market" basis. The neighbor can always offer to pay me not to invoke the new zoning rule, in which case a different "market" will emerge under quite different institutional arrangements.

To think that this model of institutional innovation can equally regard the city council – or the office of the city attorney – as an institution is to deny to the model any meaning at all. What does it mean to say one is going to model a change in the city council? What one models, or tries to explain or to predict, are changes in the rules whereby the city council operates, or the rules that it passes down which define my legal position *vis-à-vis* my tree-growing neighbor. A city council, or an agricultural experiment station, or a university, may be referred to as "institutions" by newspaper writers but that usage will do nothing to avoid serious analytical confusion.

Organizations such as the city council, or an experiment station, or a university, obtain their meaning from institutions. That is, their existence and operation depend upon a set of institutions that defines what they will do, how they will do it, how they will relate to the outside world, and how they will remunerate their employees. It is institutions, as initially defined by Ruttan and Hayami, that give meaning, scope, and responsibilities to organizations. But they cannot accept their own original definition of institutions (as rules and conventions), and then continue to maintain that public agencies are also institutions.

2   *The engine of institutional innovation*   The Ruttan-Hayami model of induced institutional innovation is driven by differential economic returns emanating from changes in resource endowments and technical change; it is a response to exogenous disequilibria in market processes. The potential flaw in this model is that it is institutional arrangements that define income and cost streams; one has a model of change driven by something (economic rent) that only gets its meaning and magnitude from that which one is trying to understand and to model – that is, institutions and how and why they change. Put somewhat differently, the current institutional structure defines which costs must be reckoned by individuals as they go about their daily life. The induced institutional innovation model relies on the cost and benefit streams arising from the existing setup as an engine of change, and as the empirical basis for confirmation.

Consider the Ruttan-Hayami test of the new wage structure in Philippine rice production. The authors regard the new wage bargain as an induced institutional innovation that restored the earlier equilibrium between marginal returns and marginal factor costs. I have earlier suggested (note 4) that economic theory offers no support for their claim that the marginal product of labor falls simply because of population growth and the attendant increase in the availability (supply) of landless labor. In fact, what happened is that farm operators, by virtue of the more abundant labor supply, were now able to disregard the very real costs that would fall on unemployed landless workers by the implementation of a new wage institution; it is the prevailing institutional structure that allows the farm operators to define a new legal relation that will obligate the landless laborers to engage in free weeding in order to be permitted to work in the subsequent harvest, and to receive their traditional share. The farm operators were able to establish a new legal relation *vis-à-vis* landless laborers that deprived the latter of sharing in the harvest unless they had previously worked – for free – in the weeding operation.

The farm operators had the requisite political power to alter unilaterally the terms of the wage contract. Ruttan and Hayami (1984, p. 207) admit as much in their discussion of the new tenancy arrangement when they state that a lower wage rate was "implied by the increase in population pressure against the land." It was this lower wage, coupled with increased yields, that provided the new economic rents that drove an institutional innovation toward subtenancy. The so-called "operators' surplus" that was now available for the leasehold tenants, or for the landlord and tenants under subtenancy, came partly, it would appear, from the share that had previously gone to laborers.

It is not sufficient to invoke the usual caveat that the "private and social costs" may have differed, for it is precisely a matter of the private interests of the farm operators and the private interests of the landless laborers. Ruttan and Hayami claim that changes in tenure and the wage contract were

> supplied, in response to the changes in demand generated by changing factor endowments and new income streams, through the individual and joint decisions of owner-cultivators, tenants and labourers. But even at this level it was necessary for gains to the innovators to be large enough to offset the risk of ignoring the land reform prohibitions against subleasing and the social costs involved in changing the traditional harvest-sharing arrangements. While mobilisation of substantial political resources was not required to introduce and extend the new land and labour market institutions, the distribution of political resources within the village did influence the initiation and diffusion of the institutional innovations. (p. 213)

The induced institutional innovation model would therefore seem to suggest that landless laborers "jointly decided" with the farm operators suddenly to be required to donate unremunerated labor to the weeding operation so that they might continue to share in the harvest as they had for many years. Also notice that the "mobilisation of substantial political resources was not required to introduce and extend the new land and labour market institutions." This is plausible since it would seem intuitive that the two changes under discussion clearly benefited landlords and new tenant operators at the expense of landless laborers. No mobilization was required for the simple reason that the losers in this induced institutional innovation had no effective ability to oppose it. Ruttan and Hayami seem to recognize this when they note that "the distribution of political resources within the village did influence the initiation and diffusion of the institutional innovations." Finally, this is a model that seems to regard it as a wonder of efficiency that landowners and tenants were both smart enough (and brave enough) to subvert the law in the interest of more "efficient markets." Of course the economic gain had to be large enough to overcome this risk of lawlessness.

The issue here is a model of institutional change that can ignore certain relevant costs (those borne by landless laborers) when seeking to explain and justify as efficient an institutional change in a wage arrangement between a limited number of farm operators and a large and growing population of landless laborers. It is a model of institutional change that seems to ignore as mere transfers the distributional implications of new institutional arrangements created by sheer imbalance of economic power. In attempting to condone the new institutional structure, this model fails to deal with the fundamental analytical issue: efficient with respect to what? By endogenizing institutional innovation in this manner one is left precisely where conventional welfare economics leaves us – able to comment on changes that seem to be efficient, but unable to comment on the important distributional issues that are at the core of institutional innovation.

The Model as a Reflection of Economic Reality

In the previous discussion I have focused on the induced institutional innovation model in terms of its logical consistency; that is, does it provide – on its own terms – a structure and a logic that will allow it to explain and to predict changes in institutions in a way that will be analytically satisfying to economists? I now want to turn to a somewhat external view of the model in terms of its relation to the world which it claims to explain and to predict. The Ruttan-Hayami model of institutional change represents an interesting meld of Marxian and neoclassical motivations. Marx considered technical change to be the primary source of institutional change, and the induced institutional innovation model extends this to incorporate ". . . changes in factor endowments and product demand." (Ruttan and Hayami 1984, pp. 204–5). Marx found this view comfortable with his overriding notion of a class struggle based on the ownership of the means of production; capitalists own the means of production, workers own only their labor power. Capitalists introduce new technology which is a threat to labor; institutions are creatures of the state (which is a creature of the capitalists) and so institutions are constraints that can only be changed with great struggle.

The neoclassical underpinning in the Ruttan-Hayami model is twofold. First, and consistent with the Hicksian-inspired model of induced technical change,[5] institutional change is motivated by price (or price-like) phenomena that modify the present value of an expected net income stream. The second neoclassical foundation is that institutions are exogenous constraints to the maximization process, and as such they often originate in the bureaucracy.

Treating technology or new factor endowments as the primary source of institutional change is not only circular, but incomplete. It is circular because all technology encompasses institutional dimensions in terms of who owns the new technology, who controls its use and benefit stream, and who must bear the costs of its implementation. The meaning of some new miracle variety of rice is not simply to be found in its chromosome map, but is, instead, bound up with: (1) how the seed is provided (by the public sector, or bought from the proprietary rights holder); and (2) what other technical complements are required for the seed's effective use (fertilizer, irrigation, new tillage practices, for example).

Secondly, Ruttan and Hayami cite the new availability of irrigation water as a technical change when, in fact, irrigation projects are the very essence of institutional change. Water does not just appear at a farmer's field one day; it is there because of a complex technical and institutional constellation of canals, ditches, control gates, political maneuvering, rules about water allocation, compliance with those rules, penalties for non-compliance, and the like.[6] While water may appear as a new technique to the farmer, it is the institutional arrangements accompanying the irrigation investment that give the water economic value to the farmer.

The third and final illustration of circularity in their model is that resource endowments are defined by institutional arrangements (property rights being central here). To say that institutions change in response to new resource (or factor) endowments is to say that new institutions appear in response to new institutions – not a very interesting prospect. There is no analytical interest in why farm operators are able to impose a new wage arrangement with landless laborers; there is only interest in proving that, with proper estimation techniques for imputed wages, one can show that individual entrepreneurs will innovate – in response to new income opportunities – new and presumably more efficient institutional arrangements.

Finally, it is incomplete to regard technical change as the primary source of institutional change – and to regard institutions as constraints on new technology. The rapid technical change in computing technology – both hardware and software – is a function of an institutional structure that included patents and copyrights. In the absence of a set of rules and legal relations regarding ownership and control of that new knowledge, the investment climate would not have been nearly so conducive to rapid change. The same thing might be said about the growth of the nuclear power industry in the United States without the Price-Anderson Act.[7] A clear understanding of institutions as collective action in restraint, liberation, and expansion of individual action would preclude any possible belief that institutions are only understood analytically as constraints on technical change. Institutions, because of what they are, define the social and economic environment within which new techniques can be introduced, controlled, and used. Because institutions define and protect income streams (property rights) it is impossible to have new technology introduced without congenial and appropriate institutional arrangements.[8]

III   THE NORTH MODEL OF INSTITUTIONAL CHANGE

A   *The Model*

One of the primary shortcomings of the model of induced institutional innovation arises over the treatment of institutions as both rules of organizations, and as the organizations themselves. The writings of Douglass North reflect an awareness of the confusion that can result from this failure to distinguish fundamentally different things.[9] He also has done more than most economists in attempting to refine the contemporary operational notion of an institution. Like many others, North notes concern that at various times the term "institution" has been used to refer to organizations (banks as financial institutions), to the legal rules that define the economic relations between people (private property), and to a person or a position (the presidency) (Davis and North, 1970). Davis and North define several terms that will find use here. The institutional environment is a set of "fundamental political, social, and legal ground rules that govern economic and political activity (rules governing elections, property rights, and the rights of contract are examples of these ground rules)." (p. 133) An institutional arrangement is an "arrangement between economic units that governs the ways in which these units can cooperate or compete. The institutional arrangement is probably the closest counterpart to the most widely used definition of the term institution." (p. 133)

North is conventional, however, in his idea of the outcome of institutional change: either it is directed toward improving the efficiency of the economy, in which case the initiating party is made better off and no one is made worse off;[10] or it is merely redistributional in nature such that the gain to one party (or group) is offset by a loss to others. In the first class of institutional change, that which is directed toward (and perhaps even motivated by) the purpose of increasing the net social dividend, he sees four possible sources of new income: (1) economies of scale; (2) externalities; (3) risk; and (4) market failure (Davis and North 1970). These four causes are endogenous to the North model of institutional innovation, while the purely redistributive case is exogenous.

> That change . . . might take the form of an amendment in the constitutional rules governing the disposition of private property, it might reflect an expansion of the franchise, or it might come from some shift in the community's utility function that alters their preferences between public and private solutions to problems. (p. 138)

Returning to the institutional changes that will increase net social dividend:

> economic institutions are innovated because it appears profitable for individuals or groups in society to undertake the costs of bringing about such changes. The purpose is to capture for the innovator some profit unattainable under the old arrangements. The essential requirement for initiating an institution (or a product) is that the discounted expected gains exceed the expected costs of the undertaking; only when this condition is met would we expect to find attempts being made to alter the existing structure of institutions and property rights within a society. (North and Thomas 1970, p. 3)

North and his frequent collaborators, Lance Davis and Robert Thomas, have devoted considerable attention to the rise of Europe and the western world. This is not the place to comment on the adequacy of the North model to explain much of modern economic growth.[11] Closer to home, the North model has been used by others to explain institutional innovation with respect to mineral resources in the western United States (Libecap 1978). Libecap focuses on the net gains to be received by mine owners as a result of new legal arrangements regarding ownership and control of mining claims. He notes that:

> On the benefit side greater precision in the law increases the probability a mine owner will maintain control of his claim. That is, greater definition and enforcement of his private rights reduce ownership uncertainty. First, as individual rights and property boundaries are more clearly defined, trespass and theft can be more readily detected and proven; second, state protection of private rights can be more easily obtained as the procedure for doing so is made clear; and third, violators of private claims are more apt to be found guilty when the obligations of enforcing officials are exactly described. (pp. 340–1)

Libecap also notes the costs of this institutional change as including learning about the appropriate legal response to new and unprecedented conditions, the transaction costs of influencing legislators and judges, and the necessary taxes to support the administrative machinery. He concludes by suggesting that "mine owners will push for greater precision in the legal rights structure as long as there are private net gains from doing so." (p. 341)

The North–Libecap approach would seem appropriate to model a situation in which there are few, if any, existing institutional arrangements in place to organize a new economic activity (mining in a frontier territory); there was an institutional vacuum. Great uncertainty existed regarding who owned what, and how one would go about establishing that ownership. The need for greater precision in the institutional arrangements was obvious on economic efficiency grounds since the prevailing chaos led to great entrepreneurial uncertainty, redundant behaviors, and lower-than-optimal investment in mining.

A similar story could be told about the evolution of the prior appropriation doctrine in western water law. In that case, the prevailing institutional arrangement imported from England was the riparian doctrine where one's use of water from a contiguous stream was sufficient to establish a prima facie case for ownership. But in the arid reaches of the western United States rivers might lie several miles (even hundreds of miles) from high-quality irrigable land. It was necessary to undertake great capital investment to move the water to suitable land. Such investments were impossible without an institutional arrangement – the prior appropriation doctrine – to insure that once the investment was made, and water put to beneficial use, a riparian owner of land could not take it away. Institutional innovation is a necessary precondition for the development of irrigation technology.[12]

These instances of institutional innovation, consisting of examples regarding more productive mining and agriculture, are not the only types of institutional innovation. According to North and Thomas, "Institutional arrangements may also be created, either by voluntary groups or by the government, which are designed to capture gains for individual groups at the expense of others (or, in short, to redistribute income)." (1970, p. 7) It is this realization that lies behind the rise in the concern for rent-seeking behavior. However, rent-seeking behavior can, if couched in appropriate neoclassical terminology, give the appearance of a gain in efficiency. It is precisely this possibility that underpins my previous criticism of the induced institutional innovation explanation of the new wage and tenancy institutions in the Philippines; an institutional change was initiated by farm operators (as rent seekers) that was justified by Ruttan and Hayami as restoring a new market equilibrium in defiance of the land reform code that they regarded, if only implicitly, as an impediment to efficiency.

B   A Critique

The model of institutional innovation developed by North, and used by him and his colleagues to explain the rise of the western world, starts with the familiar distinction between those actions that will increase the net social dividend, and those that merely redistribute income. The first of these is usually thought to be good, while the latter is often regarded as not in the interest of economic efficiency. More will be said in a subsequent chapter on the continued usefulness of this distinction. The desire to make his view of institutional innovation endogenous can also, unfortunately, explain its major weakness. By making institutional change endogenous, North has failed to recognize that the prevailing institutional structure gives rise to a constellation of costs and benefits that only obtain meaning and magnitude from that very institutional structure. Externalities only have meaning against the status quo constellation of entitlements. People are exposed to risk because of the prevailing institutional arrangements; change that structure, and the level and incidence of risk will change. Market failure as a source of institutional change can only have meaning within an institutional environment that defines the market. Likewise with scale economies; the cost curves that depict increasing (or decreasing) returns to scale only obtain their meaning from the prevailing institutional setup that defines what is a cost – and who must bear that cost.

It is begging the question to say that market failure induces institutional change, for the simple reason that the concept of a market is used to define what is efficient, and if things are efficient then there is no incentive to change. The problems discussed previously in the context of induced institutional innovation may make it appear as if the market is responding well to new situations, when in fact the favorable economic and political position of the farm operators *vis-à-vis* landless laborers is the real cause of institutional change. If the landless had more political clout then the transaction costs to the farm operators would be too high to allow the change that they (the farm operators) sought. In that instance there would be no institutional change and the status quo would be defined as efficient. By looking only for revenue-driven causes of institutional change, called new profitable opportunities, the North model misspecifies why and how institutions change, and it misses other plausible explanations for the purposeful realignment of institutional arrangements, and choice sets.

IV AN EXPANDED VIEW OF INSTITUTIONAL CHANGE

The three views of institutional change discussed previously are driven by similar causes. They seek to explain changes in the institutional environment (and so the economy) by appeal to increased income-earning opportunities or the improvement of overall economic efficiency. Each of the three models operates within the conventional view that there are only two types of economic choices to be made in a society – those that increase economic efficiency and those that redistribute income. This conventional view holds that private property rights and more fully developed markets increase economic efficiency while collective property rights and government activity only detract from economic efficiency, and – more seriously – seem only to redistribute a fixed net social product. It is maintained by the proponents of this approach that institutional change will occur when the benefits of change (to those who can initiate change) exceed the costs of change. In contrast to this model, one can think of many changes that might increase income and even net social product but for the "wrong" people, and therefore the change is never undertaken. I will elaborate this possibility in a subsequent chapter.

The three views part company somewhat in explaining the lack of institutional change. The property-rights school suggests that in the absence of change things must be optimal as they stand; if they were not optimal they would surely change. The induced institutional innovation view, and the North model, seem to give more scope for political interference preventing change that would otherwise increase efficiency. However, the most compelling shortcoming of these views of institutional innovation is their failure to start with the recognition that efficiency, however defined, is dependent upon the institutional structure that gives meaning to costs and benefits, and that determines the incidence of those costs and benefits. A model of institutional change that is driven by the quest for economic efficiency is circular. This circularity is the result of the fact that it is institutional arrangements that define what is regarded as efficient. A view of institutional change that fails to offer any legitimate rationale for change other than that of narrowly construed economic gain trivializes most collective action; it is further trivialized by the belief that all collective action either contributes to efficiency, or simply redistributes income.

Perhaps some of the difficulty in modeling institutional change rests with the fact that inadequate attention has been paid to the meaning of institutions, and to their role in the socioeconomic system. Even to settle on the definition of institutions as rules and conventions that define individual choice sets leaves open the issue of how best to conceptualize their role, and to understand the pressures that come for institutional change. Because institutional change is the *raison d'être* for public policy it seems appropriate to consider the policy process in a general way; out of this will come an avenue for exploring further the role of institutions, and the process of institutional change.

I suggest that there are three levels pertinent to this process: a *policy level*, an *organizational level*, and an *operational level*.[13] In a democracy the policy level is represented by the legislative and judicial branches, while the organizational level is represented by the executive branch. It is at the policy level that the general statements about the sort of world we want to live in are debated and ultimately formulated. The implementation of these aspirations is accomplished by the development of organizations and of the rules and laws that define how those organizations will operate, but also what they will do in a programmatic sense. The rules and laws that link the policy level to the organizational level may be called the institutional arrangements.

Now consider the operational level. At this level one finds the operating units in society – the firms and households whose daily actions result in certain observed outcomes. The range of choice open to these actors at the operational level is defined by institutional arrangements at both the policy level and at the organizational level. An example of the former institutional arrangements would be the details of the income tax code. An example of the latter type of institutional arrangements would be administrative rules such as work conditions in factories.

The behaviors observed at the operational level – the patterns of interaction – result in outcomes that will be regarded by the citizenry as either good or bad. If air is too dirty, if urban sprawl is deemed excessive, if the homeless seem to be increasing in number, then there will be a collective response through the political process and there will be efforts to change the institutional arrangements that define individual choice sets at the operational level. That is, citizen input will be directed at the policy level to seek a new constellation of rules and laws (institutions) that will alter the domain of choice for firms and households.

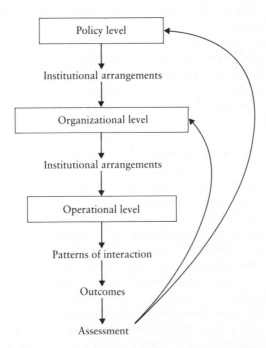

Figure 2.1   The Policy Process as a Hierarchy

This hierarchy is depicted in Figure 2.1. It is at the policy level that a society will make several determinations. First there will be decisions regarding the boundary between market and non-market processes. This determines the locus of control for many economic decisions. Second, there will be decisions taken with respect to the allocation of net benefits from various economic endeavors. Here one has tax policy that will determine the distribution of income among members of the society. The third policy-level decision concerns the conditions under which change is called for in the prior two types of collective decisions. That is, the first two are the essence of decision making about property rights and the economic benefits that shall accrue to rights holders.

Public policy is about two central concepts: (1) deciding socially acceptable institutional arrangements (entitlement structures) that both constrain and liberate individual action at the operational level; and (2) searching for the boundary between autonomous (market-like) and collective decision making. The first choice will be dominated by concern for what sort of world we want to have, who will participate in that choice, and the weighting of the preferences of the respective constituents. The second choice will be dominated by concern for the operating efficiency of alternative entitlement structures, and by the possible costs of a mistake. States, as manifestations of the hopes and interests of their citizens, retain authority over these two types of choices. There are no divinely inspired guidelines about entitlement structures, or about the boundary between atomistic and collective decisions. These are, of necessity, culturally and situation specific.

The alternative types of property regimes would be defined at the policy level in figure 2.1, and the institutional arrangements that give them meaning would be developed there and at the organizational level. These institutional arrangements will then define choice sets for economic actors – either households or firms – at the operational level. When the resulting patterns of interaction give rise to certain outcomes – a certain urban shape and form, a particular level of air quality, a stock of housing options for the homeless – then there will be general acceptance or rejection of these respective outcomes. If change is desired by some they will attempt to influence those at the policy level or at the organizational level to design new institutional arrangements. Of course decision units at the operational level can promulgate their own institutional arrangements, but public policy is, largely, about the kind of hierarchy depicted in figure 2.1.

With this general picture in mind we can now turn to a more elaborate explanation – and analysis – of institutional arrangements, and ultimately of institutional change.

NOTES

1   These three views do not exhaust the range of models concerned with institutional change, but do seem to reflect the dominant views within

economics. The obvious omission – Marx – is explained by the realization that Marx had but one engine of institutional change (or lack of change) and that was class struggle. While the interests of class are clearly relevant to institutional change, as we will see momentarily, I do not believe that the Marxian model warrants separate treatment; it is implicit in at least one of the models to be discussed here.

2 An alternative reference of earlier work in this genre is to be found in Binswanger and Ruttan (1978).

3 In spite of this definition of institutions, they earlier confuse the issue by stating that public sector "institutions" such as agricultural experiment stations "obtain their resources in the political market place and allocate resources through bureaucratic mechanisms." (Ruttan and Hayami 1984, p. 204) Hence, Ruttan and Hayami believe that institutions can both be the "rules of a society or of organizations" and at the same time be those very organizations. I will return to the analytical import of this confusion between institutions as rules, conventions, and entitlements, in contrast to institutions as organizations defined by those rules, conventions, and entitlements.

4 There is a curious phrase here to which we will return momentarily. It is asserted that the "more abundant labor supply" was partly responsible for lowering the marginal product of labor. Neoclassical economic theory regards the marginal product of labor to be determined not by the *supply* of labor but by the labor power (human capital) of the individuals *actually employed*, and the capital with which they mix their labor. The *supply of labor* is quite irrelevant to the marginal productivity of those actually employed. If the authors mean that more workers were actually employed in harvesting, to the point that they got in each other's way, then the marginal productivity of each would be less than previously. But why would otherwise "economic" farm operators not hire the proper number of harvesters as determined by the going rate of remuneration? Indeed it suggests that the greater abundance of landless laborers provided a convenient opportunity for the farm operators to modify the wage contract (an institution) so that the real harvesting wage was significantly reduced.

5 For this model see Binswanger and Ruttan (1978).

6 See Bromley (1982a, 1987) and Bromley, Taylor, and Parker (1980).

7 This legislation established limits of liability to electric utilities in case of a nuclear accident. By limiting the risk exposure, the government made it possible for utilities to obtain financing to allow construction to proceed.

8 New pharmaceutical products could hardly be expected to appear without institutional arrangements regarding the rights to the income stream arising from that particular technical item.

9 While I refer to the model in this section as the "North model", Douglass North has in fact collaborated with two individuals in particular. See, for instance, Davis and North (1970, 1971), North (1981, 1983), and North and Thomas (1970, 1971, 1973, 1977).

10   He admits, however, that in practice this ideal is rarely attained.
11   Although there are, apparently, some who question the North analysis (Ringrose 1973).
12   There is, now, great concern in the western United States over water allocation. All of the "prior appropriators" used the scarce water for irrigated agriculture and recent urban growth has placed new demands on a limited water supply.
13   This hierarchy is attributable to Ciriacy-Wantrup (1971).

3
The Nature of Institutions

The law, in its majestic equality, forbids the rich as well as the poor to sleep under bridges, to beg in the streets, and to steal bread.

Anatole France, *Le Lys Rouge*

One of the major concerns in chapter 2 was that the term *institution* has not been carefully and rigorously defined, and that *institutional arrangements* have not been carefully located in the economic system by those writing about institutional change. That will be the primary task of this chapter. I will also illustrate the way in which institutions define the nature of transactions at the operational level of an economy. Finally I will be concerned with the normative content of institutions to the extent that institutions determine what is a cost or a benefit, and for whom these costs and benefits are pertinent.

I THE PRACTICE OF INSTITUTIONS

All human activity requires certain regularizing conventions that facilitate social processes; the calendar and the clock are just that sort of convention. Time is a social convention that provides regularity and structure to our daily lives. In any social setting there is a need for a set of behavioral norms to define acceptable actions for the members of the polity. These behavioral norms may be secular, or they may be religious. Individuals of the Jewish and Muslim faiths do not eat pork, and they usually prefer food which has been prepared in certain ways. Catholics, at one time, were under some compulsion not to eat meat on Fridays. Some religions discourage dancing, the playing of cards, smoking, and the consumption of alcohol. Other religions are silent on alcohol, and some permit – even encourage – multiple wives.

Daily life is replete with rules that are both positive and negative sanctions concerning behavior. While the constraining nature of these institutions receives the bulk of the attention, their reciprocal nature insures that restraint for one is liberation for another. I can no longer burn leaves from my yard in the autumn, nor can I allow my dog to roam the neighborhood off of a leash. At the same time my asthmatic neighbor no longer need suffer from the smoke I generate, I no longer must repair the damage to my shrubs from roaming dogs, nor need I reclaim my yard from the unwelcome depositions of a time when all dogs ran free. Speed limits indicate how fast I may drive, and how fast I can expect other motorists to drive. Food and drug stipulations assure me that my cheese is indeed cheese, my meat is indeed meat (and reasonably safe), and that the malaria pills I take are – within certain probabilities – safe.

The distinctive architecture of Paris, with its mansard roofs, is a reminder that institutions can give rise to behaviors that produce certain outcomes which over time become not only the norm, but also symbols of great beauty and admiration. The mansard roof is a clever response by the architect François Mansart (1596–1666) to a rule that buildings in Paris could not exceed five stories in height. Owners of buildings, always in need of more space in an increasingly crowded urban landscape, proved amenable to innovative architecture that managed to hide an additional story under the "roof." While the building inspector might suggest that they had, indeed, six stories, the owners could quite correctly reply that they had only five stories and the roof. How could the roof constitute a story?

Other institutions are more subtle, but no less important. In Great Britain, and most of her former colonies, one drives an automobile on the left-hand side of the road. In the majority of other nations one drives on the right. It really does not seem to matter on which side of the road people drive as long as they all do it on the same side. The choice of a side of the road for driving holds no important economic consequences, but it does regularize behavior. Other regularizing institutions exist, and they are called habits or norms. Elderly people are usually treated with some deference, very young children warrant special attention when near the street, and in most countries individuals respect the sanctity of queues.

The economist's interest in institutions arises because this regularizing aspect in individual and group behavior represents the very essence of interpersonal transactions of an economic sort, and because institutions define the status quo against which any collective action must be regarded. If it is considered the norm that people be allowed to smoke in public places then collective action to alter that behavior will be viewed by smokers as an invasion of their presumed right to smoke. Regularized behavior, whether or not it is officially sanctioned by legal processes, over time takes on the aura of a right. In earlier times expectorating was quite acceptable behavior, and loud belching was the ultimate compliment to a cook. Few today would choose to exercise their presumed right to expectorate or to belch in public, but neither would they be likely to complain about their loss of freedom for this new situation. Other forms of regularized behavior do become codified in a variety of ways. In early landlord–tenant relations it soon became the norm (the convention) that the renter would need to pay a deposit to protect against damage to the dwelling – a performance bond, as it were. Soon this practice appeared in most rental contracts and it became the duty of the tenant to make the deposit. Conversely, it was the right of the landlord to receive it (Schmid 1986). Similarly, the landlord had a duty to return the deposit if the dwelling were vacated in satisfactory condition, and the tenant had the right to expect that proper behavior would result in the return of the deposit.

The contentious nature of institutions is to be found less in their existence than in their modification. Indeed, as I will show, it is institutions that enable daily life to proceed with a minimum of repetitive negotiation; institutions reduce transaction costs. But, it is also the existence of institutions that provides the regularizing dimension of daily human contact that becomes the status quo, and that therefore becomes the focus of attention when collective decisions must be taken to respond to new scarcities, new tastes and preferences, and new opportunities.

As mentioned in chapter 2, the term "institution" is also used to denote other aspects of daily life. Schools, hospitals, and churches are often referred to as institutions; marriage is called an institution. It will be helpful to suspend reference to these other kinds of institutions so that attention can remain fixed on the concept of institutions as the rules and conventions that define choice sets from which individuals, firms, households, and other decision-making units choose courses of action.

II THE CONCEPT OF INSTITUTIONS

A number of economists are now devoting increased attention to the study of institutions, and Oliver Williamson (1985) has offered one account of the intellectual traditions that underpin this revived interest in the new institutional economics. Williamson starts with two behavioral assumptions that are congenial to economists and they will be retained here: (1) bounded rationality; and (2) opportunism. The former implies a limited ability of individuals to be perfectly rational in the face of non-trivial information costs, while the latter refers to the seeking of self-interest with guile. Williamson is then concerned primarily with "the economic institutions of capitalism, with special reference to firms, markets, and relational contracting." (1985, p. 16). Williamson is interested in the rules and conventions that elicit patterns of behavior of individuals and firms engaged in various transactions – whether market transactions or hierarchical transactions. He sees the firm as a governance structure relying on rules and conventions, just as the market relies on rules and conventions.

My interest in institutions is compatible with that of Williamson and others, but I ask a different question. My concern is with the normative content of institutional arrangements, and with the evaluation of institutional change, while Williamson is more behaviorist in his assessment of institutions and the behaviors they elicit. Williamson is concerned with the institutional structure of markets and hierarchies as that structure guides and sanctions certain behaviors, and as that structure evolves to reduce transaction costs. I am concerned to explore the way in which the prevailing institutional arrangements have evolved in the face of certain economic conditions, and how any given institutional structure defines the status quo economic conditions. More importantly, I am concerned with the way in which institutional arrangements define for us what is considered efficient. My primary purpose here is to explore how the concepts of – and judgments about – efficiency and optimality are dependent upon the status quo institutional structure which defines what is a cost and for whom. I refer to this as the *normative content* of institutions since it is the basis of economic policy regarding the efficient or the optimal policy. While this issue may be obvious to many economists, it bears emphasis so that policy analysis will be conducted in light of this fact.

I follow rather conventional practice by regarding institutions as

sets of rights and obligations affecting people in their economic lives. Some of these rights and obligations are unconditional and do not depend on any contract (other than the fictitious "social contract"); these may or may not be inalienable. Others are acquired voluntarily, by entering into contracts. Some contracts are explicit, others are implicit in conventions recognized by both parties. Contracts may relate to the exchange of goods or services or money or authority in varying proportions. A system of institutions can thus be described more or less equivalently in the legal kind of parlance I have been using, as the set of rights and obligations in force; or in the parlance of sociology and social anthropology, as a role-system or status-system; or in the parlance of economics as defining: (i) what markets exist, taking market in the broadest sense, to include all voluntary exchange; and (ii) how economic relations are regulated in areas where markets do not exist. (Matthews 1986, p. 905)

Institutions can be demarcated into two classes: (1) conventions; and (2) rules or entitlements.

A   Institutions as Conventions

As suggested earlier a convention is a regularity in human behavior that brings order and predictability to human relationships. In his book *Convention* Lewis offers the following:

A regularity R in the behavior of a population P when they are agents in a recurrent situation S is a *convention* if and only if it is true that, and it is common knowledge in P that, in any instance of S among members of P: (1) everyone conforms to R; (2) everyone expects everyone else to conform to R; (3) everyone prefers to conform to R on condition that the others do, since S is a coordination problem and uniform conformity to R is a coordination equilibrium in S. (Lewis 1986, p. 58)[1]

The matter of conventions is particularly germane to coordination situations, in which a coordination equilibrium is defined by Lewis as a "combination in which no one would have been better off had *any one* agent alone acted otherwise, either himself or someone else." (p. 14) Schotter, in his work on social institutions, believes that the concept of convention requires recognition of conflicting interests and so introduces entitlements when he says:

Although social institutions are predominantly concerned with solving social coordination problems, they are not necessarily self-policing and may require some external authority, such as the state, to enforce them. For instance, a system of property rights is a social institution in which the behavior of individual agents is circumscribed to conform. It defines a regularity in behavior that is socially agreed to. Yet this institution is not in equilibrium because each person has an incentive to steal from others. As a result, some external authority must be instituted to enforce these rights – the state. (Schotter 1981, p. 11)

All citizens have a general interest in some secure structure of property relations, and yet each also has an incentive to deviate from that situation of law and order. Schotter then proceeds to define a social institution as a regularity "in social behavior that is agreed to by all members of society, specifies behavior in specific recurrent situations, and is either self-policed or policed by some external authority." (p. 11) These definitions from Lewis and Schotter contain some disagreement over terms such as institutions and conventions, with Schotter modifying the Lewis concept of convention to include what I am treating as rules or entitlements. There is also mention of preferences and agreements, yet references also to enforcement via policing. It may seem puzzling how people can mutually agree to something, and yet require policing by an external authority.

There is, quite clearly, a difference between a situation that all persons agree with, and one that all accept. When Schotter refers to situations that are agreed to by all it conjures up notions of discussion, consideration, weighing of alternatives, and then, ultimately, agreement with something to which all will be bound. Lewis maintains that while some conventions can indeed arise from this active form of the word agree, many also arise by default; drivers in the United Kingdom have never been asked to reach agreement regarding on which side of the road they shall drive. They conform to a social convention by accepting it. There is reason to understand the essential difference between regularities in human preferences and behaviors that can be regarded as a social convention, and regularities in human behaviors that arise from a structured set of legal relations. In what follows, therefore, I will divide the term "institution" into two parts, the first encompassing Lewis's notion of convention, and the second encompassing the notion of a rule or an entitlement. That is:

A *convention* is a regularity in human behavior in which everyone prefers to conform to R on the expectation that all others will also conform to R. A convention is a structured set of expectations about behavior, and of actual behavior, driven by shared and dominant preferences for the ultimate outcome as opposed to the means by which that outcome is achieved.

On the other hand:

An *entitlement* is a socially recognized and sanctioned set of expectations on the part of everyone in a society with regard to *de jure* or *de facto* legal relations that define the choice sets of individuals with respect to the choice sets of others.

I will therefore be regarding institutions as falling into these two categories: conventions, depicting social institutions that arise to coordinate behaviors derived from shared preferences over outcomes but indifference over means; and entitlements, depicting social institutions that arise to regularize behaviors in the face of discordant preferences over either social ends or means.

B Institutions as Rules or Entitlements

John R. Commons defined an institution as "collective action in restraint, liberation, and expansion of individual action." (1961, p. 73) Commons, who initiated the term "working rules", suggested that such rules indicate what

> individuals *must* or *must not* do (compulsion or duty), what they *may* do without interference from other individuals (permission or liberty), what they *can* do with the aid of collective power (capacity or right), and what they *cannot* expect the collective power to do in their behalf (incapacity or exposure). (1968, p. 6)

Another definition is that institutions are "sets of ordered relationships among people which define their rights, exposures to the rights of others, privileges, and responsibilities." (Schmid 1972, p. 893) These definitions of institutions help to clarify the point that schools, corporations, and futures markets obtain their meaning from institutions; such organizations only exist because there is a set of working rules which *defines* them. A corporation only exists as a separate legal entity by virtue of a set of working rules (entitlements) which defines what is, and what is not, a corporation. The same holds for futures markets, for schools, and for hospitals. Institutions define certain organizations or social programs, but these programs and organizations are best thought of not as being institutions, but as being defined by institutions.

Within the class of institutions there are two kinds of working rules of relevance to social organizations: (1) those that define an organization *vis-à-vis* the rest of the world; and (2) those that spell out the internal nature of the organization. These two types of institutions are found in the enabling legislation, the constitution, the by-laws, the charter, or the administrative rules of organizations. With respect to the earlier example of a corporation, the first type of institutions articulate the necessary steps which must be followed to become a corporation, and to remain one. The second type of institutions articulate how officers are appointed, how the financial records shall be kept, how administrative decisions are made, and so on. The former institutions define the corporation *vis-à-vis* the larger society, the latter give it structure.

III   INSTITUTIONS AS LEGAL RELATIONS

Because institutions are collective rules that define socially acceptable individual and group behavior, they are sets of dual expectations. The concept of an institution is one of mutualities, of correlates, of dualities. This correlative nature was recognized at the turn of the century by the legal scholar W. N. Hohfeld who postulated four sets of dualities which he considered *the* essence of legal relations among individuals in a society. The correlates were picked up by John R. Commons who used slightly different terminology to form the basis of his analysis of collective, economic, and social relations under the jurisdiction of the United States Supreme Court. Before turning to these four fundamental relations, it is necessary to draw a distinction between *legal relations* and a *legal system*.

It is axiomatic that no society can function in the absence of social order. The institutional arrangements or working rules of that going concern create the social order that allows it to function and to survive. The ways in which those institutions are promulgated and enforced constitute the legal system of that society. It is not necessary that the legal system have courts, lawyers, and jails. It is sufficient that the society have a structured set of rules and sanctions that results in social order. These need not be codified rules, nor do they need to be secular rather than religious. What matters is their recognition on the part of the members of the collectivity. When this happens there is a *legal system*. It is a legal system in the broadest interpretation of the term "legal." The societal recognition of a specific set of ordered relations among individuals is a legal relation.

When discussing the four fundamental legal relations, imagine two individuals, Alpha and Beta. Recall that since legal relations are also group specific, imagine Alpha to be a person (an individual) and Beta to be all other persons; one social entity (Alpha) may be an individual or a group against another social entity (Beta) which may be an individual or a group. The four fundamental legal relations are shown in table 3.1, with only a slight modification from the Hohfeld terminology.[2]

In the Hohfeld scheme a *right* means that Alpha has an expectation or assurance that Beta will behave in a certain way toward Alpha. As an example, Alpha has an expectation that Beta will not take raspberries from her garden. A *duty* means that Beta must behave in a specific way with respect to Alpha. As above, this means that Beta will not take raspberries from Alpha's garden. Notice that the dual of Alpha's

Table 3.1 The Four Fundamental Legal Relations (after Hohfeld 1913, 1917)

	Alpha	Beta
Static correlates	right privilege	duty no right
Dynamic correlates	power immunity	liability no power

legal position is Beta's legal position; Alpha has the right, Beta has the duty. The second correlate is that of *privilege*. Here, Alpha is free to behave in a certain way with respect to Beta. As an example, Alpha is free with respect to Beta to sell Blackacre to X, Y, or Z. The dual of privilege is *no right*. Here Beta has no recourse if Alpha behaves in a certain way with respect to Beta. As immediately above, Alpha is free with respect to Beta to sell Blackacre to X, Y, or Z. In a primitive setting, privilege would mean that Alpha is free to give or to sell a hunting tool to X, Y, or Z without the consent of Beta. This is also Beta's no right in that Beta has no right to interfere with the transaction. Alpha is free to give or to sell a hunting tool to X, Y, or Z without the consent of Beta.

The difference between the right/duty correlate and the privilege/ no-right correlate can be further clarified in the context of current public policy issues. Consider the issue of solar collectors. If my neighbor may allow her trees to grow to a height such that my solar collector would become useless, she has *privilege* and I have *no right*. If the law protects me against the incursion of shade, then I have *rights* and she has *duties*. It is my *right* to expect that "my sunlight" will not be interrupted, and it is her *duty* to see that such does not occur. These are static correlates that define legal relations at a particular time.

Turning now to the dynamic aspect, *power* means that Alpha may voluntarily create a new legal relation affecting Beta. That is, if Beta makes an offer, Alpha can close the contract and force Beta to comply. *Liability* means that Beta is subject to a new legal relation voluntarily created by Alpha. As with power, if Beta makes an offer, Alpha can close the contract and bind Beta. Finally, *immunity* means that Alpha is not subject to Beta's attempt voluntarily to create a new legal relation affecting Alpha. If Beta sells or gives away Alpha's canoe, it remains Alpha's. *No power* means that Beta may not voluntarily create a new legal relation affecting Alpha. Again, if Beta sells or gives away Alpha's canoe, it remains Alpha's.

The above scheme is symmetrical with respect to the position of Alpha and Beta. The legal relation is identical regardless of the position from which the relation is viewed (Alpha or Beta). The difference lies "not in the relation which is always two sided, but in the positions and outlook of . . . [Alpha and Beta] . . . which together make up the two converses entering into the relation." (Hoebel 1942, p. 955)

Two other considerations are important. First, individuals belong to more than one sub-group in a society with each sub-group having its conventions and entitlements that both liberate and constrain behavior. Hence it may be that any one individual is subject to several sets of overlapping legal (formal or informal) relations. In primitive societies males are members of warrior groups, decision-making groups, kinships, as well as the larger tribe or band. Females may have similar layering of memberships. The legal standards of the larger group supersede those of the sub-group, though the same sorts of correlates apply in all groups. In contemporary terms, we belong to a variety of organizations and associations that have their own constellations of legal relations.

Second, the four fundamental legal relations are reducible into two further categories which are either active or passive. The right/duty and the power/liability relations are active in that they represent imperative relations subject to the authority of the state. On the other hand, the privilege/no-right and immunity/no-power relations are passive in that they are not themselves subject to direct legal enforcement. Instead, they set the limit of the state's activities in that they define the types of behavior that are beyond the interest of the state. As seen in the privilege instance, the state declares that it is none of its direct concern if Alpha sells Blackacre to X, Y, or Z. In a sense, these legal relations are statements of "no law."

Hoebel makes the point that in our legal system every right that Alpha has upon Beta is reinforced by accompanying pressure on courts to compel Beta to perform his/her duty. While there may be court analogues in primitive settings, it will more often happen that the aggrieved person (or kin) must enforce the right. If this is done in a socially sanctioned manner (within the law) then they have the legal privilege to apply the conventional sanction.

IV   INSTITUTIONS AND MARKETS: THE ECONOMY
AS A SET OF ORDERED RELATIONS

It is often easy to imagine that market processes, because they are so conducive to the purposeful and volitional behavior of millions of buyers and sellers, are vast unstructured arenas in which anything goes. Nothing could be further from the truth. The essence of markets is order, predictability, stability, and reliability. These ideas of predictability and order, however, should not be confused with rigidity. To have structure and reliability in process is quite different from structure and reliability in outcomes. Markets provide order and stability of process, which then, combined with the maximizing behavior of millions of autonomous participants, results in a wide variety of outcomes. It is the ordered relations of market processes that are of concern here. I am interested in the legal preconditions that enable atomistic economic agents to engage in transactions without ever coming face-to-face with other market participants, often without close inspection of the items being exchanged. The convention of a uniform currency relieves the seller of concern for what will be received, although the buyer faces no such certainty with respect to quality of what has been purchased. And yet the exchange process works well enough to insure that buyers usually get what they thought they purchased.

To some, markets imply a meeting place of potential buyers and sellers; others regard the market as the outcome of a large number of transactions, while others regard it as a metaphor for a large number of exchange agreements. I will consider a market to be a regularized medium for the exchange of benefit (or income) streams. Markets are about the exchange of entitlements to future benefit streams. When I order a fine *canard à l'orange*, I give the restaurant a certain sum of money (a part of the restaurant's benefit stream) in exchange for a sumptuous meal that will bestow benefits on me. The duck, while marvelous, is merely a means to an end – my enjoyment at the time, and the pleasant reflections thereafter. If markets are about the exchange of benefit streams, it follows that markets must be defined by the ways in which those benefit streams are defined, transmitted, and enforced. It is this aspect of markets and exchange processes that will be of concern here.

An interest in the legal foundations of the economy is concerned with the issues of law, of predictability, and of regularity in human interaction. Social groups find their cohesion in information – information about shared values, information about the likely actions of others, and information about the consequences of certain acts committed by any members of the group including ourselves. Language is an information system. The interest here is not just in language, or only in the information that langauge contains and imparts, but rather with a particular functional dimension of language and concepts. That functional dimension pertains to the establishment of a system of expectations among members of society regarding the actions of others. Small groups, and I leave aside concern for a precise definition of "small," can establish and maintain a system of expectations based on shared trust. But social interaction cannot be limited to small groups, and so language and information must be established that will inform and guide individual behaviors that hold implications for the larger society. That is, law must be seen both as language and as concepts. It is in this sense that I will use, throughout, the term "law."

In what follows, law and legal arrangements will be understood to mean that set of language – and so information – that imparts expectations regarding the actions of members of a polity. Law places boundaries upon expectations, and gives a certain structure to human interaction. Law need not be written (codified), nor must there be lawyers. All that is needed is a set of terms that defines a structure for human interaction, and a shared understanding of the means for resolving disputes within that structure when compliance is not universal.

A market has previously been defined as a process whereby control over future income streams is transferred among participants. Notice that a market need not have a particular location, nor is it necessary that something tangible be exchanged. Markets are concerned with changes in ownership and control of future streams of benefits and costs. Simple markets are those that occur contemporaneously, and where full value is exchanged. More complicated markets occur over time and space, and may involve delayed payment. When such realistic dimensions intrude, there must be language that defines the objects being exchanged (since the buyer may not actually see the object being purchased), there must be language that defines the terms agreed to, and there must be language that defines what either party might do if other conditions are not met. That is, there must be a contract.

The requirements of any market are therefore, at minimum, ownership of the things to be exchanged, and information. More complicated markets entail more elaborate features. The role of the legal foundations of an economy is to provide a predictable structure within which exchange activity might occur and flourish. This legal foundation is required whether the economy is organized along lines that give the government a dominant role, or whether it is organized so that the private sector is the dominant active agent.

The difficulty comes with the realization that no economic system, whether market oriented or command oriented, can thrive if locked into an inflexible structure that does not recognize the exigencies of new technology, new scarcities, or new preferences on the part of buyers. This flexibility is said to represent one of the main benefits of market processes as opposed to command processes. It is wrong, however, to attribute this flexibility to the existence of markets rather than to the real cause, which is a legal environment that recognizes new opportunities, and that allows individual agents (individuals or firms) to capitalize on those opportunities. Markets do not cause adaptation to new conditions; they allow responses to the situations that are permitted by the legal foundations of the economy. The social problem is to craft a legal structure that offers both predictability and flexibility; a structure that establishes order, yet allows for change. It is important to understand that predictability of institutional arrangements is not the same thing as inflexibility.

With it understood that the legal foundations of the market consist of the conventions and entitlements that define choice sets of independent economic actors, it is now possible to introduce two terms that will be central to the remainder of the book. Both refer to transactions, but with critically different roles in a market economy. Most of economics is concerned with the domain of commodity relations; that is, with the buying and selling of goods and services. This domain of economic activity will here be referred to as *commodity transactions*.

The second domain of economic activity concerns the very order, structure, stability, and predictability of the regularized market processes through which commodities move. In this domain there are transactions over the "rules of the game." These transactions will be called *institutional transactions* to emphasize that they are about the institutional structure that defines the economy as a set of ordered relations. It is the institutional transactions that yield a particular structure of institutional arrangements that defines the domain over which commodity transactions will occur.

By recognizing both commodity transactions and institutional transactions, the economist will be able to see markets as manifestations of the legal foundations of the economy, and economics will then be seen not only as the study of the exchange processes that are defined by those foundations, but also as the study of those very foundations. The failure to understand the domain of institutional transactions can give rise to misleading conclusions about the domain of commodity transactions – particularly with reference to conclusions about the existence and normative significance of economic efficiency.

It is institutions that: (1) define the choice domain of independent economic actors in the status quo; (2) define the relationship among individuals; and (3) indicate who may do what to whom. Since institutions define the choice sets of individuals and groups, they are at the core of choices and behaviors. It is the aggregate of institutional arrangements that determines, at a particular moment, economic conditions. That is, there is a prevailing structure of norms, conventions, rules, practices, and laws that shape or define the choice sets of individuals and groups in any economy. In a centrally planned economy these are the quotas of inputs, the production plans, the accounting prices, the shipping schedules, the supply of dwellings, the availability of jobs, and the like. These institutional arrangements define the space within which individuals and groups are free to exercise decision-making latitude. In a market economy these institutional arrangements would consist of a different constellation of constraints and opportunities – the tax laws, wage rates, contractual obligations for workers, product liability for commodities, health insurance premiums and coverage, and the like. This is a bundle of norms, conventions, habits, practices, customs, laws, and administrative rules that define choice domains: I can change jobs, I cannot drive 90 miles per hour; I can build a house on a particular piece of land, I cannot build a cement factory; I can hire workers for my factory, I cannot refuse to hire them only because they have red hair, or hazel eyes, or happen to be male, or embrace an unfashionable religion.

So the institutional environment defines the choice domain (the choice set) within which I – and others in society – may operate. But economic conditions also influence the structure of institutional arrangements. When nuclear power was first proposed for the commercial generation of electricity the insurance companies would not consider coverage for the utilities. A law was passed to limit the liability from a nuclear accident to $500,000 and so the insurance companies would agree to issue policies to the utilities. An economic condition, a technical possibility, created the demand for a new law (an institution) that in turn made the economic environment conducive to nuclear power plants. The economic condition creates a need for a new institutional form, and that new institutional form then creates the new economic environment. Without the new institution the economic conditions would clearly differ from the situation with the new institution.

Both commodity transactions and institutional transactions are at the core of a dynamic economy. An individual or a group of individuals with an interest in a particular outcome will undertake efforts to modify existing institutional arrangements. Such efforts, if they reach fruition, will entail institutional transactions that create new economic opportunities. A new constellation of commodity transactions is the manifestation of those new opportunities. Of course institutions can also retard the realization of new economic opportunities – a topic to be taken up in a subsequent chapter. The idea of circular causation between economic conditions and institutional arrangements allows a more realistic and dynamic notion of the economy, at the same time recognizing its fundamental order and stability. Rather than viewing institutional arrangements as external and alien to the economy, the structure proposed here allows the recognition that there are, in actuality, two levels of choice in economics. One level concerns the allocation decisions made within the constraints of given choice sets, while the other concerns the very structure of those choice sets.

A market economy is often characterized, at the most basic level, as consisting of a circular flow of goods and services moving in one direction, and money moving in the other. This is depicted in elementary texts as resembling figure 3.1. In this characterization households sell labor to firms in exchange for wages and salaries, while firms sell goods and services to households in exchange for money. The interest here is in several new concepts to understand the economy as a set of ordered relations. These new concepts include *decision units*, *choice sets*, the difference between the *nominal and real boundaries* of decision units, and the nature of entitlements that define the flows between firms and households, as well as those entitlements that define one firm *vis-à-vis* another, or one household *vis-à-vis* another.

A Decision Units

By convention, or by conscious collective action, human society consists of units that undertake actions, and that take decisions regarding their

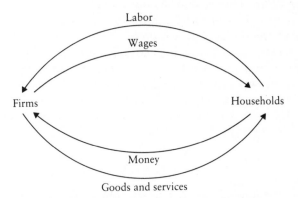

Figure 3.1 The Flow of Economic Activity

daily conduct. The individual is a decision unit of great significance in economics; other decision units are the family, and the firm (Ben-Porath 1980). The formation of decision units arises out of physiological necessity (as in the family), out of economic and social convenience (the kinship group), out of economic advantage (the firm), or out of the need for protection (the militia). Institutions, as the working rules of going concerns, define these decision units *vis-à-vis* other decision units, and they give structure and regularity to the internal workings of such units.

The firm, a dominant decision unit in economics, is defined by a constellation of contracts. It is a socially sanctioned organizational entity that has authority to make decisions in whatever manner it chooses, and for its own reasons. The firm is a centralized contracting agent that engages in a team production process. It is a specialized surrogate market in that allocative decisions within the firm are made on its own internal calculus. Outside of the firm, price movements guide resource flows; inside the firm these market transactions are replaced by entrepreneurial direction. As Coase pointed out, the reason for the existence of the firm can be found in the necessity of avoiding the costs of carrying on all transactions, every day, in a market. Team production will become a firm if it yields an output larger in value than the output possible through separable production in decentralized markets. But this larger value must be sufficient to cover the costs of organizing and disciplining members of the team. If this joint value is not adequate to cover these extra costs, the activity will occur across decentralized markets. Simply put, firms arise to reduce transaction costs (Coase 1937; Williamson 1985). A point to be made throughout this book, however, is that institutions determine the nature and magnitude of transaction costs. Therefore, the notion of the firm as a reflection of transaction costs is seen to be subject to some analytical ambiguity. In particular, the social justification of the firm rests, in the Coasian sense, on the efficiency with which complex production processes can be organized and coordinated by a decision unit. But with the recognition that institutions define what is regarded as efficient, one is reminded that the choice domain of the firm – its nominal boundary – is itself a policy variable of some interest. This will be elaborated in the subsequent sections.

B   *Choice Sets*

Choice sets are familiar in economics. The consumer has a possible consumption bundle in some set X, which represents a consumption (or choice) set. The consumer has preferences on the various bundles x in X (which is closed and convex), and these preferences are assumed to order the set of various bundles. With the proper assumptions there is a continuous utility function for the consumer that will represent those preferences over the consumption (or choice) set. The set of all feasible bundles is simply that set of all possible bundles that the consumer finds affordable. Let Y represent the consumer's income, and let $p = (p_1, \ldots, p_n)$ be the price vector for the goods in the bundle. Then, the set of affordable bundles (the budget set) is given by:

$$B = \{x \text{ in } X; \ px \le Y\}$$

The idea of constraining a consumption set by available income rarely elicits much comment; those with higher incomes will have greater choices open to them, and hence in one sense will have more freedom to act. The rich will have in their budget set winter months in Spain and Switzerland, while the poor must content themselves with an occasional pint of ale at the local pub. This differential material freedom is not viewed as an infringement on the rights or freedom or liberty of the poor, and so utility-maximizing behavior of rich and poor alike proceeds. The ability to choose from within budget sets to maximize utility is taken as sufficient evidence of the freedom implicit in market processes. With the proper assumptions this independent maximizing behavior is said to lead to the collective condition of Pareto optimality.

But the root idea of a consumption set X, that contains all the possible bundles x, deserves more careful attention when the concept of institutional arrangements is under consideration. Institutional transactions modify choice sets by expanding them for some members of society, and restricting them for others. Those for whom a choice set has been reduced in scope will often suggest that his or her rights or freedom or liberty have been constrained. Note that a choice set can be a consumption set X for consumers, or a production set Z for firms. The institutional structure of a society determines the nature and scope of both X and Z. For consumers, new products will expand the consumption set $(X^* > X)$, just as new techniques will expand the firm's production set $(Z^* > Z)$. Likewise, the discovery that a new chemical compound in X^* is carcinogenic, and must now be prohibited, will lead to a new production set $(Z' < Z^*)$. At the same time that the firm's production set is redefined to exclude the carcinogenic compound from use, the consumption set of consumers is redefined (actually expanded) to reflect the absence of that compound in the food that will be eaten. The relevant consumption set is now X' (where $X' > X^*$).

My inability to continue to burn leaves in the autumn means that my consumption set has been modified from M to M^* (where $M > M^*$), but that the consumption set of my asthmatic neighbors has been modified from N to N^* (where $N < N^*$). My range of choice has been reduced, that of my neighbors has been enhanced. Institutions as collective action in restraint, liberation, and expansion of individual action are the essence of the definition of consumption and production sets. That collective action which results in modifications of choice sets (either consumption or production) must always proceed from a given structure of institutional arrangements. It is against the status quo that patterns of interaction will lead to outcomes deemed to be unacceptable. One obvious remedy is for the various parties to attempt to strike a mutual bargain that will improve the situation. However, note that any bargain will always be made from within the existing structure of institutions that defines choice sets. An alternative avenue open to disputants is to attempt to modify directly the institutional arrangements that define those choice sets. Rather than my asthmatic neighbors having to buy out my ability to burn leaves, they have the option of going to the city council to obtain a new institutional arrangement that would prevent me from burning leaves without first getting their permission; this may entail the possibility of me having to buy out their objection. If they should refuse to sell then I am constrained from burning leaves, and they are liberated from the unwanted smoke.

Some economists will object to this interference of the city council in what could be a potentially Pareto-improving bargain among neighbors.[3] That matter will be taken up in a subsequent chapter. The issue now is simply to point out that liberation for one party is constraint for another, and that to advocate bargaining among parties to a dispute is to take the status quo institutional setup as the appropriate one against which change is to be judged. The Buchanan (1959) position on this attempts to deny that the status quo has any special claim on our attention; it is simply what exists. But his insistence on Wicksellian unanimity for any change – driven by the methodological concern to avoid Pareto-inferior changes – has the practical implication of giving a degree of sanctity to the existing institutional arrangements. Most importantly the very concept of Pareto-improving (or Pareto-inferior) changes is itself a function of the institutional arrangements under question.

C   Nominal and Real Boundaries

The production and consumption sets of decision units define possible and feasible actions open to firms and consumers, respectively. When a firm uses in its production process a chemical compound that is found to be carcinogenic then its choice holds important implications that are beyond the recognized "boundary" of the firm. Indeed, externalities are said to exist when decisions made by a firm (or consumers) hold important implications for other firms (or consumers) beyond the recognized boundaries of the firm (or household), and there are no contracts for those impacts. The existence of contracts implies the existence of formal arrangements for compensation in the event of the infringement of presumed rights (transboundary problems).

The emphasis here is on contracts since a firm is defined in terms of contracts that permit the firm to acquire control over certain important factors of production. When services are used by the firm – or when disservices are visited upon others by the firm – in the absence of contractual agreements and compensation, atomistic wealth maximization will be inefficient as defined by the prevailing institutional arrangements. Since the firm is defined by the domain over which it has a constellation of rights, there is an incongruity between the nominal domain of the firm, and the real domain of the firm. The nominal domain is that which is presumed by the firm, and that which is defended in legislative and judicial proceedings concerning the firm's managerial autonomy from the larger society. The real domain of the firm encompasses all of the valuable services used – and disservices created – for which contracts may or may not exist.

The firm is defined as a decision unit with reference to the range of choice for command decisions (extra-market control) and not with reference to the physical (or even economic) relationship between services that enter through one door, and products and social impacts that leave through another. It is the position of the boundary of the firm – that frontier which divides market processes from command processes – that is of relevance for collective action about the choice sets of both firms and consumers.

Collective action to alter the status quo will invariably arise from instances where there is a divergence between the internally presumed (nominal) boundary of decision units, and the real boundary of those decision units as reflected in the scope of costs visited on others in society. The notion of boundary problems may often appear as just that in a literal sense. And here it seems appropriate to introduce the distinction between choice sets that are feasible and those that are perceived to be feasible. Consider again the example of solar collectors on roof tops. If a home is purchased with the presumption that a solar collector will be added to the south-facing roof, the new owner will have made several important financial calculations on the basis of that belief. This constitutes the perceived feasible set. However, if the purchaser has not carefully ascertained the local ordinances concerning trees, it may turn out that the south side of the house will soon be shaded by a neighbor's ever-taller trees. In this instance the homeowner is left with little choice but to attempt to bargain with the neighbor about the height of the trees. If the neighbor is unsympathetic to the new owner's entreaties, then solar collectors are not a feasible choice. There is an incongruence between the new owner's perceived feasible set and the actual feasible set.

Another example – also of increasing relevance – concerns the presumed "right" of a landowner to perform certain modifications to the landscape. Until recently, the presumption has been that a swampy area occurring on a person's land was of no great significance to others, and that if the owner desired to fill the wetlands, few would take notice. However, in many places the ecological importance of wetlands has been realized; they are an important habitat for certain plant and animal species, and they act as filters for many nutrients which might otherwise reach nearby lakes and streams. Because of this new knowledge many local jurisdictions have enacted ordinances that require landowners to acquire permits prior to draining and filling wetlands. In this way the interest of others in those lands is given effect by the new institutional arrangements.

In a well-known case, the Wisconsin Supreme Court has ruled that a landowner does not have the absolute right to drain and fill wetlands so as to construct a dwelling. The court ruled that:

> The changing of wetlands and swamps to the damage of the general public by upsetting the natural environment and the natural relationship is not a reasonable use of that land which is protected from police power regulation . . . It seems to us that filling a swamp not otherwise commercially usable is not in and of itself an existing use, which is prevented, but rather is the preparation for some future use which is not indigenous to a swamp. Too much stress is laid on the right of an owner to change commercially valueless land when that change does damage to the rights of the public . . . The Justs argued their property has been severely depreciated in value. *But this depreciation of value is based not on the use of the land in its natural state but on what the land would be worth if it could be filled and used for the location of a dwelling.* While loss of value is to be considered in determining whether a restriction is a constructive taking, *value based upon changing the character of the land at the expense of harm to public rights is not an essential factor or controlling.* (*Just v. Marinette County* 1972)

The pertinent issue here is missed if one focuses on restrictions for the Justs, or worries that the court does not understand the concept of opportunity cost. The issue is simply that one party was bound to lose in this instance of incompatible uses of the wetlands (Schmid 1987). If the Justs were free to proceed, those with an interest in wetlands and lake quality would have had to bear unwanted costs; if the Justs were enjoined (as they were) then it is they who must bear unwanted costs. If the court had found in favor of compensating the Justs for this restriction on their choice set then it implies that they had a right to impose costs on others and can only be enjoined if their loss is bought out. But if they had been free to proceed, who would have bought out the loss of the others? It is not sufficient to protest that the Justs, after all, owned the land on which they wished to build. To do so is to beg the ultimate question of the social sanctions of ownership, the divergence between nominal and real boundaries, and the ability of an owner to impose costs on others.

V THE NORMATIVE CONTENT OF INSTITUTIONS

The interest here in institutions arises because of their central role in defining the economy as a set of ordered relations, and therefore in their role as determining individual choice sets. This matters for the obvious reason that judgments about economic efficiency are functionally dependent on the way that institutional arrangements define who must bear which costs, and who may reap which benefits. The domain of institutional transactions is concerned with the respecification of individual choice sets; notions of efficiency and equity are central to the design of economic policy, and to judgments about the efficacy of possible policy outcomes. But it must be kept in mind that efficiency and equity as analytical concepts are themselves defined by the institutional setup. The structure of institutions provides the theoretical (as well as the legal and political) rationale for the disregard of certain costs that attend particular economic activities. This is what I mean by the normative content of institutions.

The conventional approach, characterized by the Marshallian-Edgeworthian-Pigovian economy, is a world in which individual agents compete for private goods – that is, for goods that are rivalrous in consumption. In the course of that consumption of private goods certain spillovers may occur, thereby driving a wedge between private and social benefits. A similar story could be told about the input space for firms.

This economy is one of private scarcity, functioning markets, and occasional externalities.

But the substance of economics goes beyond this picture of bargaining over private goods with incidental side effects sometimes present. Instead, a more careful examination reveals the economy to be one of pervasive visitation of unwanted costs – costs that are either of a collective consumption nature, or privately borne. In this world not only do people come together to trade at the margin, balancing willingness (and ability) to pay against changing marginal increments to satisfaction, but individuals – across both space and generations – visit costs and benefits on others. The good marginalist is inclined to view this visitation of costs as an aberration, believing that such events can be corrected with taxes and bounties, or with a clearer definition of property rights to allow markets to work better where none existed before.

If the occasional visitation of unwanted costs was an accurate description of the world at the time of Marshall, Edgeworth, and Pigou, it is not so today. Problems of air quality, groundwater quantity and quality, energy exploration policies, coastal habitat problems, urban sprawl, wilderness designation and management, the management of other public lands, private forest land management, soil erosion, locally unwanted land uses (LULUs), surface water problems, marine fisheries, habitat/species preservation, mineral exploration, and the management of toxic and hazardous materials are all characterized by the presence of joint costs. This inextricable binding together of numerous parties by the visitation of unwanted costs creates a special conceptual challenge, for the obvious reason that not all parties for whom these matters are of interest are able to enter consensual bargains to have their wishes expressed or their interests protected. The physical realities of many of these economic problems preclude the thoroughgoing individualization of ownership and control that is the essence of contemporary economic analysis. The difficulties in assigning clear ownership and control to individuals of, say the airshed or the high seas are well understood. Even if that were possible, it would beg the ultimate questions of who has the socially sanctioned rights to undertake specific actions, who has the exposure to unwanted costs, and who must bear the burden of proof in order to be relieved of such costs.

Consider a world in which independent economic agents engage in a variety of activities, yet the actions of one hold uncompensated cost implications for another. If those costs are transmitted via the physical media rather than via the price mechanism, they are termed "technological externalities." Conventional wisdom would recognize this as a problem of market failure. It is characterized, traditionally, by a divergence between private costs and benefits, and social costs and benefits. There are two dominant views regarding the solution to this externality problem. One view is to tax the offending party an amount equal to the marginal social damages inflicted on others, thereby internalizing the offsite costs. Another view is to create an opportunity for the two competing uses to bargain over who will be made to bear the joint costs. The first view is associated with Pigou, the latter with Coase.

The Pigovian solution requires the involvement of an authority outside of the two interacting firms and this will usually mean the government. Even after the imposition of the optimal tax there will remain some actual physical interdependence (joint costs), but the efficient level of joint costs will have been realized by the tax. Coasian opposition to the strict application of Pigou's tax on the offending activity centers on the idea that joint costs indeed require two agents in close proximity; jointness is a function of the physical proximity of two competing activities. In other words, many externalities would not exist if the two parties would only keep their distance. Indeed the current debate over acid rain policy takes on its nature and scope because the taller smokestacks have altered the situation of joint costs in two ways.[4] First, the taller stacks remove the harmful material from the immediate vicinity. Second, the pollutants are spread over such a wide jurisdiction that the resultant costs to any single party are less than the transaction costs necessary to seek corrective action.

The Coasian solution is to recognize the dual nature of these costs, and to establish a situation in which both parties might negotiate. Notice that this bargaining can only occur after the antecedent rights structure has been determined. The negotiated solution results in a situation in which there will remain some relations involving scarce resources that lie outside of this bargained solution – and that market forces, left to themselves, cannot internalize. Buchanan and Stubblebine (1962) regard this situation as one of Pareto-irrelevant externalities. That is:

> Buchanan and Stubblebine suggest that the mere desire to alter the behavior of the imposing party (B) does not imply the ability to accomplish this change. They define a Pareto-relevant externality as one in which the extent of the activity can be altered by the parties so that the victim (A) can be made better off without the imposing party (B) being made worse off. That is, there are mutual gains from trade . . . We see, therefore, that a marginal externality can be potentially relevant – since the victim may seek for it to be eliminated – but still be Pareto-irrelevant – since it is impossible for both parties to gain

from an adjustment of the status quo. When the economy is at a Pareto-optimal point we can only conclude that all remaining external effects are Pareto-irrelevant, even though there are surely many that remain potentially relevant. (Bromley 1986, p. 50)

If the Coasian prescription is followed there are two possible outcomes. The first is one in which no bargain can be struck between the two competing uses and so the status quo remains unmodified. Demsetz (1967) would suggest that this absence of a bargained outcome is itself optimal and that the status quo structure was Pareto optimal.[5] Others would see this outcome as simply an artifact of the status quo structure of presumptive rights that forced the victim of unwanted costs to approach the source of those costs to offer payment for relief.[6] The fact that there was no change may indeed be Pareto optimal, but such a conclusion strips Pareto optimality of any policy relevance. The other possible outcome is one in which the two parties indeed strike a bargain so that the victim pays the offending party to reduce offsite costs somewhat, or the emitter compensates the victim for bearing the disutility of the situation. As above, there would remain some joint costs that were not part of the bargain; the externality would have been optimally internalized. If the existing institutional (or rights) structure were different, another different optimal outcome would occur.

A bargained outcome in the Coasian tradition is much less common than is the failure of the parties to reach some agreement – either because they did not try, or because they tried and failed. Dahlman (1979) argues that this inability to move beyond a particular status quo outcome is a function of the existence of transaction costs. These costs are central to the concept of externalities. Indeed, Dahlman notes that:

> . . . It is not possible to specify any class of transaction costs that – given individual wealth-maximizing behavior under well-specified constraints that include exchange costs – generate externalities that constitute deviations from an *attainable* optimum; second, that the concept of externalities – insofar as the word is intended to connote . . . the existence of an analytically proven market failure – is void of any positive content but, on the contrary, simply constitutes a normative judgement about the role of government and the ability of markets to establish mutually beneficial exchanges. (1979, p. 143)

Dahlman's view is that the relevance of externalities is to be found in the existence of transaction costs; such impediments to bargaining are thus a necessary condition for the persistence of unwanted costs being visited on others. Notice that transaction costs are not necessary for the persistence of physical interdependence among economic agents, for even when costless bargaining occurs there remains physical interdependence that is "not worth" eliminating. Dahlman suggests that there is no transaction cost that can generate a Pareto-relevant externality. Put somewhat differently, Pareto-relevant externalities cannot exist on the basis of transaction costs since those costs must exist in a model of the attainable optimum. It is the presence of transaction costs that prevents the attainment of the perfect Pigovian world, and transaction costs are quite capable of rendering the Coasian world optimal as it stands – otherwise it would change. That is, the Pigovian solution requires an omniscient central controller who can view the world as a unified firm and generate a schedule of taxes and bounties that will render all remaining technological externalities Pareto irrelevant. This is the Pigovian Planner.

In the Coasian approach there is the ubiquitous Walrasian Auctioneer, the *deus ex machina* of competitive markets, attempting to move toward some equilibrium in which optimality will be found. However, the presence of transaction costs implies that it may not be possible to move from the status quo – in which case existing allocations and cost incidence are considered to be optimal.

Dahlman criticizes these two stylized solutions to so-called "market failure" problems. The contemporary relevance of market failure is with reference to some Pareto optimum. Dahlman considers a properly specified and well-behaved general equilibrium system which, for every initial endowment, yields a unique general equilibrium price vector. Given current entitlements (and so endowments, including the ability to impose unwanted costs on others), the economist is able to specify a unique Pareto-optimal solution. Admit ubiquitous externalities into this system and let the Walrasian Auctioneer generate a new equilibrium price vector. In general the new price vector, and its associated allocation of resources, will differ from that attained in the world without externalities. Hence, one obtains the standard conclusion that externalities prevent the attainment of a Pareto optimum, and the accompanying distortion is considered to be bad. It is here that government "intervention" is often suggested as a solution.

Since a world with zero transaction costs is, by definition, also a world without Pareto-relevant externalities, the first model from above is one without transaction costs. But the second model, with Pareto-relevant externalities, is the one with transaction costs. Indeed, it is the very existence of transaction costs that differentiates the two models.[7]

Dahlman concludes that the conventional prescription of searching for the combination of taxes and bounties that will make the second model resemble the first – and using government as the vehicle for that process – is misdirected for the simple reason that the first model is not attainable; it is a scientific fiction. Another way of stating the same thing is to suggest that the search for Paretian perfection is a quest for a fictional target. Schmid has commented on the important difference between *Pareto irrelevancy* and *policy irrelevancy* (Schmid 1987).

Dahlman suggests that this problem is not unique to externality matters; the early concern with monopoly was judged against a world of perfect competition (which is the first model discussed above). More recently those concerned with market structure have adopted as a norm something called "workable competition" and, now, "contestable markets." The literature on international trade measures current performance – in the presence of tariffs and certain barriers – against a perfect world that has no barriers (Krueger 1974). But how relevant for policy is a perfect world of zero transaction costs? Dahlman argues:

> If we include costs of transacting in the constraints that describe the conditions under which economic agents perform their individual wealth maximization, we would then describe an attainable optimum, and this is the one we should use in judging optimality and welfare problems. (1979, p. 153)

Cheung (1970) offers a variation on this same theme. He starts by questioning the very term "externality", preferring instead to focus on the nature of contracting among various interests to a resource conflict. Thus Cheung broadens the issue from one of the willingness to contract (which is a function of the transaction costs that are of interest to Dahlman), to the legitimacy to contract. Thus, there are two possible explanations for the persistence of joint costs: (1) the costs of delineating and enforcing the limits of exclusive rights are too high and so there is an absence of willingness to contract; or (2) contracts may not exist to define exclusivity because exclusive rights are not regarded as being legitimate.

Consider first the situation in which the various parties to a joint-cost situation have the legitimacy to contract. In this case the matter is simply one of the costs of arranging bargains. The costs of forming exclusive rights to contract can be thought of in two stages. The first stage would be the costs of gathering information about the rights in question, the costs associated with bargaining over the nature of the emerging rights, and finally the costs of enforcing the contracts that have been arranged. These costs will vary according to the resource situation. For instance, on a high-seas fishery the sheer dispersion of the various agents would make this aspect very expensive indeed. If the contracting process has been successful, then the second stage is one in which existing exclusive rights are transferred over time. There are costs associated with this transfer process, just as there are costs associated with the original definition of exclusive rights. Cheung notes that the income that can be derived from an exclusive right, or the gain from enforcing that right, depends on the existence of transferability in the market place; for without transfer the higher options may not be realized. Hence, the lower the costs of contracting for transfers, the higher will be the gain of enforcing exclusivity. The cost of enforcing exclusivity depends also on the existence of transfer and its associated costs.

Both stages then – establishment of exclusivity and the transfer of existing exclusive rights – entail transaction costs. The absence of exclusive rights can imply two quite different conditions. The first, just discussed, is that the costs of establishing exclusivity may exceed the perceived benefits attaching thereto. It is here that those who find compelling reasons for volitional exchange will advocate actions that have as their purpose the reduction of transaction costs – in a sense wishing to lower the barriers to individual contracting. But one cannot conclude that the existing situation is one of market failure; in the absence of a market, where it requires the purposeful actions of the state to permit the establishment of market processes (by lowering the transaction costs that now preclude a market), it would be a mistake to label the status quo as a situation of "market failure" for the simple reason that no market exists. As Demsetz has suggested, the absence of markets may itself be optimal on efficiency grounds (1967).

So the nub of the matter is the structure of entitlements that exist – or are presumed to exist – in situations of joint costs. It is this structure of entitlements that underlies the presumed legitimacy of any particular negotiation over joint costs. The answer to the question of legitimacy of entitlements is to be found in the nature of the relevant social welfare function – a subject to be explored extensively in chapter 5.

VI INDIVIDUALS, MARKETS, AND COERCION

The discussion so far has been concerned with the practice and nature of institutions, and with the normative content of institutions. On the subject of the normative content of institutions, one of the basic propositions within economics is that institutions, by being constraints on choice sets, represent fundamental diminutions in the range of choice open to individuals. Collective action, and the institutional transactions that occur there, are usually regarded as resulting in infringements on the range of choice open to individuals. Much of the earlier discussion in this chapter has been concerned with the usual desire to allow bargaining as opposed to seeking institutional change; bargaining among volitional agents is perceived to enhance the freedom of the atomistic economic agent, while institutional change that alters choice sets within the market arena is seen as coercion of the individual. This belief is largely a function of the historical evolution of modern economic thought.

As a science develops it is important that it be consistent with the prevailing social ethos in which it will function. Even for astronomy, hardly a policy science, the experiences of Copernicus and Newton are instructive. But for a science of individual and group behavior it would be incongruous if the received wisdom did not, at the very least, accord with generally held beliefs about social interaction. In that sense, science – but especially social science – is a belief system much like art, music, and even religion (Harris 1979). The prolonged intellectual and social ferment in Britain that accompanied the Industrial Revolution – a period that happens to coincide with the development of modern economic thought – can be understood in this light.

One does not overturn existing social and economic relations simply because the relative prices of wool and corn undergo change. These changes in the social milieu require a general recognition that there might be a better way to organize economic life, and that reorganization will require some attendant social changes. The market is embedded in society rather than conversely. The discussions of eighteenth-century Britain had been concerned with the rights of individuals versus the rights of the monarchy and the emerging government; indeed it was really about separating governance from the monarchy, and then crafting the nature and structure of that governance. The *tour de force* that we know as Adam Smith's most famous work, *Inquiry into the Nature and Causes of the Wealth of Nations*, came at a time in history when there was great intellectual interest in the prospect that societies might prosper with greater freedom for individual choice – a freedom that was sought against the severe restrictions of church, monarch, and class. Smith offered 'justificatory theory" in the sense that he provided – like Keynes 160 years later – a logically consistent set of axioms and conclusions that both met the test of cultural compatibility in the evolving social scene, and provided practicing economists with a body of thought which then allowed, in the Kuhnian sense, the widespread practice of "normal science."[8]

The essence of Smith's vision is that individual self-interest, not beneficence or altruism, was responsible for the industry and energy that would lead to greater aggregate wealth. The importance and the sanctity of the individual decision maker was stressed in both philosophical and political thought and writings of the time, as well as in the economic theory then emerging. Small wonder that now, 200 years and a plethora of material wealth later, the sanctity of individual choice is at the center of economic thought and theory. In the extreme this view holds that while collective action (usually by government) implies coercion, there is no coercion in markets. And it is said to be precisely the absence of coercion that releases the entrepreneurial energies of the masses. Simply put, it finds expression in the Reagan-Thatcher idiom of the 1980s – that is, to "get government off our backs."

Many economists sincerely believe that markets are free of coercion, and that markets are the guarantor of political freedom. For instance, Milton Friedman (1962) argues that the market is both a direct component of freedom, and a necessary (though not sufficient) condition of political freedom. This connection between the market and freedom is said to be established by private enterprise and the fact that individuals are free not to enter into any particular exchange. Freedom of the individual to deny any particular exchange is seen by Friedman as insuring maximum freedom for the individual. It is said to assure unanimity in all interpersonal transactions since no one individual is forced into any particular transaction. This consensual and unanimous aspect of voluntary bargains is at the heart of much of the usual faith in the market. A related position, most often espoused by Buchanan, is that collective action implies political externalities unless it is accompanied by Wicksellian unanimity (1959, 1972a, 1972b).

A careful assessment will reveal, however, that there is no logical support for the familiar proposition that markets are coercion free while non-unanimous collective action is coercive. Both markets and collective action simultaneously constrain and liberate the individual, and there is no way within economic theory to sustain an argument that the coercion of collective action is different from the coercion of markets. The apparent freedom, or absence of coercion, of the market turns out – on closer inspection – to beg more than it answers. For it must be kept in mind that individuals are not free *not* to enter some transactions. Friedman hinges the case for a lack of coercion in markets on the freedom not to enter *any particular transaction*. That is, I am free to buy any of the nine brands of toothpaste that happen to be on the shelf, or to buy none at all. But if I happen to like a different brand of toothpaste – one that cannot obtain scarce shelf space because of any number of reasons – then I am not free to buy that brand of toothpaste. Of course, neither am I forced to buy any of the nine that are on the shelf; I always have the option of using baking soda, or going without. The toothpaste example is not very momentous, and the peculiar tastes of each of us cannot be perfectly catered to either by a market or by a state planner. That is not the issue.

The matter here concerns the logical ability to affirm individual freedom (the absence of coercion) by the mere fact that I can choose to avoid any particular transaction (the purchase of toothpaste). Macpherson would argue that freedom is present when I have the opportunity to avoid all transactions, not just any particular transaction.[9] To the extent that the rich have more choice in avoiding certain transactions – such as hiring their labor out to owners of capital – then they are less coerced than the poor, who have little choice but to arise every morning and stand in a work queue hoping that the jobs do not run out before they get to the head of the queue. There is another comment upon markets and freedom:

> By claiming as we so often do, that our free economy maximizes everything at once – the enjoyment of freedom itself, present living standards and future progress – we render freedom a poor service. We are implying that we are really making no sacrifice for freedom. We are getting it cheap, almost as a by-product. The truth is otherwise. Freedom has its cost and it is our good fortune that we are able and willing to pay it . . . The nature of the coin in which we may have to pay will not always be the same. It may be efficiency, it may be immediate progress, it may be stability or equality. Gains in all these could perhaps be had – of this too we can never be sure – at the cost of a little freedom here and there. (H. C. Wallich, cited in Hutchison 1964, p. 128)

I will address the matter of markets, collective action, and coercion from three perspectives. The first will concern the matter of individual will and intent.

A   *Will and Intent*

The case for freedom and markets is made by Hayek when he points out that coercion should be regarded as a restraint on what an individual may do when that restraint is the result of the will of other individuals, and that "we should not regard as coercion the restraint on what an individual can do imposed upon him by 'physical circumstances.'"

(Viner 1961, p. 231) Because one's "physical circumstances" can quite easily be regarded as their situation in the market, it is natural for those who prefer markets to point out that any change from the status quo by collective action, unless it has unanimous assent, constitutes coercion. Viner, in commenting on Hayek, notes that Hayek suggests that:

> Freedom is thus defined as freedom *from* subjection to the will of others, and not as freedom *to do* anything in particular, or for that matter to do anything at all, in the sense of power or ability or opportunity to do it . . . It is to enable him to maintain a sharp distinction between "coercion" as meaning willed restraints on others and the restraints from "physical circumstances" that Hayek puts so much stress on what A "wills" with respect to B as distinguished from what impact A's behavior has on B regardless of whether A had B in mind or not. (Viner 1961, p. 231)

Here we can see the essence of the problem. If A *wills* some restraint on B then that would comprise coercion. If conditions are such that A can behave (in my terminology A has *privilege*) in a manner that is seriously detrimental to the interests of B – but is oblivious to B's suffering, or absent-mindedly harms B – that is not coercion. Those who defend markets and the status quo would suggest that when B seeks relief from this intolerable situation the *presence of will on the part of B*, coupled with B's necessity to seek some official sanction to be relieved (usually in the form of government action), comprises the essence of coercion. For if B had only the *will* to alter A's behavior, and rather than relying upon the state had attempted to bargain with A over the interference and had failed, then the status quo would be reaffirmed as efficient and B would simply be out of luck; the freedom of the market would be confirmed. As a defense of minimal government and *laissez-faire*, Hayek's selective perception of coercion seems purposeful – if not very logical.

This matter of will and intent is germane to situations of joint costs. The conventional view of externalities is that they are unintended side effects of some other direct action; the steel mill makes steel but as an unintentional by-product it also fouls the air. Collective action to reduce that pollution is then argued to be coercion of the firm. But another view of the matter would reveal a different answer. When the steel mill is planned the owners/manager *know* the recipe for steel, and they know that it will entail a certain quantity of coal being burned and the smoke from that combustion must go somewhere. How this part of the production process can be dismissed as unintended is curious to some (Schmid 1987, p. 41).

Those who see collective action and institutional change as untoward intrusion into the free choice of firms or individuals to do as they wish seem to commit several other conceptual errors that require elaboration. Most economists will find the greater benefit in the widest possible scope for free-market activity as opposed to government regulations. That is, unless there are compelling indications of market failure things will simply go better, or economic efficiency will be enhanced, if firms are free to do as they wish in the unrelenting discipline of competitive enterprise. This metaphor of the market carries great analytical weight, in spite of little consideration for the evolution of markets.

B   The Evolution of Markets

Today's markets did not simply appear *de novo* but rather represent the product of decades of institutional change. Consider a time in which it might be supposed that individuals lived in a Hobbesian state of nature in that there were no institutions of property, of contract, or of general behavior. Call this time $t = 0$. Since in $t = 0$ there is no government, by definition there cannot be coercion by the state. But neither can there be markets for the simple reason that there are no operational concepts of property, or of contract, nor is there a uniform medium of exchange. Each individual in $t = 0$ has his own notions about what is his, about how he would like to structure contracts, and about what ought to constitute the relevant currency. Assume that the onset of exchange is seen to be impeded, first of all, by the lack of a common currency. Because there are different interests to be served in this decision, because the various members of society have differential gains and losses depending upon the currency decision, there is no unanimous decision possible. To pick one medium of exchange over the n other possibilities is to serve the interests of some, and to impinge upon the interests of others.

But a common currency is required and so a coercive decision is necessary; we are now in $t = 1$. The coercion in $t = 0$ has made it possible for a currency to be identified and for large quantities to be manufactured for distribution to the members of the group. As the currency works its way into the society it is noticed that the process of exchange is not working as well as some thought that it would. It is concluded that the absence of property rights in physical objects is responsible for the low level of exchange activity. Since physical possession is currently the sole basis for ownership in this society, individuals are reluctant to relinquish possession without security of obtaining something in return. The decision that some form of property is required is not met with universal acclaim however, since those without many physical possessions at the moment are fearful that they will be left less well off than if the initiation of property rules were to occur at some other time. Unfortunately there is no ideal time to transform physical possessions into legally sanctioned property since there will be gainers and losers regardless. A property structure is finally arrived at, with the practical effect that some are coerced into a situation that is not in their private interest, even though the aggregate well-being of the community is understood to be enhanced thereby.

The institutions of currency and property bring us to $t = 2$ where we await the full flowering of enterprise and exchange. Once here however, the citizens realize that the mere existence of the concept of property does not prevent some members of society from believing that physical possession by whatever means is still acceptable behavior. It is now apparent that some form of policing is required, the funding of which must come from every member of society. Once again coercion of the individual is seen to be a necessary ingredient to get the group organized so that market exchange might replace the more primitive autarky. It is clear that none of the members would willingly offer financial contributions to support the police force, even though they might privately admit to its need.

The coercion of the individual in the form of taxation now takes us to $t = 3$. Those who had promised that the growth of markets would free them from the unwanted coercion of Hobbesian war are finding it ever more difficult to convince their libertarian neighbors that all will soon get better. The members of the community notice that thoroughgoing exchange has still not been realized, and begin to chafe under the tax burden, the imposition of a common currency, and the redefinition of their preexisting rights to the objects that had been acquired through their superior strength. Complaints of government interference are heard in the land. Soon a respected scholar realizes that the absence of laws of contract is impeding the full flowering of the market – by which means alone the people shall be made both free and rich. Once a complete commercial code has been crafted, a code that includes the essence of free contract, the engine of enterprise and exchange begins to hum to life; we now enter $t = 4$. But of course the uniform commercial code has affected different members of society in quite different ways. Those who were advantaged by the status quo that they knew in $t = 3$ begin to fuss once more about the coercion of the state. But they also notice something – namely that those who were born in $t = 4$ find nothing very strange about the particular institutional structure in place as they partake in the market; indeed those who regard $t = 4$ as the status quo marvel that their ancestors ever thought they could have a market economy without a common currency, without laws of property, without the policing of those laws, and without a uniform commercial code. As $t = 4$ progresses some notice that life would be even better if only they could alter the laws of contract in a certain way. Such modifications in the status quo are not, as we might suppose by now, uniformly appreciated. Indeed, there is bitter contention among the members of the group; the ones who find the status quo comfortable complain about do-gooders, rent seekers, and the interference of the state. Those who stand to gain by the modification appeal to the argument of making the market work even better – of getting yet more output from the community's scarce resources.

The story ends here, but the reader is free to carry the allegory as far as desired. My concern, in spinning this particular story, is to emphasize that "coercion" is not of much analytical help in considering market processes as opposed to the collective action of the state that alters the choice sets of members of society. To suppose that the market and its discipline remove elements of coercion from daily life is to believe that markets descended on the world one day without compromising status quo interests and entitlements. The market is no guarantee of freedom, nor does it insulate individual participants from coercion. The point is *not* that markets are either more or less coercive than collective action that modifies choice sets; the point is simply that individual market choice occurs from within a *budget set* that is defined both by existing institutional arrangements, *and* by one's income position. To suppose that a budget constraint is less impinging on the individual's range of choice than is a particular collective decision regarding acceptable individual behavior is to strain for distinctions that are not differences.

The presumed benevolence of a budget constraint, as opposed to a collective rule, is that the budget constraint is the result of impersonal and universal forces that are the end result of millions of atomistic decisions taken by free and willing individuals. In contrast, rules and conventions (institutions) redefine choice sets through the willful and purposeful actions of those seeking to improve their own economic position, or to restructure society in some way that differs from the status quo. The essence of collective choice, which then acquires the connotation of coercion, is the redefinition of individual and group choice sets which are then enforced by the coercive power of the state. This coercion will invariably be cast as the state (or government) interfering with the rights of the individual. However, this conception of the problem as one of the citizen versus the state is fallacious and must be modified to reflect the fact that all collective action is more properly modeled as a three-part relation. That is, Alpha stands to Beta in some particular relation that is recognized and sanctioned by the state. It is false to assume that the essence of institutions is simply the state against Alpha (or against Beta). Those who often lament government interference will usually have in mind a dyadic relationship in which they view themselves as one party to the dispute, and the state as the other. On this dyadic view it is all too easy to conclude that the government is acting to interfere with one person's freedom. But institutional arrangements – and the legal correlates that give them substance – are not dyadic but are, rather, triadic.

In an increasingly complex world, where population growth is contributing to increased crowding of individuals into confined spaces, it follows that individuals will increasingly impose unwanted costs on others. That is, the *real boundaries* of individual actions exceed the *nominal boundaries* of recognized *decision units*. My inability to paint my house chartreuse is also my protection that the house across the street will not be painted purple. My inability to let my dog roam free is also my protection against unwanted depositions in my front lawn – or the freedom to avoid the cost of a fence. My inability to establish a tavern in my home is my protection that a neighbor will not start a church in hers. There can be no presumption here that aggregate freedom is either lesser or greater than in the absence of these institutions that define choice sets. It is not correct to look at a particular instance in which a choice set is modified by collective action and conclude that the individual's freedom has been impaired.

The consideration of urban zoning may be instructive in this matter of coercion and freedom. Those who find more virtue in the operation of unfettered markets will suggest that zoning is coercive and distorts true property values by preventing landowners from undertaking those land uses that will maximize their own private wealth – and by extension, aggregate wealth.[10] But there is more to zoning than the simple story of the state against one landowner. Zoning is, instead, an example of collective action in which all landowners are simultaneously constrained *and* liberated.[11] That is, all owners of land in a particular geographic area are similarly affected by zoning laws; all have their choice sets diminished in a similar fashion, but that restriction on the range of choice for some activities is, at the same time, an expansion of choice for other activities. When some offensive activities (junkyards, brickworks, dog kennels) are prevented, this very prevention constitutes an expansion of choice with regard to quiet and dust-free garden parties, and a peaceful night's sleep.

When individuals complain about the restrictions of zoning laws it will often take the form of lamenting about laws that preclude, without public compensation, a property owner's development plans. Those who advance this argument are convinced that their property has been taken without compensation in defiance of the Constitution. However, if one of those (Alpha) who complains about the inability to undertake certain activities should happen to have an immediate neighbor (Beta) who suddenly decides to open a loud and offensive gravel pit – an event of drastic consequence to Alpha's peace and quiet and ultimately his or her land value – the denial of that opportunity to the ambitious neighbor (Beta) under zoning law constitutes the effective protection of existing property rights that most individuals would claim they desire. Does Alpha seriously mean to suggest that the public purse ought then to be tapped to compensate the would-be gravel vendor (Beta) for his inability to ruin Alpha's land value? If Alpha's grand development schemes must be bought off by the public purse, why not Beta's?

Alpha either is sanguine about having his/her land values destroyed by the noise and grime of a rock crusher, or is not bothered by the prospect of a large number of individuals with great development schemes being bought off by those who wish to be spared such contiguous affronts. The latter alternative, by the way, looks very much like extortion to a local community seeking to maintain quiet neighborhoods and stable residential land values in the face of brickyards, discotheques, and dog kennels. What is missing from this view of the world is the fundamental recognition that property rights are triadic; there is the rights holder, there is the thing and its value (property), and there are all other citizens. Those who are most frequent in their criticism of government have, instead, crafted a dyadic view of the world – the right holder and government. While this makes it convenient to complain about government intervention, it overlooks the fact that restriction for Alpha is liberation for Beta. The fact that the state is the intermediary in that *restriction cum liberation* does not obviate the truth that Beta's freedom to choose ends where Alpha's nose begins.

Those who consider market processes to be the preferred mechanism for resolving collective choice problems find many instances of coercion in state action, and fail to find coercion at all in market transactions. In the current terminology, market transactions take place within choice sets by consensual bargainers. All that is required is that the prevailing choice sets be considered ideal, and that the current distribution of income be good enough. Conventional market processes proceed from the assumption that income is distributed among the populace in an acceptable manner; if it were not, wouldn't it be changed?[12]

But this selective perception of coercion is an incomplete picture. If I very badly wish to install a solar collector on my roof but am threatened by the tall trees on a neighbor's lot to the south, in the absence of city rules concerning her creation of shade on my roof, I have little choice but to attempt a bargain with the neighbor. It is my *willingness to pay* against her *willingness to sell*. Since she has the protection of the status quo, I must outbid her. Since I am bound by my income constraint, and she is bounded only by her love of those shade trees, it is not hard to see that I am indeed coerced by the status quo and my necessity to meet her reservation price for those trees. For if the status quo were in my favor, and she wanted to plant tall trees, she would have to bid against my desire to utilize solar energy. Under this alternative condition it is her income which is the constraint. If she cannot match my reservation price then it is I who can coerce her. To say that there is no coercion in bargained exchange is to ignore the status quo structure of institutional arrangements (entitlements) that define the very domain within which all volitional exchange operates.[13]

This matter of government intervention can be further regarded by referring back to the wetlands case of *Just* v. *Marinette County*. Recall that the owner (Just) of some marshlands bordering a lake was prevented from filling it so as to construct a dwelling; such prevention being justified by the local authorities so as to prevent irreparable damage to the lake and downstream rivers. The landowner was seeking an enhanced income stream through modification of the status quo. The county – as the agent for others – successfully argued before the court that the owners possessed no right to alter the landscape from its natural state in order to reap higher income. The owners of the land bought marshlands, and after the denial of the permit they still owned marshlands. Government, acting as an agent for others, had not deprived them of any income stream which they had not always had. The restriction merely prevented them from enhancing their income through a modification of the natural environment. The court ruled that their original choice set was intact, as was that of those who cared about water quality and the aesthetics of the shoreline. It is perhaps unfortunate that the owner's hoped-for choice set could not be realized, but that must be laid at the feet of the owners in their entrepreneurial optimism – and opportunism – not to the pervasive interference of government.

When a farmer undertakes the control of crop pests with the aerial application of chemicals, then the spillovers from that action may hold important implications for the choice sets of others; similarly with the dumping of factory wastes into a fishing stream. When the farmer discharges the laborers who formerly controlled the weeds in his fields and replaces their function with chemical sprays, he is taking a decision that the prevailing institutional structure indicates he has the right to take. Where industrial union contracts have been written to redefine workers' rights in their future income stream, such a summary dismissal would be more difficult. When this institutional change came about, the workers were able to redefine their own choice sets, as well as those of the factory owners. Those who cite government interference bear the burden of also defining the situation in which the state refuses to assist the redefinition of choice sets for the workers as government interference with the interests of workers. To do nothing to alter the status quo is, in fact, to support the status quo, and the workers might reasonably regard *that* situation as government interference in their lives as much as employers lament government interference in the way they choose to run their particular business.

The chemical-using farmer is also able to influence choice sets if his actions kill the birds or the butterflies valued by someone else. If the rights in this case are unclear – as they surely are at the moment – then the farmer is able to impose costs on others. Because there is no property structure for this instance, some are made worse off by the farmer's actions. Not only are farm workers now unemployed, but those who like birds are made worse off. If the latter individuals were able to obtain a ban on the use of such sprays they would be able to modify the choice set of the farmer; perhaps the farmer will be led to rehire his erstwhile laborers. But to imagine that the farmer's use or non-use of chemicals has anything at all to do with the substantive freedoms he enjoys is going rather too far. Before that particular pesticide was available, and the farmer practiced another method of pest control, he would not have been described as unfree. Once the pesticide became available few would seriously suggest that the farmer now had more freedom. Hence, it is difficult to sustain an argument that the banning of a particular pesticide now reduces the farmer's freedom.

The task, then, is to reconcile claims that markets are coercion-free ways in which human interaction might be organized, while collective action that is brokered and enforced by the state is the essence of coercion. The burden of the argument in favor of putatively free bargaining over the heavy hand of the state is that the individual is able to act in a way that is fully consistent with his or her own preferences – constrained only by (the minor inconvenience of) a budget constraint. It is, after all, individual preferences that are said to be sacred in a market economy; it is from the expression of such preferences that one might deduce the optimal social strategy. Can we, employing economic concepts, conclude that individual utility is more seriously affected by a change arising from collective action than from a change arising in markets?

C   Collective Action, Budget Constraints, and Coercion

Imagine that a consumer faces two possible consumption sets. Set x^* is characterized by:

$$x^* \subset X$$

while set x is characterized by:

$$x \subset x^* \subset X$$

where: $x^* = \{x_1, x_2, \ldots, x_n\}$, $x = \{x_1, x_2, \ldots, x_{n-1}\}$, and $x + x_n = x^*$

The consumer prefers consumption set x^* to set x. Let $x^m < x^*$ be attributable to circumstances arising from market phenomena. For instance, assume that a price increase for x_n is of sufficient magnitude to cause the consumer to abandon consumption of x_n. Let $x^c < x^*$ be attributable to collective action that precludes the continued purchase of x_n. Assume, in this case, that a federal panel believes x_n to be carcinogenic and so its continued availability is made illegal. The consumer can no longer purchase x_n under either situation; the logical problem is to determine if the utility of the consumer is affected by the means whereby x_n is no longer in the consumer's choice set. The utility loss to the consumer from the absence of x_n in the choice set is the same, but does it matter why the good is no longer in the choice set? That is, can one prove that:

$$U(x^*) - U(x^m) > U(x^*) - U(x^c) \qquad (3.1)$$

Alternatively, one must prove that:

$$U(x^m) < U(x^c) \qquad (3.2)$$

Changes in consumer welfare must be "inferred from observable attributes of household consumption behaviour and the hypothesis of utility maximization." (Boadway and Bruce 1984, p. 39) There are two accepted measures for estimating utility changes at the individual level. The first measure, compensating variation, seeks to determine the magnitude of income that must be given to the individual that would

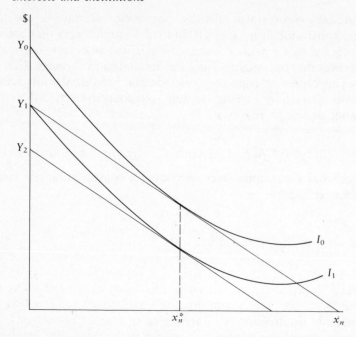

Figure 3.2   Welfare Loss from Absence of x_n from Consumer's Choice Set

just compensate for the utility loss arising from the removal of a particular element from the status quo choice set. The second measure, equivalent variation, asks how much the individual would pay in order not to be deprived of this particular element. This can be represented graphically as in figure 3.2. Here the vertical axis represents the individual's total income, minus that which must be spent on consumption of the item plotted along the horizontal axis. The point Y_0 represents the money value of current utility while purchasing nothing of good x_n. The price of x_n is shown by the budget line. When x_n^* of x_n is purchased (the optimal amount of x_n given its price) it is seen that the individual has spent $Y_0 - Y_1$ for that quantity of x_n, and still retains Y_1 that can be devoted to the consumption of other goods and services.

If good x_n should for some reason be prohibited as a result of collective action, the effect on the individual is reckoned as follows. First shift indifference curve I_0 downward until it intercepts the status quo budget line at Y_1. Secondly, shift the status quo budget line downward until it is just tangent to I_1. The intercept of this new budget line on the vertical axis denotes point Y_2. Next determine the money value of this prohibited good by ascertaining the money equivalent of the lost satisfaction of no longer having good x_n in the choice set. The individual would require, as compensation for its prohibition, the magnitude $Y_0 - Y_1$; this is called the compensating variation (CV). If one wanted to know how much the individual would be willing to pay not to have x_n banned then the magnitude $Y_1 - Y_2$ becomes relevant; this is the equivalent variation (EV). It is the money equivalent that the individual would pay in order not to be deprived of the opportunity to purchase x_n.

It should be noted that the utility loss of a price increase in x_n that drives the consumer away from the purchase of x_n would be reckoned in exactly the same way as above. There are no means within economic theory to distinguish between the utility loss arising from a good that can no longer be purchased because it is too expensive, and the utility loss arising from a good that has been banned by collective action. In short, it is impossible to test the proposition that $U(x^m) < U(x^c)$.

There is, it seems, general agreement that when CV and EV differ, it is preferable to measure EV when the individual is faced with a presumed loss in welfare, and to measure CV when the individual is faced with a possible gain in welfare. That is, do not ask how much individuals would pay to avoid a loss in welfare but rather ask how much they would require in compensation to be restored to their status quo level of satisfaction. In instances of welfare gains, ask not what they would willingly forgo to avoid the gain, but rather how much they would be willing to pay in order to experience the gain.[14] But regardless of the particular welfare measure chosen, the methodological approach remains one of asking the income equivalent of goods that may or may not appear in the individual's choice set. In this regard, there is no analytical difference between a good whose price has increased so much that it is no longer affordable to the individual, and a good that has disappeared from the market for reasons of collective action. In either instance, a good will not appear in the consumer's budget set, which is the feasible subset of the individual's choice set (Varian 1978). Since the evaluation of a consumer's gains or losses is conducted via the mechanism of whether or not a particular good falls in or out of a budget set, the practical impact of collective action that removes an element from a budget set is no different from a market event that removes a good from a budget set.

VII SUMMARY

Institutions have two dimensions: either as consensual arrangements or agreed-upon patterns of behavior that comprise conventions, or as rules and entitlements that define – with both clarity and obvious sanction – individual and group choice sets. The economy as a set of ordered relations obtains its structure and operational character from these rules and conventions. The very existence of these institutions, however, forms the basis of the concept of efficiency. That is, the magnitude and incidence of costs and benefits is an artifact of the prevailing institutional structure. Because market processes are used as the norm against which to reach conclusions about what is efficient, and because institutional arrangements give scope and meaning to market processes, it is institutions that determine what is efficient. For any particular structure of resource endowments and wealth positions – which are, by definition, determined by the institutional structure – there is an efficient allocation in production and consumption space.

Economics as policy science is constantly faced with the problem of what is best to do in any particular situation. One finds comfort and intellectual guidance in the concept of economic efficiency and Pareto improvement. Yet economic change is driven by individual and group perceptions about the status quo *vis-à-vis* some alternative state in which things will, presumably, be better. This perception of change is energized not by aggregate wealth measures, but by individual calculations of potential gain. The economist's job is, quite often, to determine the extent to which these notions of individual gain come at the expense of others or represent, at bottom, an improvement in the economic condition for all. A correct answer to this question requires that more attention be devoted to efforts to determine indications of social preferences to guide individual and collective actions.

Costs and benefits obtain their meaning from institutional arrangements, and hence economic change that obtains its motivation and legitimacy from the prospect for economic gain as defined through market processes is tautological. Economic change will occur when the benefits of change exceed the costs of change; otherwise the status quo is efficient.

The interest in economic change and its rationale has recently been manifest in a renewed concern for institutions and institutional change, and one often sees reference to something called "efficient institutions." North and Thomas note that those countries with "efficient institutions" grew and prospered, while those with "inefficient institutions" did not. Does this suggest that efficient institutions are simply a constellation of rules and conventions that contribute to greater monetary wealth? If so the tautology is affirmed.[15] The issue is not one of being efficient or inefficient in the abstract, but of being efficient or inefficient with respect to a particular purpose or objective. If monetized net national income is the sole operative objective then certain institutional arrangements (such as encouraging the free and unfettered discharge of industrial wastes into air and water) are efficient for that purpose. On the other hand, if a clean environment *and* net national income are relevant objectives, then a different institutional structure (one that implies a different form of garbage disposal) is the efficient institutional setup. It is not possible to define efficiency without first specifying the objective to be pursued. Those who claim that stricter environmental protection is inefficient (or contributes to inflation)[16] have a particular objective function in mind that happens to assign no benefits to a cleaner environment. Efficiency and efficient institutions have no meaning without reference to an objective function. Likewise, benefits and costs are meaningless concepts without reference to an objective function.

Finally, the argument that markets are arenas in which coercion is absent cannot be sustained by a careful consideration of market processes. Collective action that alters institutional arrangements modifies individual choice sets, just as do changes in prices and income.

NOTES

1   Lewis allows for a "few exceptions" by subsequently modifying this definition to read "almost everyone . . . ."
2   Hohfeld used the term "demand right" rather than "right," "privilege right" rather than "privilege," and "no demand right" rather than "no right."
3   The positions of Brennan and Buchanan (1985), Buchanan (1959, 1972a, 1972b), Cheung (1970), Coase (1960), and Demsetz (1967) are perhaps most obvious in this regard.
4   I am indebted to Paul Barkley for this observation.
5   It should be obvious that a state of extreme income disparity, wherein one party has the bulk of the wealth, and the other is on the verge of starvation, can be described as Pareto optimal. That is, there is no alternative distribution of the goods that will make one party better off (the poor man) without making someone else worse off (the rich man). Pareto optimality can be seen, therefore, to be a rather suspect decision rule.
6   For instance, see Bromley (1978, 1982b, 1986), Mishan (1974), and Samuels (1971, 1972, 1981).
7   See also the discussion by Schmid (1987, pp. 202–10 and pp. 234–5).
8   For a discussion of justificatory theory see Macpherson (1973).
9   For a detailed discussion of the view that markets do not imply coercion see "Elegant tombstones: a note on Friedman's freedom" in Macpherson (1973).

10   See Siegen (1970).
11   Indeed it is this universality of treatment under zoning that explains its survival of the Constitutional prohibition of taking without compensation.
12   Actually, the assumption is more properly stated as income being *optimally* distributed rather than being merely *acceptably* distributed.
13   The Willig (1976) conclusion that willingness to pay will approximate willingness to accept compensation and so make these two different bargains equivalent holds only when the item being bargained over represents a "small" fraction of the consumers' income. Energy expenditures in many climates would seem not to qualify under this condition.
14   EV is also said to be more consistent in giving measures of original utility changes.
15   In a more recent treatment of institutional change North indeed relates the notion of efficient institutions to those that produce the greatest output (North 1981, footnote on p. 7).
16   See Miller and Yandle (1979) for a treatment along these lines.

4
Preferences, Choices, and Institutions

Conventional economics is not about choice, but about acting according to necessity. Economic man obeys the *dictates* of reason, follows the *logic of choice*. To call this conduct choice is surely a misuse of words, when we suppose that to him the ends amongst which he can select, and the criteria of selection, are given, and the means to each end are known . . . Choice in such a theory is empty, and conventional economics should abandon the word.

Shackle, *Decision, Order, and Time in Human Affairs*

The role of institutions in defining individual and group choice sets was discussed in the previous chapter. When institutional arrangements change as a result of collective action it is important that the nature of that transition be understood as it affects the choice domain of atomistic agents. Finally, the issue of individual preferences and choice warrants special treatment. Specifically, it is important to differentiate between preferences as revealed by decisions taken from within existing choice sets, and preferences over alternative choice sets.[1]

I PREFERENCES: REVEALED AND OTHERWISE

Since the 1940s philosophers of science have been virtually unanimous in rejecting the notion that the goal of science is prediction as opposed to explanation (Caldwell 1982). In spite of this, the accepted approach to the understanding of individual preferences and choices is usually concerned more with prediction than with explanation. By failing to explain individual preferences it follows that there is an inadequate basis for assessing the reaction of individuals to modifications in their choice sets. Revealed preference theory seeks to represent the underlying preferences of individuals from nothing more than observed behavior; tramps prefer to sleep under bridges, and criminals (at least those modeled in the prisoners' dilemma) prefer long rather than short sentences.[2]

Paul Samuelson, in his early work on the theory of revealed preference, indicated that his purpose was to "develop the theory of consumer's behaviour freed from any vestigial traces of the utility concept." (1938, p. 71) Ian Little elaborated this by stating that one of his main aims was to demonstrate "that a theory of consumer's demand can be based solely on consistent behaviour . . . [and hence] . . . it must be possible to explain that behaviour without reference to anything other than behaviour." (1949, p. 90) If a meteorologist claimed to explain the weather without reference to anything other than the weather it would be amusing. In explaining choices, Sen was so amused that he offered the following:

> On this interpretation the use of the word 'preference' in revealed preference would appear to represent an elaborate pun . . . . Preferring x to y is inconsistent with preferring y to x, but if it is asserted that choice has nothing to do with preference, then choosing x rather than y in one case and y rather than x in another need not necessarily be at all inconsistent. What makes them look inconsistent is precisely the peep into the head of the consumer, the avoidance of which is alleged to be the aim of the revealed preference approach. (1982, p. 56)

Sen argues that the logical property of completeness (or connectedness) of binary relations is important in the context of revealed preference theory. Connectedness of preferences requires that when two choices are available (x and y) the individual either prefers x to y or y to x, or is completely indifferent as between the two. If the person chooses x rather than y it is presumed that x is regarded to be at least as good as y. It is not admissible to assume that the person has no idea which to choose and thus x is chosen simply because a choice is required at that time. Sen draws attention to the story of Buridan's ass which starved because it was unable to decide between two stacks of hay. The usual interpretation is that the ass was indifferent as between the two, but if that were true it would have made no difference which stack was eaten since the loss of going without the other would be zero. The ass was not at all indifferent between the two or it would have immediately consumed one or the other.

> Choosing either haystack would have appeared to reveal a view that that haystack was no worse than the other, but this view the ass was

unable to subscribe to since it could not decide what its preferences should be. By choosing either haystack it would have given a wrong signal to the revealed preference theorist since this would have implied that he regarded the chosen haystack to be at least as good as the other. (Sen 1982, p. 62)

If there is (or was) true indifference then either choice is acceptable and there will be no regret. However, this is not the case if the underlying preference relation is unconnected (or incomplete) over this pair. That is, incompleteness exists if the chooser can say neither that x is preferred to y, nor that y is preferred to x, nor that he is indifferent between the two options. Buridan's ass starved, therefore, not because of indifference but because of incompleteness – the absence of another choice that was really preferred. The ass was revealing something quite apart from indifference; his behavior indicated something about preferences. The obvious point to be drawn about the concept of revealed preference is that there is often less to observed behavior than meets the eye. Consider the familiar example of revealed preferences that is modeled as the prisoner's dilemma problem.

There are two prisoners apprehended for a minor crime, but in fact suspected of a far more serious antisocial act. They are isolated and told that if they both confess to the major crime they will be convicted of the major crime, but to show his appreciation the prosecuting attorney will ask for only ten years (not twenty) in prison for each. If neither confesses, each will be convicted of the minor offense and be sentenced to two years in prison. If only one confesses to the major crime then the confessor will go free and the other, who remained silent, will go to prison for twenty years. The negative numbers in table 4.1 can be regarded as the payoff to the two prisoners of the various choices open to them.

Table 4.1 The Prisoner's Dilemma

	Prisoner 2 Confess	Prisoner 2 Not confess
Prisoner 1 Confess	$-10, -10$	$0, -20$
Not confess	$-20, 0$	$-2, -2$

It is clearly in the interest of each of the prisoners to confess, regardless of what the other will choose to do. That is, by confessing prisoner 1 reduces his sentence from twenty years to ten should prisoner 2 also confess. If prisoner 2 does not confess, then prisoner 1 goes free rather than getting a two-year sentence. Rational self-interest leads both to confess, whereas had both not confessed they would have been sentenced to only two years each. Can it be that rational self-interest gives each an additional eight years in jail? Sen suggests the possibility of each prisoner acting not on rational self-interest but rather out of a commitment not to let the other person down, regardless of the implications for himself. Here neither would confess and they both draw a two-year sentence. The revealed preference theorist looks down on this game and is not encouraged. It must be assumed that each prisoner prefers at least one of the outcomes from not confessing over that available from confession.

> That is, he prefers either the consequences of his not confessing given the other prisoner's non-confession, or the consequences of his not confessing given the other prisoner's confession. But in fact neither happens to be true. The prisoner does not prefer to go to prison for twenty years rather than for ten; nor does he prefer a sentence of two years to being free. His choice has not revealed his preference in the manner postulated. (Sen 1982, p. 64)

If other-regarding behavior on the part of the prisoners is assumed then this would not be surprising. That is, assume that the prisoners had so much concern for the sufferings of each other that they would willingly choose non-confession on the basis of joint welfare. But this is not being assumed.

> Each is assumed to be self-centred and interested basically only in his own prison term, and the choice of non-confession follows *not* from calculations based on this welfare function, but from following a moral code of behaviour suspending the rational calculus. The preference is no different in this case from that in the earlier example, but behaviour is. And it is this difference that is inimical to the revealed preference approach to the study of human behaviour. (Sen 1982, p. 65)

Sen notes that there are contractual agreements that might allow the prisoners to agree to the optimum choice. But it is much more important to understand those situations in which contractual agreements are impossible. This would be the case where no binding agreement exists, yet the two prisoners decide not to confess. The problem is that if both prisoners behave as if they were maximizing a different welfare function from the one that they actually have, they will end up being better off in terms of their actual welfare function. That is:

To take the extreme case, if both prisoners try to maximize the welfare of the other, neither will confess . . . since non-confession will be a superior strategy no matter what is assumed about the other person's action. The result of each trying to maximize the welfare of the other will, therefore, lead to a better situation for each in terms of his own welfare as well. It is not necessary that the prisoners in fact have this much concern – or indeed any concern – for the other, but if they behave *as if* they have this concern, they will end up being better off in terms of their real preference. This is where the revealed preference approach goes off the rails altogether. The behaviour pattern that will make each better off in terms of their real preferences is not at all the behaviour pattern that will *reveal* those real preferences. Choices that reveal individual preferences may be quite inefficient for achieving welfare of the group. (Sen 1982, p. 66)

The matter of individual preferences and choices then comes down to the range of options open to an individual when it is time to make a decision. While the prisoners' dilemma may seem contrived in terms of daily choices, it is not different in terms of the necessity of deciding from within a choice set defined by the status quo.

The concern here is to explore the relationship between preferences and choices, and between those situations in which goals or objectives dominate preferences, and those in which preferences are dominated instead by means or instruments. Following Shubik, I emphasize that there is a critical distinction between choices and preferences. Preferences refer to a state of mind, and to outcomes or prospects. On the other hand choices refer to an act, a decision, or a strategy. "Only by working through the intervening deterministic, probabilistic, or game-theoretic processes . . . can . . . [one] . . . translate . . . preferences among *outcomes* into preferences among *strategies*." (Shubik 1982, p. 82: emphasis in original)

II PREFERENCES AND CHOICES

I will explore two basic games – the isolation game and the coordination game – in order to illustrate how preferences for outcomes, working through institutional arrangements and so the structure of payoffs, will determine preferences among strategies or choices.

A   The Isolation Problem: Prisoners' Dilemmas and Dreams

The isolation problem is best known as the prisoner's dilemma. Recall from above that two prisoners are apprehended for a minor crime, but actually suspected of a more serious one. The two suspects are isolated and told that if they both confess to the major crime they will be convicted of the major crime and sentenced to ten years in prison. If neither confesses each will be convicted of the minor offense and be sentenced to two years in prison. If only one turns state's evidence by confessing to the major crime then the confessor will go free and the other, who remained silent, will go to prison for twenty years. The numbers in table 4.1 represent payoffs in the sense of prison sentence under each option.

It can be seen that under this institutional structure each prisoner, by confessing, can reduce his sentence from twenty years to ten years if the other prisoner should also confess. If prisoner 1 should confess and prisoner 2 does not (perhaps out of loyalty to his colleague), then prisoner 1 goes free rather than getting a two-year sentence. Under the structure of the game as determined by the prosecuting attorney – or the relevant legal situation that defines the terms of such plea bargaining – the self-interest of each leads both to confess, whereas had both not confessed their respective prison sentence would have been only two years each. It is precisely this incentive structure that reflects the preferences of the legislature; preferences shaped institutional arrangements that would facilitate the process of extracting confessions from suspects of major crimes. Plea bargaining is the observed behavior in response to the institutional arrangements in place – the rules of the game – that provide an incentive structure conducive to the extraction of a confession from suspected criminals; that is the *raison d'être* for such institutions. The objective (preference) of the state is to extract confessions, the objective (preference) of the suspects is to minimize their own time in jail. By defining the incentive system accordingly, and by isolating the suspects so as to preclude communication, prisoners are led to "rat" on their colleagues. The outcome for the prosecuting attorney is exactly coincident with her preferences, but the outcome for the suspects is not at all coincident with their preferences – which one must assume is to minimize time spent in jail.

Imagine now a time, before plea bargaining, in which the state had not so cleverly discovered how – short of torture and threats of imminent death – to induce suspects to make choices that are inimical to their preferences. Imagine a similar situation in which two suspects are apprehended for a minor crime, but thought to be – and in fact are – guilty of a far more serious one. The prosecuting attorney does not have the option of relying on torture or death threats to aid in the extraction of confessions, nor can she promise leniency in return for cooperation. The sentence for the minor crime is two years in jail, and for the major crime ten years. The suspects are isolated as before, and interrogated. Confession to the more serious crime will add eight years to the sentence of each, regardless of what the other suspect says. If each is strictly self-interested the non-confession option is the best choice; the suspects have no incentive to rat and so each is given the more lenient sentence for the crime in which they were in fact engaged when apprehended. The more serious crime, which they also committed, remains unsolved. I call this game, depicted in table 4.2, the "prisoner's dream."

Table 4.2   The Prisoner's Dream

	Prisoner 2	
	Confess	Not confess
Prisoner 1 Confess	– 10, – 10	– 10, – 10
Not confess	– 10, – 10	– 2, – 2

The isolation game can thus be seen to have two different outcomes, depending upon the institutional arrangements in place. The rules of the game determine whether or not it is a prisoner's dilemma or a prisoner's dream. The preferences of the prisoners are invariant across the two games: they wish to minimize their respective sentences. The preferences of the prosecuting attorney can certainly be assumed to be concerned with solving crimes in both instances. The difference in the outcome of the two games has nothing to do with preferences and everything to do with choices; it is the institutional structure that defines the environment of choice – or what I have already termed *choice sets*. Choices are made from the pertinent choice set, and those choices will vary even with the same underlying preferences.

This story of preferences and choices reflects choice sets defined by the institutional environment in which the members of the decision group operate; the prisoners were making choices from within choice sets defined for them by the rules of prosecution and the customs of interrogation. Another story can be told about preferences and choices in which the institutional arrangements are autonomously evolved by the members of the decision group.

B　The Coordination Problem with Durable Autonomous Institutions

The pure coordination problem is one in which the separate interests of the various parties are in perfect agreement, and the resulting actions are of no consequence to others not part of the decision group. This pure form, explored by Schelling (1960), Lewis (1986), Runge (1981), and Ullmann-Margalit (1977), is exemplified by the case in which two parties coming for a meeting have somehow failed to specify at which of three possible train stations (I, II, or III) they will wait for the other party. Given perfect indifference of the two individuals as to which station is the meeting place, this is the pure coordination problem in that the only thing that matters is that they meet at one of them. The coordination problem is found in that both parties must guess correctly in order to meet; they must attempt to read the other's mind regarding which of the three possibilities that party will choose. If each forecasts correctly, they meet; if not, they fail to meet. This situation is depicted in table 4.3.

Table 4.3　The Pure Coordination Problem

		Individual B	
	Station I	Station II	Station III
Individual A Station I	1,1	0,0	0,0
Station II	0,0	1,1	0,0
Station III	0,0	0,0	1,1

The pure coordination problem is then made more complex by introducing the possibility that the two individuals will need to meet again in the future. Imagine them to be completely indifferent about which station. They then simply pick one at random, thereby establishing a convention: when A and B are to meet at a train station it will be at station number x (where x may be I, II, or III). If the meetings become a regularity then it seems more realistic to assume that the two parties indeed have preferences regarding which station is to be the meeting ground. This may arise because the stations are different distances from the home of each, or one particular station is more aesthetic than the other two. When preferences of the individuals participating in an event are allowed to differ then a pure coordination problem is transformed into a *mixed coordination problem*.

Consider a man and a woman who, more than anything, wish to spend time together. On a particular day they are faced with three possible activities: (1) work in the garden; (2) go sailing; or (3) have a picnic in the nearby forest. The possible levels of individual satisfaction for these three activities are shown in table 4.4. The off-diagonal elements, which imply that the man and woman are not together, are trivial here since going their separate ways has been ruled out.[3] In this setting the payoffs to the individuals are a function of their lexicographically ordered preferences. That is, they first wish to be together, and secondarily to participate in an activity that individually brings them pleasure. The man is willing to sacrifice his first choice (sailing) in order to be with the woman, and the woman likewise relents on gardening for the sake of being with the man.

Table 4.4 The Mixed Coordination Problem

	Garden	Woman Picnic	Sailing
Man Garden	4,9	0,0	0,0
Picnic	0,0	9,7	0,0
Sailing	0,0	0,0	11,4

This game has been referred to as the "battle of the sexes" which, it would seem, is a misnomer. It is more accurate to refer to it as the "lovers' game," since compromise over specific activities is willingly undertaken in order to satisfy higher-order preferences of being together. If the nature of the relationship should change such that both parties attached more importance to what each individually preferred then it would become a true battle of the sexes. But as long as the two want to spend time together this is the mixed (or two-stage) coordination problem in which the higher-order problem is to be together, and the second-order problem is to pick the preferable activity, constrained by the condition of being together.

The analogy to the train station problem is direct; the higher-order problem is to be together, whereas the second-order problem (given the different preferences for the three train stations, should such differences exist) is to meet at one that represents a compromise. As long as preferences are identical there is no struggle over the outcome; all that matters is that each meeting place be clearly agreed upon. In the case where preferences do differ, it is possible to imagine several possible conventions arising: (1) meet at the same station each time; (2) meet at each station in sequence; or (3) let the two parties alternate selecting the meeting spot. When preferences intrude, the convention in an autonomous game becomes more complex, but patterns of regularity will nonetheless evolve. Such conventions are autonomous and self-enforcing. They are autonomous because they arise from the internal dynamic of the several agents, and they are self-enforcing because no independent agent has any incentive to modify the convention. Such conventions can be regarded as coordinating institutions because they arise from situations in which all parties gain from the consistent coordination of behaviors.

These two examples concern a small group of agents (a decision unit) working out institutions for coordinating their actions. Moreover, it is assumed that the choices ultimately taken are of no consequences to other individuals. These examples of the pure and mixed coordination problems represent situations in which conventions, once developed, are expected to come under little pressure for change. However, there are numerous settings in which stable conventions, because of new circumstances, are put under pressure to be modified. Even in the case of autonomous innovation of institutional arrangements, there will be a transition into coercion, either requested and imposed by the group itself,[4] or intruded by an external agent. Consider now a second class of coordination problems in which autonomous conventions that were once sufficient come under pressure and evolve into an autonomous innovation of institutional arrangements to preserve the original coordinated outcome. This would reflect the transition of conventions into entitlements.

C   The Coordination Problem with Vulnerable Autonomous Institutions

Consider a village surrounded by rich agricultural land and a large number of farmers all engaged in the production of a reasonable variety of products. Imagine that there are five large farmers, each specializing in a particular commodity, who decide that they would like to take their produce to the village and establish a market; assume that all of the other farmers within market distance are just large enough to satisfy their own subsistence needs and therefore they do not have an interest in the village market. Since there is no village market at present it becomes quite important that each farmer choose a day for the trip in which his prospects for abundant sales are maximized. If only one farmer shows up with a wagon of, say, potatoes the potential business will be less than if one brings potatoes, another brings tomatoes, a third brings onions, a fourth brings cabbage, and a fifth brings chickens. If only their actions could be coordinated the potential gain to each will be greater than if the potato farmer goes on Monday, the tomato farmer goes on Tuesday, the onion farmer goes on Wednesday, the cabbage farmer goes on Thursday, and the chicken farmer goes on Saturday. If each went on their own preferred day they could sell some of their products; however, the crowds of buyers will certainly be larger, and hence total agricultural sales will be higher, if there is one day at which potential buyers could obtain a greater variety of goods.

The conditions exist for each individual farmer to improve his market prospects by searching for a convention among the other four that would have them all go to the village on the same day; a Pareto-better situation is possible from coordinated action. Each farmer has an incentive to coordinate his actions with those of the other four, and to arrive at a convention that each will find mutually beneficial.

Notice that each of the farmers may have had some *a priori* preferences about which day he would proceed to the village, but his economically optimal choice is to go on the day that would reap the greatest net economic benefit, and this is a function of what the other farmers choose to do. Consider now a situation in which the buyers of tomatoes begin to fuss that tomatoes do not last the week, and wouldn't the tomato farmer consider coming to the village on Wednesdays as well as to continue to come on Saturdays along with the other four? Alternatively, if he will not come on both Wednesdays and Saturdays, wouldn't he come only on Wednesdays? The possibilities are depicted in the payoff matrix of table 4.5.

Notice here that the value-maximizing solution is for all farmers to come to the village on Saturdays. However, the prospect of the tomato farmer coming twice per week offers him an opportunity to improve his net position per week from 9 to 10, 11, or even 12, but by doing so he will cause the net position of the other four farmers to fall to 15, 26, or to 22; this fall is explained by the extra costs to them of a second market day per week that are not offset by higher sales.

Table 4.5   Net Payoffs in a Vulnerable Coordination Problem

| | *Other farmers* | | |
	Wednesday	Saturday	Both
Tomato farmer Wednesday	3,25	4,15	4,17
Saturday	5,12	9,31	6,20
Both	10,15	11,26	12,22

The highest-valued outcome for the five taken together remains to come to the village on Saturdays only, even though the tomato farmer could improve his own position by switching to two days per week regardless of what the other farmers decide to do.

In the two previous coordination problems the members of the group were bound together by a lexicographic ordering and so the autonomous institutional arrangements were durable. Here there is an opportunity for individual defection from the convention, even though total net benefits to the group of five will actually fall. How might situations of vulnerable coordination be stabilized from within the decision group? The deterioration in the stability and total net value of the village market can be autonomously deterred in two possible ways. These are: (1) the preferences option; and (2) the incentives option.

The Preferences Option
The matrix of net economic benefits in table 4.5 depicts the financial outcome to the tomato farmer and to the other four farmers under three possible market situations; Wednesdays, Saturdays, or both Wednesdays and Saturdays. It would be a mistake to assume that net economic payoff is all that matters to these five farmers. Their underlying preferences have some bearing on the marketing strategies chosen. To let personal preferences outweigh monetary considerations does not imply that the farmers are somehow irrational. Rationality says nothing about maximizing income or profit but rather speaks to maximizing behaviors that are simply consistent with preferences. If economic gain weighs more heavily than preferences based on other considerations then farmers are rational to follow what is economically optimal. If other considerations weigh more heavily than economic gain then they are rational to follow these other considerations (Ullmann-Margalit 1977).

Imagine a matrix of preference indices for the five farmers showing their feelings with regard to alternative market days. Such aggregation across the four farmers can be effected by using their independent rankings in some ordinal sense, and then performing an order-preserving transformation on them.[5] Table 4.6 depicts the preferences of the participants regarding three market possibilities. These preferences should be understood to reflect the desirability of particular outcomes for each of the five individuals in full awareness of the reactions that each of the four others have regarding particular choices. That is, the tomato farmer is now aware that should he choose to go to the village on both Wednesdays and Saturdays the other four farmers would probably be quite displeased. Following Hirschman (1970), they might exercise "voice." Since the tomato farmer is assumed to care about his standing in the community the views of the others are important to him. Hence, despite the possibility of an income gain he finds that his underlying preferences are decisive in his choice of days on which to go to the market. The farmer is choosing to maximize utility even though economic gain is not maximized by the choices selected.

Table 4.6   Preferences for Market Day

	Other farmers		
	Wednesday	Saturday	Both
Tomato farmer Wednesday	2,2	1,4	0,2
Saturday	1,0	4,6	1,2
Both	2,1	2,3	3,3

The Incentives Option

The strength of underlying preferences in coordinating group behavior will be a function of the size and cohesiveness of the group. In rather small groups, where identity is known and reputation is important, then preferences will be dominant. This is an example of the *weak lovers' game* from above. Members of certain groups do care about their standing and reputation within the group. However, in those instances where underlying preferences will not be decisive in coordinating behavior within a group of interacting individuals (a decision unit or decision group), it will be necessary to turn to other incentives.

In the village market situation imagine that the other four farmers undertake efforts to ensure that the restless tomato farmer stays in line. One option is for them to convince the village council to impose a tax on net proceeds if someone attempts to market goods on both Saturdays and Wednesdays. But this option which is external to the group of farmers is not the first place to look for the restoration of coordination; instead, consider the other four farmers with respect to the structure of economic payoffs to see if there are some economic incentives that will reinforce the status quo. Do they have an aggregate willingness to pay sufficient to keep the potential defector in line? If they could agree to tax themselves $1 each and give it to the potentially wayward tomato farmer they could restore the former stable equilibrium of a Saturday market. Notice that this is a situation of the tomato farmer having the ability (in my terminology he has *privilege*) to act without regard to the interests of the other four; the only way they can have their interest protected is to bribe the tomato farmer. This situation is depicted in table 4.7, with the original payoffs indicated as before, and the post-tax/incentive payoffs shown in brackets [ ].

Table 4.7   A Vulnerable Coordination Problem Modified by Autonomous Incentives

| | Other farmers | | |
	Wednesday	Saturday	Both
Tomato farmer Wednesday	3,25	4,15	4,17
Saturday	5,12	9,31 [13,27]	6,20
Both	10,15	11,26	12,22

Assuming perfect knowledge about others' behavior, notice that the other four farmers pay no tax for the Wednesday option since the tomato farmer would never choose that option over either the Saturday option, or the Wednesday and Saturday option; it is only these latter two choices that pose a problem for the other four farmers. Likewise, since it is only necessary that the other farmers secure an incentive structure that will ensure the stability of Saturday-only choices by the tomato farmer, it is this single cell that is modified by the new structure of incentives. The net economic position of the other four farmers is seen to fall by 4, which represents the side-payment from them to the tomato farmer to ensure that he will choose to go to market on Saturday only.

The previous case illustrates the situation in which autonomous institutions can arise to reinforce agreements that make the aggregate of all members of a decision group better off economically, yet imply that one (or more) of the members of the decision group loses from the agreement. Where preferences are dominant the economic gains from defection are insufficient to countermand the evolved convention. However, where economic returns are dominant over preferences, reinforcement requires that *institutional transactions* within the decision group occur to modify choice sets of the members.

It is possible that the other four farmers would be unable to effect a changed incentive structure sufficient to offset the temptation of the tomato farmer to defect. Consider a situation in which certain transaction costs are important. By transaction costs I mean: (1) the costs of all five farmers gaining information about the marketing desires and options of the others: (2) the costs of reaching agreement among the five farmers; and (3) the costs of monitoring and enforcing the agreements that are reached. These transaction costs will reduce the net ability to pay of the other four farmers and so will impede their ability to bribe the tomato farmer not to defect. If these transaction costs are assumed to be $4 it can be seen that the four farmers are unable to offer enough to keep the tomato farmer from going to market on both days. The new payoff structure is derived as follows:

Status quo net income to the four farmers	31
Transaction costs to the four farmers	− 4
Minimum necessary payment to tomato farmer	− 2
	25

Given the economic surplus between the optimal and second-best choices for the other four farmers ($31 − $26), their maximum willingness to pay to preserve the optimum is $5. It takes $2 to make the tomato farmer indifferent between staying with Saturday-only markets, and switching to both days. This leaves a surplus with the other four of $3, with transaction costs being $4. Hence the potential offer from the four, plus the transaction costs, total $6 and reduce their net position from $31 to $25 (table 4.8). Clearly, they are better off to avoid attempting collective action to effect an institutional change, thereby allowing the tomato farmer to defect and to go to market on both days. Notice that the choice to defect on the part

Table 4.8   A Vulnerable Coordination Problem with Transaction Costs

| | *Other farmers* | | |
	Wednesday	Saturday	Both
Tomato farmer Wednesday	3,25	4,15	4,17
Saturday	5,12	9,31 [11,25]	6,20
Both	10,15	11,26	12,22

of the tomato farmer has reduced the total value of the marketing event for all five farmers from $40 to $37, even though the tomato farmer obtains a larger share of the total dollar amount than under the Saturday-only convention. That is, he obtains 30 percent of the total net value by defecting ($11 of $37) as against only 23 percent of the status quo convention ($9 of $40).

The other four farmers have one more avenue open to them, and that is to seek the assistance of an external agent, in this case the village council; this is the coordination problem that requires the imposition of institutional arrangements from outside of the group and it changes the structure of the game. It is a situation observed in the prisoners' dilemma problem in which the nature of the institutional arrangements and the resultant payoffs place a higher priority on defecting than on maintaining agreements.[6]

D   The Coordination Problem with Imposed Institutions

When the members of a decision group are unable to innovate new institutional arrangements to preserve value-maximizing (and coordinated) outcomes then it becomes necessary to look elsewhere for the proper institutional transactions; this is referred to as imposed institutions. However, the term "imposed" requires some qualification. Note that it is only imposed because of the status quo rights structure that has the interest of the other four farmers at the mercy of the whims of the tomato farmer. Had the status quo been one that prevented defection – that is, had the status quo been one that is about to be explored here as a "new" institutional arrangement – then a change to allow defection would also be imposed from outside of the group.

It would have to be imposed since the other four farmers would lose by the new institutional structure, just as the tomato farmer loses by the imposed institutional arrangement explained below.[7]

The imposed institutional change to be explored here comes from action of the village council, which has three options: (1) a bargained solution among all five farmers; (2) a tax imposed selectively on certain marketing options; and (3) a strict mandate declaring which shall be the market day.

The Negotiated Solution

Imagine that the four farmers are able to enlist the aid of the village council in their efforts to prevent the defection of the tomato farmer. The total value of the Saturday-only option has already been demonstrated ($40 versus $37) and so the problem comes down to the level and incidence of transaction cost. If the other four can persuade the council to pay these costs then a solution similar to that with zero transaction costs is possible. But, of course, someone must pay these costs and so this represents a mere shift of cost incidence from the farmers to the village council, and ultimately to those who support the village with their taxes.

Consider the situation in which the village council, because of its existing administrative structure, can accomplish the same task as could the dispersed farmers for $3 (as opposed to the $4 that the farmers would incur). The village council is a more cost-effective agent for the group. The council, by incurring the costs of $3, could effect the same results as could the dispersed farmers for $4, but since the incidence of these costs no longer resides with the four farmers this outcome is identical to the earlier solution of the costless world. Imagine, rather, that the council collects from the four farmers the exact cost of its role as their agent. Now the net position for the four farmers is reckoned as:

Status quo net income to the four farmers	31
Transaction costs paid to the council	− 3
Minimum necessary payment to tomato farmer	− 2
	26

Here the net position of the four farmers who prefer Saturday-only markets, and of the tomato farmer who prefers to market on both Saturdays and Wednesdays, renders them all indifferent as between whether or not the tomato farmer markets only one day per week, or both days. This is shown in table 4.9. The above solution illustrates the possible outcomes when the incidence of transaction costs is not

Table 4.9   A Vulnerable Coordination Problem with Reduced Transaction Costs

| | *Other farmers* | | |
	Wednesday	Saturday	Both
Tomato farmer Wednesday	3,25	4,15	4,17
Saturday	5,12	9,31 [11,26]	6,20
Both	10,15	11,26	12,22

relevant to those involved in the negotiated convention, or when a third party is a more cost-effective participant in the negotiations. Here, as earlier, the village council has acted as a facilitative mechanism to protect not only the interests of the four farmers, but the total value of the market as well. It is possible that the level of transaction costs incurred by the village council would be as large as those incurred by the four farmers acting independently ($4) in which case there would be nothing to prevent the defection of the tomato farmer.

The Tax Solution

It is still possible that the persistent four farmers could convince the village council to impose a tax on anyone wishing to market produce more than once per week in the village; after all the market results in traffic congestion and other costs to the village. If the tax scheme were followed it would yield a payoff structure as shown in table 4.10, where a tax of $3 is assumed for those who plan two marketings per week.

Table 4.10   A Vulnerable Coordination Problem Restored to the Status Quo with a Tax

| | *Other farmers* | | |
	Wednesday	Saturday	Both
Tomato farmer Wednesday	3,25	4,15	4,17 [4,5]
Saturday	5,12	9,31	6,20 [6,8]
Both	10,15 [7,3]	11,26 [8,14]	12,22 [9,10]

The Mandate Solution
The final option is one that must be invoked in cases where neither preferences nor economic incentives will be decisive. Imagine that the other farmers manage to convince the village council to restrict markets to but one day a week. Further assume that Saturday will continue to be the chosen day since the total value of the market (that is, the aggregate net benefits to the five farmers) is greatest for the Saturday-only option. In both the incentives and mandated options the economic interests of the tomato farmer have been sacrificed to the group interests of all farmers. The interactive effects of having all five farmers at the market on the same day, but only once a week, represent positive external economies to the group, although one of the members is made worse off than otherwise.

Notice that the situation being depicted here is analogous to those situations of common property resources where any individual member of the group may have an economic incentive to defect from the evolved management convention (or entitlement structure). In grazing situations the convention is the stint, the agreement to withhold animals from the pasture at agreed-upon times. Here it is an agreement to go to market one day per week, and when the others go. But the concepts are the same, and the solutions open to the group are similar. In the market-day example an evolved convention, when put under pressure, will be transformed into an entitlement structure (where the tomato farmer has a duty to go to market but once a week – and when the other four go), or the farmers will dissolve as a decision group and each will do as he wishes given the rights structure. It is easy to imagine that over time it would be economically optimal to hold more than one market day, and for the farmers to pick and choose as they wish. Additionally, as transportation costs fall other more distant farmers may become relevant players in the game. However, the constrained choice of but one market day was, at one time, economically efficient for the group (and for the villagers) even though the tomato farmer and his customers had other wishes.

The issue under consideration here is that aggregate income is maximized in the face of constraints on individual economic agents – an idea that often gets lost in the celebration of *laissez faire*. *Laissez faire* does not mean that each does what he/she wishes; anarchy is not the road to aggregate economic well-being, or to maximum social welfare. It has been illustrated here that what started out as a situation of convergent choices for a market day based on aggregate net income evolved, under new economic conditions and potential opportunities, into a situation in which one participant wanted to defect; that defection constituting a Pareto-inferior outcome since one person's gain (that of the tomato farmer) was more than offset by the losses of the other four. It is economically efficient for the tomato farmer to be prevented from going to the village on the second day. The institutional transactions that originally resulted in the agreement to (the convention of) Saturday as the sole marketing day, and the subsequent institutional transactions that resulted in the evolution of a more formal entitlement structure, are examples of institutional transactions that contribute to economic efficiency. This is illustrated in conventional terms by figure 4.1. The two production possibility frontiers reflect the two institutional arrangements, with the exterior one representing the Saturday option, and the interior one representing the two-day option. The one-day market is seen to be everywhere superior to the alternative on productive efficiency grounds, but the two are Pareto non-comparable in a distributional sense.

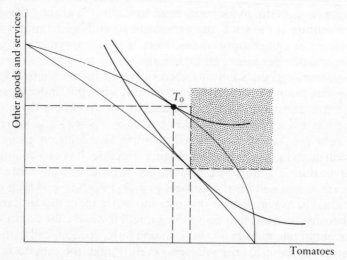

Figure 4.1   Institutional Arrangements and Allocative Efficiency

Now imagine that the tomato farmer, being persistent, managed to prevail on the village council and to obtain the right to begin a Wednesday market, even though aggregate economic efficiency was not well served thereby.[8] Figure 4.1 shows a situation that I will, in chapter 5, describe as a redistribution of economic advantage. It is, in the more conventional terminology, rent-seeking behavior in that the tomato farmer has used scarce resources that could otherwise go to the production of tomatoes, to negotiate with the village council to be allowed to come to market twice per week. Because the other farmers lose thereby, as do consumers since the Saturday-only market maximizes value, this situation is not properly characterized as merely redistributing a given social dividend (pure income redistribution) since scarce resources are required to effectuate the change. It is properly regarded as a redistribution of economic advantage in the direction of the tomato farmer, and away from the other merchants and consumers.

Now consider a different phenomenon that I will call *reallocating economic opportunity*. One starts with the need to disaggregate the social welfare function to understand that the social position of tomato farmers is now a policy objective, where this was not so before. That is, start with the idea expressed in figure 4.2 in which the social importance of the class of all farmers is no longer undifferentiated, but rather the tomato farmer is to be singled out for special notice.

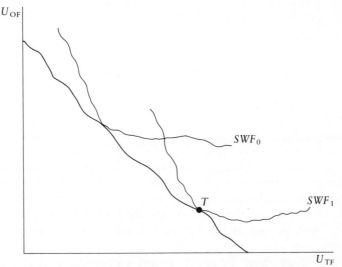

Figure 4.2   Two Possible Social Welfare Functions

The recognition of a new social welfare function (SWF_1) has its practical importance in the identification of new social indifference curves, now reflecting the fact that the income level of tomato farmers is of policy relevance, along with the other items that were formerly incorporated in the social utility function and, therefore, in social indifference curves. Point T in figure 4.2 maps into point T' in figure 4.3. Point T', lying on the interior production possibilities frontier of figure 4.1, and also lying on the new social indifference curve U_1, depicts the new efficient point.

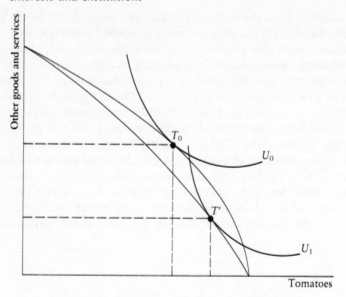

Figure 4.3   Productive and Social Efficiency

Point T' cannot be considered inefficient, for it (T') has as much claim to efficiency as does T_0 in figure 4.1. The difference is that economic efficiency is properly understood to reflect the most effective way of attaining collective goals or objectives, whatever they may be. If all that matters is efficiency within the village market then economic efficiency is defined in terms of the net income arising from a market policy of but one day per week. If tomato farmers and their customers become a special social concern then economic efficiency can no longer simply be reckoned as the net monetized income from the village market.

This change from T_0 to T' is not inefficient, it is not merely redistributing income, nor is it rent seeking. T' represents an economically efficient *reallocation* of economic opportunity. The economy is at a new socially efficient point (T' in figure 4.3) that recognizes the new social welfare function (SWF_1 of figure 4.2), and this yields a new social utility function and social indifference curve in figure 4.3 (U_1 as opposed to U_0). By giving appropriate attention to the possible nature of the social welfare function and social indifference curves it is possible to offer new insights into collective action that modifies choice sets. Such analysis would move beyond the simplistic orthodox dichotomies where all institutional changes either are in the interest of allocative efficiency, or merely redistribute income. Reallocating economic opportunity is entirely consistent with social efficiency, and there are, not surprisingly, both efficient and inefficient ways to effect that reallocation. This will be developed more completely in chapter 5.

III SUMMARY

The matter of preferences, choices, and institutions is central to the study of collective action and public policy. Individuals have preferences over the institutional arrangements that define their choice sets, and they have preferences over choices made from within those choice sets. The economist's job is to attempt to understand the structure of individual and aggregate preferences over the nature of institutional arrangements, and then to understand preference for choices from within those sets. This will imply a more careful consideration of individual and collective expressions of who counts – that is, of the social welfare function pertinent to any collectivity.

It also implies that more attention must be paid to the subtle yet important distinction between policy instruments and policy objectives. A policy objective is found in the utility function of the relevant decision maker(s), whereas policy instruments are not reflected there. Social efficiency must be understood to be defined with respect to objectives. Most economists will feel comfortable with the position that for each particular institutional structure – by which is meant the structure of resource endowments – there is at least one efficient resource allocation plan. That means, equally, that efficiency must be measured against something, since benefits and costs only obtain their meaning from the purposes being sought. Social efficiency can be measured as the extent to which social objectives are achieved with the minimum necessary sacrifice of valuable inputs – however denominated.

The conventional approach has been to treat only monetized gains and losses, since these presumably reflected – or at least could be made commensurate with – volitional exchange values arising from markets. Moreover, some believed that this approach made economists objective policy scientists. However, a belief in the market, and the social significance of exchange prices observed there, is as much a value judgment as is a belief in the social beneficence of central planning. This should not be taken as a defense or a denigration of either of these mechanisms for organizing economic activity. But the fact that they are both predicated upon a belief system cannot be denied. As economists become more conscientious in recognizing the critical distinction between policy objectives and policy instruments, it will become easier to understand that institutional transactions, and so institutional change, are capable of increasing productive efficiency, of distributing income in some socially more desirable manner, of reallocating economic opportunity to achieve social efficiency in line with social objectives, or of redistributing economic advantage to suit the whims of those who are able to manipulate the state in their behalf. These situations will be elaborated in the following chapter.

NOTES

1 Field (1979) has written on the difficulty in applying models designed to address the former question to those issues pertinent to the latter question.

2 In criticizing the "new household economics" of Gary Becker, it has been observed that: "Any actual choice can be accommodated in the conventional theory of consumer behavior because of the indeterminacy of the preferences that give rise to it. Even holding expectations constant through the assumption of perfect information will not take up enough slack, for there is no way to pin down tastes within the theory. Moreover, there seems to be no other theory in which economically exogenous tastes are endogenous. There is no prospect of a psychological theory of preferences that will enable us to identify changes in them independently of the identification of beliefs, either. This is the source of the apparent empirical emptiness of the conventional theory of consumer behavior. Therefore, matters are worse than Becker supposes. It is not just that there is no psychological theory of tastes independent of the assumptions of economic theory; there cannot be one." (Rosenberg 1985, p. 53)

3 Non-zero entries could easily be put in the off-diagonal cells without changing the nature of the choice problem as long as the diagonal cells dominated.

4 Cheung (1983) tells the story of boat pullers along China's canals and rivers prior to the communist regime. A group of laborers would hire themselves out to the owners of boats and appoint one of their own to whip them and monitor their effort as they pulled.

5 If the process still leaves some readers concerned simply substitute "Old McDonald" for the other four farmers and imagine that this farmer produces potatoes, onions, cabbage, and chickens. Then the game is between the tomato farmer and Old McDonald, and such two-person comparisons should be less worrisome.

6 Imagine that the two suspected criminals, just like the farmers, had reached an agreement about behavior. However, the incentive structure determined by the prosecuting attorney, or the market conditions and the resulting economic benefits, made defection from the agreement quite irresistible.

7 I am grateful to Al Schmid for this observation.

8   This would be an instance in which a Pareto-irrelevant externality for the group was nonetheless of considerable policy relevance – particularly to the unhappy tomato farmer who wished to gain, even if at the expense of the other four.

Part II

Institutional Change

5
Institutional Transactions

If the contemporary critics of orthodox theory can be
accused of not appreciating the importance of a coherent
theoretical structure and of understanding the resiliency and
absorptive capacity of prevailing orthodox theory, the
defenders of orthodoxy can be accused of trying to deny the
importance of phenomena with which orthodox theory deals
inadequately and at the same time overestimating the
potential ability of models within the orthodox framework
somehow to encompass these phenomena.

Nelson and Winter,
An Evolutionary Theory of Economic Change

I THE ECONOMY AND INSTITUTIONAL CHANGE

In previous chapters I was concerned with institutional arrangements
as they determine individual and group choice sets. In chapter 4 I
introduced the distinction between institutional transactions that
redistribute economic advantage and institutional transactions that
reallocate economic opportunity. These two classes of institutional
transactions are said to be distinct from the conventional view that
collective action and institutional transactions either increase economic
efficiency, or else merely redistribute income. In this chapter I will offer
a more complete treatment of these four kinds of institutional
transactions, and I will clarify the distinctions among them. This
material will be preceded, however, by a discussion of institutions and
the concept of efficiency.

The early work of John R. Commons centered on the idea that the
transaction is the essence of economics (Williamson 1985). In more

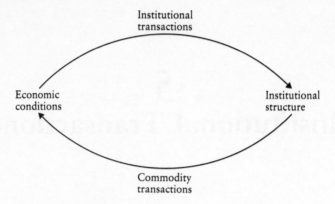

Figure 5.1 **Institutional and Commodity Transactions**

recent times the focus has seemed to shift to a dominant concern for the objects of exchange; commodities rather than people have taken center stage. I have earlier introduced the notions of *commodity transactions* and *institutional transactions* in order to suggest that economic behavior is about more than the exchange of goods and services; economics is also about the definition and delimitation of individual and group choice sets. Those choice sets are defined by, and are continually being modified by, institutional transactions. It is these institutional transactions that yield new institutional arrangements.

Just as these institutional arrangements will determine the nature and scope of commodity transactions, the economic conditions at any moment will be important in determining the institutional transactions that will occur, and hence the institutional arrangements that will emerge. When economic and social conditions change then the existing institutional structure may no longer be appropriate. In response to these new conditions, members of society will undertake efforts to modify the institutional arrangements (either conventions or entitlements) so as to bring them in line with the new scarcities, the new technological opportunities, new distributions of income or wealth, or the new tastes and preferences. Those activities undertaken in response to new economic conditions, with the intent of establishing new institutional arrangements, are called *institutional transactions*. Those activities undertaken within a given institutional structure are referred to as *commodity transactions*.[1] While I refer to both of these phenomena as transactions, the more conventional area of transactions concerns two or more economic agents coming together to bargain within a well-defined institutional environment. The relation between the economic conditions in a society at any given moment and the structure of institutions can be considered with the aid of figure 5.1.

In the domain of institutional transactions one encounters the arena in which the institutional preconditions of the market are determined. Or more properly stated, one encounters the domain in which the institutional preconditions of exchange are determined – with markets being one process whereby that exchange occurs. The obvious interest in institutional transactions is found in the fact that institutional change will occur at the level of the status quo structure of expectations, or the prevailing structure of rights, duties, privilege, and no rights which defines current commodity transactions. Institutional change is, therefore, about changes in the relations that define individuals' choice sets.

It is tautological that choices must be made from within the choice set available at that moment; you play with the cards you have been dealt. Indeed, many regard this matter as precisely the essence of economics – constrained choice. But choices and preferences are two distinct psychological entities. The issues explored here will concern the distinction between *preferences that guide institutional transactions, and preferences that guide commodity transactions*. It is here that one can explain the shared social preference for a system of, say, property rights and yet observe a preference for contravening that structure when it is in someone's private interest to do so.

The *preferences* that lead to institutional transactions are those that will give expression to particular *interests*, which then show up as *claims* against the prevailing institutional structure. The intent of such claims is, in the final analysis, to modify existing *institutional arrangements* in order to provide a new and different structure of *conventions* or *entitlements*. It is this structure of conventions and entitlements that forms the legal foundations of the market and its commodity transactions. The concern in this chapter will be to provide a model of four kinds of institutional transactions that lead to new institutional arrangements.

II   INSTITUTIONS AND EFFICIENCY, AGAIN

The primary concern in this section is with the way in which the status quo influences judgments regarding the economic efficiency of a planned institutional transaction. This will be discussed in terms of the choice problem and the status quo, and then in more general terms of institutional innovation and the efficiency implications of that change.

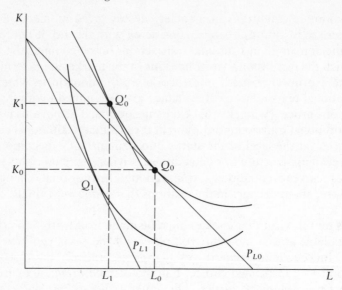

Figure 5.2　Labor and Capital Use under Two Entitlement Regimes

A　The Choice Problem and the Status Quo

The impact of the status quo on the choice problem in institutional transactions can be illustrated with an example concerning the safety conditions in coal mines. Consider an existing institutional arrangement that implies no liability on the part of mine owners for accidents that lead to injury or death to miners. To depict the efficient mix of labor and capital in the mine, consider figure 5.2. Here the status quo situation, indicated by the relative price of labor and capital depicted by P_{L0}, will imply an efficient use of each at K_0 and L_0, respectively.

Under the status quo institutional arrangement laborers must assume the full risk of work-related accidents, and hence there is no incentive on the part of mine owners to invest in costly and "inefficient" safety precautions. As long as labor is abundant relative to jobs in the mines (or elsewhere), the mine owners will have an incentive to preserve the status quo.[2] Given only this information, the economist would look at this situation and pronounce it an efficient use of labor and capital.

Now imagine a different institutional arrangement, one in which laborers hold a property right in their future labor power. This right obligates the mine owners to contribute to an annuity per unit of time worked so as to indemnify workers and their survivors in the event of an accident. In the language of entitlements developed in chapter 3, the mine owners formerly had privilege, and the laborers had no rights with respect to their (the laborers') future income stream. The new structure of entitlements is one of rights on the part of laborers, and duty for mine owners to indemnify those rights if necessary. Leaving aside for now the process by which this new institutional arrangement might evolve, the new relative cost of capital and labor would be depicted in figure 5.2 by the line P_{L1}. The efficient mix of labor and capital has been altered by this new institutional arrangement.

Those who felt that the status quo was the proper institutional structure will be quick to note that these new relative factor prices mean that mine output is reduced (Q_1 as opposed to Q_0), and that if the former output (Q_0') is to be restored, it will now require relatively more capital and less labor (K_1 and L_1).

But there is more to the story. For the first time there is an economic incentive for the mine owners to invest in safety equipment that will reduce the probability of accidents. Hence:

$$P_{L0} = \text{wages}$$

while

$$P_{L1} = \text{wages} + \text{annuity}$$

where the annuity is determined by the added costs for the miner if there should be an accident, weighted by the probability of accidents. If the mine owners can reduce accidents, there is a tradeoff in the size of the annuity that must be contributed for every hour's work in the mines. There will be a related efficiency calculation of the optimal level of investment in mine safety; the mine is now producing two products, coal and safe working conditions. Because safety can be thought of as a non-productive expenditure that must be undertaken, the investment in safety (its cost) will be balanced against the benefits of safety to the mine owner (a reduction in the required annuity contribution to the miners' fund). This is depicted in figure 5.3. Notice that increased safety in the mines can only be purchased with ever-increasing expenditures. This is the marginal cost curve of safety expenditures (MC_S). Notice also that the marginal benefits of (the demand for) increased safety (MB_S) fall as ever-greater safety precautions are undertaken. The "efficient level of safety" occurs where the two curves cross (S^*).

The solution at S^* still represents a synthesis of monetary and non-monetary benefits to the miners of increased safety as represented by MB_S. The new institutional arrangements have forced the owners of mines to be responsible for the safety conditions and the future

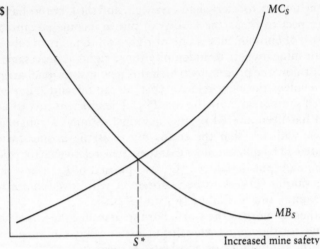

Figure 5.3 The "Efficient" Level of Safety

income-earning potential of their workers. It is this institutional change that causes the curve MB_S to be relevant. Under the prior legal situation, MB_S was simply a *claim* on behalf of the *interest* of the laborers, but it was without meaning because there was no force of law to give it effect. Under the new institutional structure, where mine owners are bound by law to protect the labor power of their workers, the claim reflected in MB_S becomes an entitlement. The legal situation of mine owners was, before the institutional change, one of *privilege*, while that of the laborers was one of *no right*. Following the institutional change laborers obtained *rights* over their future labor power, and mine owners obtained a *duty* to indemnify those rights. Suddenly MB_S becomes relevant to the mine owners and they are forced to search for an increased level of safety.

Some will object to the above by suggesting that there is no reason for the government to impose a new legal situation on coal mines. They would advocate, instead, letting mine owners select various combinations of safety and wages to allow mine workers to choose the wage–safety regime that maximized their utility. Several observations seem in order in response to this position. First, it would seem to place faith in the assumption that there are a large number of mine owners willing to provide a continuum of working conditions from which laborers can choose. Secondly, it assumes perfect information and costless mobility among laborers such that they can easily switch among regimes. Finally, and perhaps most seriously, it takes on faith the *laissez-faire* optimism that holds that owners of capital possess some natural right to define the working conditions of laborers who can take a particular job or leave it. To assume, because workers have the option to choose among several wage–safety regimes in some utility-maximizing fashion, that one has done the economically efficient thing is to reduce efficiency to an object of scorn. A reading of English social history during the Industrial Revolution ought to be required for all who see such wisdom in free-market solutions to working conditions.

One additional issue warrants discussion. The conventional view might be to undertake a benefit–cost analysis to determine whether greater safety in mines is efficient. If the status quo is one of unsafe mines, and it requires the agreement of mine owners (or those politicians beholden to the interests of mine owners) to make them safer, then the burden of proof is on the laborers (and those representing their interests) to show that safer mines are also more efficient mines. As long as mine owners doubt that, and are able to stall institutional change in search of yet better evidence, the status quo carries considerable inertia.[3]

The issue is one of how to define efficiency, and which point – the status quo or some alternative institutional arrangement – will provide the basis for the efficiency calculation. Who will speak for the miners? Must they have no legitimate claim unless they can bribe the mine owners to invest in greater safety? It seems worthy of analytical attention that laborers should have to purchase something which an alternative legal environment would grant to them free. Under the status quo, if they are unable to raise enough money to bribe the mine owners into providing a safer workplace, some would then quite cavalierly suggest that safety conditions must be optimal as they are. The presence of a notional demand for safety – or the inability to meet the necessary reservation price of the mine owners – is taken as sufficient evidence of the efficiency, and, by implication, optimality, of the status quo.

Of course mine owners, and other entrepreneurs, will seek institutional innovation when the benefits of change exceed the costs of change, but the status quo institutional environment defines what is a relevant cost. In the absence of action on behalf of miners by the state, those costs of an accident borne by laborers are simply not relevant to the decision calculus of the mine owners. In the Panglossian language of Buchanan and Stubblebine (1962), such inconveniences to laborers and their families are merely "Pareto-irrelevant externalities." The venerable distinction between allocative efficiency and redistribution leaves the economist without any concepts and language to describe the mine safety problem. Is it selfish rent seeking and mere income redistribution? Is it a move toward allocative efficiency?

B *Institutional Innovation and Efficiency*

One accepted approach to the matter of institutional change would be to determine whether or not the potential gainers from a change would be able to compensate those who had lost from such a change. If such compensation were possible, even though it does not actually occur, and if there is then any residual for the potential gainers after their hypothetical compensation to the losers, then the change satisfies the conditions of a potential Pareto improvement. Consider the following expression to reflect the discounted present value of the change under discussion:

$$V = -C_M + \sum_{t=1}^{T} \frac{(B_t - C_t)_M + (B_t - C_t)_L}{(1+i)^t} \tag{5.1}$$

where:

V is the net present value of the change

C_M is the initial cost for increased safety made in time $t = 0$

$(B_t - C_t)_M$ is increased net income accruing to mine owners arising from the higher morale and productivity of laborers attributable to the new safer working conditions

$(B_t - C_t)_L$ is increased net income accruing to laborers arising from the new improved safety conditions

i is the social rate of time preference

t is the time stream with final value T

If there is to be an economic surplus leading to an institutional change the following condition must be met:

$$\sum_{t=1}^{T} \frac{(B_t - C_t)_L}{(1+i)^t} > C_M - \sum_{t=1}^{T} \frac{(B_t - C_t)_M}{(1+i)^t} \tag{5.2}$$

In other words, the present-valued net benefits to the laborers must exceed the present-valued net benefits to the mine owners for having made the expenditure in greater safety. If this condition holds then it represents a potential Pareto improvement and aggregate efficiency would be enhanced by the institutional change. This condition can also be expressed as:

$$PVNB_L > C_M - PVNB_M \qquad (5.3)$$

The problem comes in ascertaining exactly how much laborers will benefit by various levels of safety, and also what will be the ultimate impact on the net benefit stream over time to the mine owners. Moreover, being content with *potential* as opposed to *actual* compensation minimizes the practical difficulties associated with the presence of transaction costs that fall differentially on the laborers as opposed to the mine owners. That is, the status quo requires that the laborers initiate the expensive and tedious process of gathering information about the costs and benefits of safety measures, the negotiation of a new safety regime, and the enforcement of that regime. It is unlikely that the mine owners would pay any of these costs, and so the workers would be required to incur additional expenses in order to alter an institutional environment that only they seem to dislike. When transaction costs are admitted to the analysis, condition (5.3) becomes:

$$PVNB_L - TC > C_M - PVNB_M \qquad (5.4)$$

This should make it clear that the presence of transaction costs will serve to act as a deterrent to change that must be initiated by the laborers. Finally, reliance on the *potential* Pareto improvement means that there is no need to worry about exactly how it is that the laborers are to acquire the necessary capital to compensate the mine owners.[4] But these operational and empirical problems are minor compared to the conceptual problem that gives inertia to the status quo structure of entitlements, even assuming the interest is confined to potential, as opposed to actual, compensation.

Consider the counterfactual status quo institutional structure, one in which laborers have an entitlement to their future income stream. The problem then is one of attempting to determine whether or not it is a potential Pareto improvement to alter that structure. There would still be interest in knowing about the present-valued net benefits from the two situations, but now it is unlikely that any initial investment comparable to the C_M from equation (5.4) would be required. That is, if the safety conditions in the mine are to be changed it would not imply the expenditure of funds to destroy the safety measures already in place. Existing safety devices would simply be allowed to deteriorate and, over time, to become ineffective. The absence of these initial costs means that the problem would be formulated as one in which safety conditions would be allowed to deteriorate if

$$PVNB_M - TC > - PVNB_L \qquad (5.5)$$

That is, if the present-valued net benefits to the mine owners, less their necessary transaction costs (since it is they who would be interested in altering the status quo), were in excess of the loss to the laborers. But how can one measure the present-valued net benefits to the laborers and the mine owners? The answer requires a brief return to the situation in which the status quo institutional arrangement is one of no safety precautions in the mines. Recall that the conventional efficiency calculation would be to see if the value to the laborers of enhanced safety was in excess of the required safety investments (C_M), plus the present-valued net benefits that would accrue to the mine owners $(PVNB_M)$. This latter component $(PVNB_M)$ may be positive or negative. If it is positive it implies that the annual operating costs of the new safety equipment were more than offset by the value of the annual increase in coal production made possible by a more satisfied workforce, and fewer shutdowns because of safety-related problems. If it is negative it implies that the annual operating costs of the new safety equipment exceeded the incremental value of coal that could be produced.

The estimation of C_M is seen to be a strict engineering problem, and the estimation of $PVNB_M$ is concerned with the economic value of the annual stream of coal produced net of the increased annual costs made necessary by the safety devices now in place. Under either institutional arrangement, that is, regardless of whether the status quo is an unsafe or protected mine, the estimate of $PVNB_M$ would be the same; there is no reason to suppose that it would differ under either institution. This can be seen by noting that it consists of two elements: (1) changes in coal output; and (2) changes in the operating and maintenance (O & M) costs of the mine. The O & M costs would increase for the safer mine constituting a cost element in $PVNB_M$, while the increased value of coal production could either exceed these new costs or fall short of them. If it is assumed that a safer mine leads to an increase in coal production because of higher morale and fewer shutdowns for safety concerns, then the change to a safe mine would yield $PVNB_M > 0$.

Starting from a safe mine and considering an institutional change to allow it to become less safe would then be seen to represent a benefit to the owner since he/she would not be required to incur the added O & M costs. There would be a concomitant cost to the owner stemming from the reduction in the value of output owing to lower worker morale and more frequent interruptions of work because of unsafe working conditions. Either way the components of $PVNB_M$ remain unchanged, although in the one instance $PVNB_M$ may be positive (since it is a *net* value), and in the other negative.

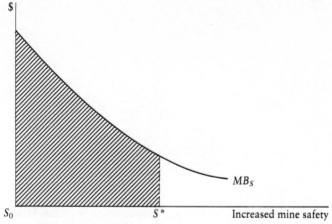

Figure 5.4   Willingness to Pay for Mine Safety

But what of the conceptual problems with $PVNB_L$? The curve MB_S in figure 5.3 represents a demand curve for safety by laborers. This reflects their willingness to pay for increased safety in the workplace and we may regard this as their private value of increased safety. Their total willingness to pay for increased safety would be regarded as the shaded area in figure 5.4. If one is considering an institutional change as regards greater mine safety then this discounted willingness to pay on the part of laborers becomes $PVNB_L$. It is this magnitude that will then be compared with the necessary investment costs (C_M) and with the magnitude of $PVNB_M$. Referring back to condition (5.3), or (5.4) if transaction costs are to be included, it is a potential Pareto improvement if those conditions are met; if not then it is inefficient to improve upon mine safety.

Now start from a status quo of a safe mine and inquire about the conditions under which it would be efficient for there to be less safety. Under this starting position the question that is relevant to the laborers is rather different from the one that was relevant under the other status quo. No longer is one interested in their demand for safety (what they would be willing to pay). The relevant question now is what they would require by way of compensation to forgo that which is legally theirs (a high degree of safety). One has, therefore, not a demand curve which will give total willingness to pay for safety, but a *reservation curve* that illustrates what they would require in compensation to give up the status quo safety regime; the reservation curve maps their reservation price at each level of possible safety, commencing with the status quo. It would look as depicted in figure 5.5.

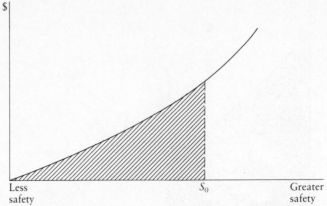

Figure 5.5   Willingness to Accept Compensation for Less Mine Safety

The reservation curve depicts how the laborers view the increased psychic and financial costs of diminished safety in the workplace, and the area under the curve is the total willingness to accept compensation for having to work in conditions that are less safe than the status quo (S_0). Unlike the demand curve for safety, which depicts how much they would be willing to pay for greater safety, the reservation curve is dependent not upon their current level of income but rather upon their more genuine (that is, unmodulated by their current income) preferences for safety. The Willig (1976) result on the similarity of the magnitude of consumer's surplus for the two situations would seem not to be pertinent here. It would be hard to argue that the amount of money at stake for the miners represents a "small" part of their total income; indeed if they hold no other job it represents the totality of their income.

Because willingness to pay for greater mine safety (WTP) is not equal to the willingness to accept compensation for less safety (WTA), the decision rule for institutional change is seen to have two different forms depending upon from where one starts.

Under the status quo of no safety procedures (or investments) in the mines the conceptual and empirical base of $PVNB_L$ is the laborers' willingness to pay for greater safety (WTP). Under the status quo of safe mines the conceptual and empirical base for $PVNB_L$ is the laborers' willingness to accept compensation in order to work under more risky conditions (WTA). This yields the following:

Case I: unsafe mine   Here the decision problem concerning whether or not there should be an institutional change to make the mine more safe would be formulated as:

$$V = WTP_L - (C_M - PVNB_M) \qquad (5.6)$$

and an institutional change would meet the potential Pareto improvement condition if:

$$WTP_L > C_M - PVNB_M \qquad (5.7)$$

Case II: safe mine   Here the decision problem concerning whether or not there should be an institutional change to allow the mines to become less safe would be formulated as:

$$V = PVNB_M - WTA_L \qquad (5.8)$$

and an institutional change would meet the potential Pareto improvement condition if:

$$PVNB_M > WTA_L \qquad (5.9)$$

Combine equations (5.6) and (5.8) (since they both equal V) to form:

$$PVNB_M - WTA_L = WTP_L - C_M + PVNB_M \qquad (5.10)$$

which simplifies to:

$$WTA_L = C_M - WTP_L \qquad (5.11)$$

This means that the two status quo institutional arrangements would end up in the same ultimate institutional arrangement only if the necessary investment cost in moving from the unsafe conditions (C_M) were equal to $WTA_L + WTP_L$. That is, equation (5.11) is satisfied only if:

$$C_M = WTA_L + WTP_L \qquad (5.12)$$

In the absence of this heroic assumption, the status quo institutional structure will dominate the choice of the new institutional structure. In other words, there is no basis to the belief that the initial assignment of property rights does not matter for the ultimate outcome. The Coase theorem requires that transaction costs be zero, and that there be no income (or wealth) effects. Even if transaction costs are assumed to be zero, the mine safety problem is essentially about the wealth effects of alternative institutional arrangements (rights structures). There will obviously be a different safety regime in coal mines if miners must pay for greater safety than if they must be compensated to accept less safety.[5]

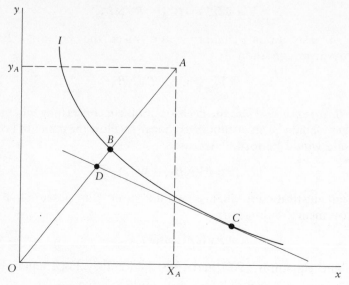

Figure 5.6   Technical and Price Efficiency

III   ON EFFICIENCY AND OPTIMALITY

In the subsequent section I will develop the theory of four kinds of institutional transactions – those that increase productive efficiency, those that reallocate economic opportunity, those that redistribute income, and those that redistribute economic advantage. That treatment will require a clear understanding of the various types of efficiency within economic theory. It will also involve a careful consideration of the concepts of the social welfare function, the social utility function, social indifference curves, and of social optimality.[6]

A   *Technical Efficiency*

Technical efficiency requires knowledge of the *efficiency production function*, or the output that a perfectly efficient firm could obtain from any particular combination of inputs. If a particular firm produces output A using inputs x_A and y_A, the isoquant I in figure 5.6 shows the various combinations of the two inputs that the *perfectly efficient firm* would require to produce the same level of output as the firm under study. Point B in the figure shows the perfectly efficient firm using the two inputs in the same proportion as the firm producing

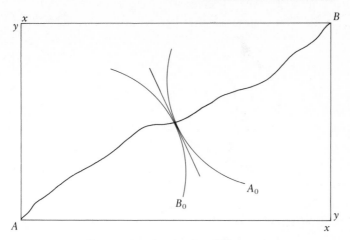

Figure 5.7   Productive Efficiency

at A. However, note that the required inputs of the perfectly efficient firm are only a fraction (OB/OA) of those required at A. Farrell (1957) has defined the technical efficiency of the firm producing at A as the fraction OB/OA, where $0 < OB/OA \leq 1$.

B   Price Efficiency

Of much more interest in economics is the relative use of x and y in relation to their respective prices. Price efficiency occurs at point C in figure 5.6. Points B and C both represent technical efficiency, but only one of them is price efficient. The costs of production at C are given by the fraction OD/OB of the costs of production at B; the fraction OD/OB represents the price efficiency of B. If the firm under study were to change its input mix until point C were reached its costs could be reduced by the factor OD/OB; this is the price efficiency of the firm.

If the firm under study (producing at A) were to become perfectly price efficient and technically efficient its costs would be a fraction (OD/OA) of their current level. This defines the overall efficiency of the firm; it is the product of both technical and price efficiency: $(OB/OA)(OD/OB) = OD/OA$. But price efficiency must also be concerned with the presumption that the observed price fully reflects all pertinent social costs, at the margin, of the use of any particular factor. If, as in the mine safety problem, the factor costs (in that case miners' wages) are not fully inclusive of relevant social costs

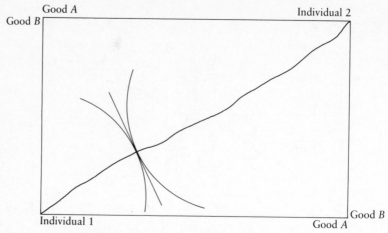

Figure 5.8   Consumption Efficiency

then one has nominal price efficiency as opposed to real price efficiency.

C   *Productive Efficiency*

Productive efficiency is achieved in an economy when for every firm the marginal rate of technical substitution among productive inputs is brought into equality with the ratio of the relevant marginal factor costs. The contract curve in input space is depicted for two firms (producing A and B) and for two factors (x and y) in figure 5.7. Every point along the contract curve depicts points of productive efficiency; each point is a Pareto-optimal combination of input use since it is impossible to reallocate the two factors without causing a reduction in output. There are an infinite number of productively efficient points along the contract curve.

D   *Consumption Efficiency*

The economy has reached an exchange optimum when the ratio of marginal rates of substitution across all possible goods and services is brought into equality with their relative prices, and these ratios hold for every consumer. Figure 5.8 depicts efficiency in exchange (consumption efficiency); again each point along the contract curve depicts a Pareto-optimal point. In line with earlier observations, recall that demand curves of relevance in matters of consumption reflect the

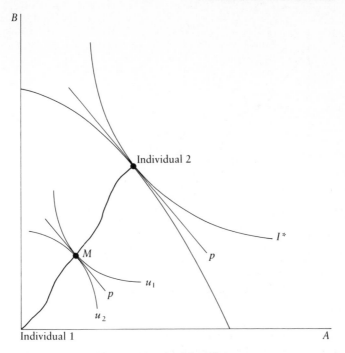

Figure 5.9   Social Efficiency

prevailing distribution of income. The efficiency in consumption must be understood to reflect a situation constrained by the possibility that income is not optimally distributed in society. An optimal distribution requires that the marginal utility of income be identical across all consumers.

E   *Social Efficiency*

Social efficiency, or the *top-level optimum* in Mishan's terminology, occurs when the domains of consumption and production are super-imposed. Given the total production of A and B in the economy, figure 5.9 shows a production possibilities frontier derived from the contract curve of figure 5.7; the points along the curve in figure 5.7 correspond to points along the production possibilities frontier in figure 5.9. The community indifference curve in figure 5.9 (labeled I^*) is congruent with the marginal rate of physical transformation of A into B (shown by the production possibilities frontier) and to the relative prices of A and B (shown by P).

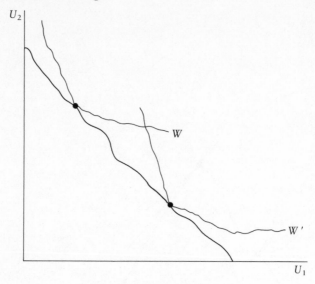

Figure 5.10   Social Welfare

Within goods space the relative prices for A and B are depicted (P), and there is a particular distribution of A and B as between the two consumers denoted by the point M. The particular bundle of A and B that is produced (and that is shown in figure 5.9) implies a particular level of aggregate utility as between the two individuals, and that utility for each will depend upon how the bundle is distributed between them. Individual 1 may not have a great deal and individual 2 may have much more; this would correspond to point M, where 1's utility is quite low while that of 2 is much greater.

Recall that the position of I^* is a reflection of the social utility that attaches to the presence of both commodities $(A$ and $B)$ in society; the slope at any point along I^* depicts the marginal utility of exchanging one for the other. The figure also depicts a relative price line that brings all of this into harmony. But, the demonstrated convergence of marginal rates of substitution, of marginal rates of transformation, and of relative prices, assumes perfection elsewhere in the economy.

F   Social Optimality

The existence of the bundle of A and B gives rise to the contract curve in goods space in figure 5.9, which then maps into a utility possibilities frontier in utility space (U_1, U_2) as shown in figure 5.10. If there were a different bundle of *A* and *B* being produced, it would result in a different position on the production possibilities frontier of figure 5.9, and consequently a different contract curve in goods space in that figure. This different structure would then yield a different utility possibilities frontier in figure 5.10.

The difficult issue in public policy is to determine the nature of the pertinent social welfare function *W*. As reflected in figure 5.10 it is a statement about whose interests count, those of individual 1, or those of individual 2. The somewhat standard practice in policy analysis is to suggest that the economist is unable to say what the social welfare function looks like, and therefore all that can be done is to show what action would be efficient and then let the politicians take actions in response to – or in recognition of – *their* perception of the social welfare function. But this passive role relegates the economist to the task of a social accountant. A more constructive role, and one to be elaborated later in this chapter, is to undertake a search for indications of the pertinent social welfare function and then to assess collective actions within the context of that ordering.

Recall that the social welfare function is a

> statement of a society's objectives in which the level of *social welfare* or well-being is represented as a function of the way in which resources are allocated. In the form in which this concept was introduced by A. Bergson, social welfare is generally made a function of the levels of *utility* of the individuals forming society. (Pearce 1981, p. 399)

The social welfare function is an aggregating mechanism for making collective decisions about what ought to be done. It is a mechanism for aggregating individual interests to arrive at collective decisions; it is concerned with whether or not it is more important to cater to the interests of individual 1 or to those of individual 2. In formal terms the social welfare function is expressed as:

$$W = f(U_1, U_2, \ldots, U_n)$$

where U_i represents the utility or happiness of individual *i*. Judgments about the social desirability of any particular action require clear knowledge of whether the relevant social welfare function is given by *W* or by *W'* in figure 5.10.

To some extent, Arrow's decisive proof of the impossibility of an aggregating mechanism that would satisfy a minimal number of reasonable assumptions has inhibited economists from playing a more central role in public policy. Arguments persist over the very existence of a social welfare function, and with respect to the belief that to talk of a social welfare function is to make interpersonal comparisons of utility. Since Lionel Robbins, economists have been apprehensive of making *interpersonal comparisons of utility* out of a fear that such comparisons entailed making value judgments. Blaug, in commenting on this fear, argues:

> statements about interpersonal comparisons of utility are not value judgments but merely untestable statements; they are either true or false.
> ... Value judgments may be untestable, but not all untestable statements are value judgments. (Blaug 1980, p. 137)

Collective decisions *are* made, and they are made frequently. To take any collective action at all is to presume a particular social welfare function, for collective action is simply a response to one or more groups' perception of what ought to be done. Moreover, collective decisions are undertaken with the explicit notion in mind of altering the position of one group of individuals with respect to another group. This recognition need not be viewed with suspicion, as it often is by some economists.

The homeless are cared for at the expense of those who must provide the financing for such programs, as are the elderly, the sick, and the handicapped. Nations have defense budgets that are too large according to some, and culture budgets that are too large for others; both situations benefit one group at the expense of others. The question for the policy analyst is one of discerning the articulated preferences coming from the political process, and then of helping to formulate programs and policies that will accomplish those objectives in an efficient fashion. The economist who does this is not compromising scientific objectivity by observing the collective expression of social goals and objectives. More will be said in this regard in chapters 8 and 9.

IV   INSTITUTIONAL TRANSACTIONS

The foregoing treatment of efficiency and optimality is offered as a prelude to the pending elaboration of four kinds of institutional transactions. Recall that conventional wisdom draws a distinction between those activities that are motivated by allocative efficiency (pie enlarging) and those that are redistributive in nature (merely redividing a fixed pie). Recently, there is increasing attention being paid to behavior that seems more serious in that it entails the use of scarce resources to compete over policies that simply redivide a fixed pie. Such activities are termed "rent seeking", and they are regarded as being unproductive. Such directly unproductive profit-seeking activities (DUPs)

> represent ways of seeking profits (income) by undertaking directly unproductive activities . . . that . . . yield pecuniary returns but produce no goods or services that enter a conventional utility function directly or indirectly. Insofar as such activities use real resources, they result in a contraction of the availability set open to the economy. Tariff seeking, lobbying, tariff evasion, and premium seeking for given import licenses . . . are all privately profitable activities. *However, their direct output is zero in terms of the flow of goods and services entering a conventional utility function.* (Bhagwati, Brecher, and Srinivasan 1984, pp. 17–18: emphasis added)

This clarification of rent-seeking behavior suggests an opportunity to explore institutional transactions in a new light. Specifically, the reference to goods and services "entering a conventional utility function" suggests a line of analysis that might illuminate a critical distinction between: (1) a situation in which a number of, say, shoe manufacturers organize to lobby for import restrictions on cheaper Italian shoes; and (2) a situation in which a number of mine laborers organize to lobby for greater mine safety. Both activities are examples of collective action to modify existing institutions and thus choice sets, and hence both activities are examples of institutional transactions. Moreover, both activities give the appearance of being strictly redistributive in that the import restriction redistributes income from consumers of shoes to domestic manufacturers, and increased spending for mine safety does not obviously increase the nation's output of marketed goods and services (mine output) but merely seems to make miners better off at the expense of consumers of coal and owners of mines. However, these two activities – as metaphors for large classes of collective action and institutional transactions – have several crucial conceptual differences that have not been fully recognized and incorporated into the theory of collective action.

At the intuitive level, the action by domestic shoe manufacturers to remove cheaper imports from direct competition is a pecuniary act intended to increase the market share and stabilize domestic profits. Collective action to restrict cheaper imports, if successful, will result in a *redistribution of economic advantage* in favor of domestic shoe manufacturers. With mine safety, this is an issue dominated by social attitudes and preferences about acceptable work conditions; satisfactory working conditions for miners in late 1900 are obviously different from those of the last century. It is possible to use conventional economic analysis to determine the efficient organization of a mine under several status quo safety regimes, but selecting a proper level of safety is a matter of social concern. Collective action to modify the safety of the workplace, if successful, will result in a *reallocation of economic opportunity* in favor of coal miners. The conceptual distinction between institutional transactions that redistribute economic advantage (import restrictions) and those that reallocate economic opportunity (mine safety) offers a way out of the usual box which holds that all collective action is either in the cause of efficiency, or merely redistributive.

I will offer a conceptual clarification of four types of institutional transactions. That is, institutional transactions will be seen to: (1) increase productive efficiency; (2) redistribute income; (3) reallocate economic opportunity; or (4) redistribute economic advantage.

A   Institutional Transactions
that Increase Productive Efficiency

The most familiar type of institutional transaction is that which alters choice sets in a way that leads to an undisputable increase in the monetized net social dividend. During the early days of gold and silver mining in the western United States there was great confusion about the exact boundaries of various claims,[7] there was uncertainty over enforcement of claims, and enforcement costs were exceedingly high (Libecap 1978). Each miner had something to gain by a more careful articulation of the property rights in minerals, even though a few of the more belligerent might prefer the anarchy of the status quo. The recognition of a need for a new institutional structure over minerals was driven by the recognized need for order and stability in the expectations and behaviors of the participants. Consider this situation as depicted in figure 5.11. Here there are two production possibilities frontiers, indicating the possible production of minerals and all other goods and services under poorly specified mining laws (A), and under the improved institutional environment (B) detailed by Libecap. One can illustrate how a more comprehensive mining law contributes to productive efficiency as the economy moves from point Q to Q^*, lowering the cost of minerals in the process. Notice that I depict social efficiency at both Q and Q^* although this is strictly by assumption.

Institutional transactions of this sort find their origin in the notion of conventions, and the coordination problem as developed in chapter 4. Here, all participants in an economic situation recognize that *some* system of property is preferable to anarchy (which is really a system

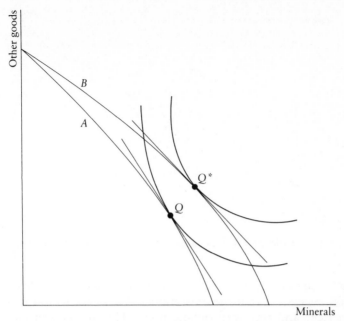

Figure 5.11   Institutional Transaction that Improves Productive Efficiency

of "might makes right"). A structure of institutions in the current example will be *informed by conventions* to the extent that all participants have shared preferences for a workable system that renders mining more efficient. But pressure on the members of the community of miners to defect from the convention increases as the potential economic benefits of defection increase. The convention will thus evolve into a structure of *entitlements* such that the rights and duties of each participant are clearly spelled out. The instability of conventions in the mining case drove the system toward a structure of entitlements. The total losses from the potential defection from the convention of just a few miners were sufficiently large that a more structured and enforceable system was required. Institutions as *entitlements* rather than as *conventions* provided the solution to the problem of anarchy in the new mining areas, and the evolved institutional structure led to clear increases in production from the mines.

B   Institutional Transactions that Redistribute Income

A different type of institutional transaction is one whose explicit purpose is to change the distribution of income.[8] Imagine a situation in which

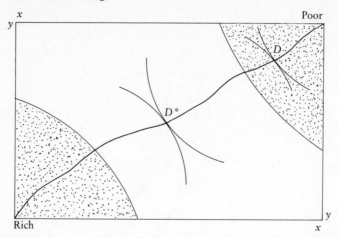

Figure 5.12   Institutional Transaction that Modifies Income Distribution

collective action is promoted to revise the income tax laws. The original concern is that the existing tax system seems too favorable to the rich, and too hard on the poor. The mechanism chosen is to raise significantly the marginal tax rate for the wealthy and remove a number of the poor from the tax rolls altogether. The impact of this institutional change can be depicted with the aid of an Edgeworth box where the monetary impacts are depicted in terms of altered consumption over time. The shaded areas in figure 5.12 represent extremities of the distributional possibilities that have been determined, through the political process, to be unacceptable. The status quo distribution is given by point D, while the new altered distribution, that will result from revisions in the tax system, is shown as point D^*.

Recall that the contract curve in exchange space maps out all points that are Pareto optimal and that the curve also defines all points that are considered efficient in exchange. Hence the various points along a contract curve are Pareto non-comparable and there is no un-ambiguous way to rank the social states defined by D and D^*. But societies are constantly undertaking actions that alter the distribution of income, and the matter can be understood by making reference to the quote above regarding DUP activities. That is, DUP activities seek to improve the economic position of someone by actions that "yield pecuniary returns but produce no goods or services that enter a conventional utility function directly or indirectly." (Bhagwati, Brecher, and Srinivasan 1984, p. 18)

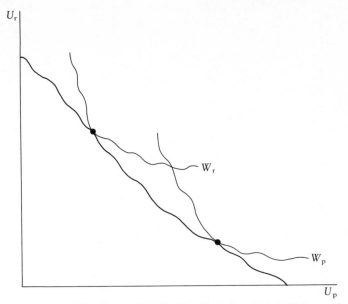

Figure 5.13   Social Welfare Functions for Two Possible Policies on Income Distribution

The issue of relevance here is that collective action to redistribute income is driven by individual and group utility functions that do clearly give weight to the net income position of different members of society. That is, members of a society are not indifferent to the income position of their compatriots and so actions that are taken to modify the distribution of income derive from individual utility functions. There are, to be sure, no conventional goods and services that enter such utility functions, but the distribution of income is a public good that clearly appears in individual and aggregate utility functions. Consider figure 5.13 in which two possible social welfare functions have been inscribed, one showing greater recognition of the interests of the poor (W_p), and another showing greater recognition of the interests of the rich (W_r).

Assume that the new tax law reflects a general recognition that the concerns of the poor now warrant more attention than previously, and hence there is a shift in the relevant social welfare function from W_r to W_p. The existence and recognition of W_p would be the engine of change that would drive the enactment of policies – for instance changes in marginal tax rates – to bring about a move from D to D^* in figure 5.12. Notice that while there are efficient and inefficient

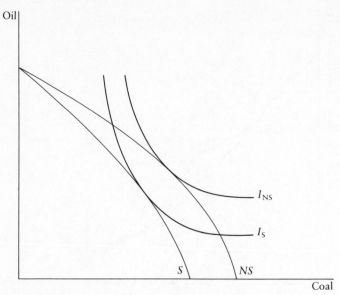

Figure 5.14 Two Safety Regimes in Coal Mining

ways – administratively – to alter the ultimate distribution of income, there is no efficient or inefficient distribution of income without a prior specification of social objectives regarding income distribution. It is this specification of social objectives that brings a shift in the relevant social welfare function from W_r to W_p.

C Institutional Transactions
that Reallocate Economic Opportunity

The third class of institutional transactions is concerned with the reallocation of economic opportunity. Recall that production possibilities frontiers obtain their meaning from the distribution of resource endowments and techniques available in an economy; the production possibilities frontier is also constrained by the prevailing structure of institutions since institutional arrangements determine resource endowments. There are infinitely many frontiers, each depicting a different structure of resources, technical abilities, and institutional arrangements in the economy. For instance in Muslim societies where women are generally not involved in the commercial sector, the production possibilities frontier will be different from a society in which female participation is more complete. The institutional arrangements that determine the nature and magnitude of the

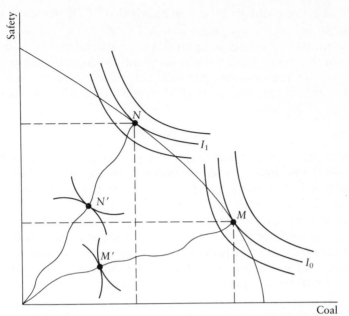

Figure 5.15   Production Relations in Coal Mining

commercial workforce will, *ipso facto*, determine the position and shape of the production possibilities frontier.

Recognizing the relation between institutional arrangements and production possibilities allows the construction of figure 5.14 in which are depicted production possibilities between coal and oil in an economy under two different safety regimes in coal mining. The two production possibilities frontiers depict the tradeoff under coal mining conditions that are safe (S), and under conditions that are not safe (NS).

It might be thought proper to inscribe social indifference curves as shown by I_S and I_{NS}, and then to conclude that safety laws reduce coal production, economic efficiency, and also social welfare. This would not be correct. To see this it is necessary to move beyond the simplicity of production possibilities frontiers and on to the domain of utility. We start by recognizing that the safety conditions in a coal mine represent the deliberate expenditure of funds for that purpose, as opposed to funds spent only for the production of coal. There is a production surface for both coal and for safety conditions. With a given total expenditure, more spent on safety means less available for mining coal. This can be depicted in familiar fashion as in figure 5.15. The figure should be understood to represent an aggregate of all coal production in a country rather than merely that of one particular mine, although the same concept applies to a single mine.

In contrast to the story of figure 5.14, greater safety in coal mining does not imply moving to a lower social indifference curve, but rather implies a different *structure* of social indifference curves. Recall that social indifference curves are derived from a social utility (*not* welfare) function of the form:

$$U = U(x, y, \ldots, m) \qquad (5.13)$$

where $(x, y, \ldots, m)$ reflects the bundle of goods and services available in society. This bundle of goods includes, in addition to coal, food, clothing, and other private goods purchased in commodity transactions, the constellation of public goods such as literacy, environmental quality, the net wealth position of members in society, the general state of human health, and work conditions of factories, farms, and mines. All of these comprise inputs into the general level of satisfaction of individuals in a society and so the position of the social indifference map must be seen as a reflection of prevailing attitudes about this full consumption set.

Citizens consume more than just private goods purchased in commodity transactions; we also consume collective goods that are purchased in institutional transactions. If social attitudes about child labor, the distribution of income, slavery, or general safety conditions in mines are such that these situations do not represent much concern, then there is one structure of social indifference curves. If, however, attitudes change and new tastes and preferences emerge about the desired consumption bundle then a different structure of social indifference curves is relevant. If working conditions in mines are not of much social significance then the relevant social indifference curves might be as depicted by I_0 in figure 5.15. As attitudes change about these matters then preferences for safety and humane working conditions will change and be depicted, perhaps, by a mapping structure such as I_1. Points M and N are both Pareto-optimal points since they lie on society's production possibilities frontier. Both are productively efficient output combinations of coal and safety, as are all possible points along the frontier. Moreover, both points are potentially socially efficient given the social objectives reflected by either I_0 or I_1. However, every point on the frontier, by being Pareto optimal, is also Pareto non-comparable.

Each of the two denoted bundles (M and N) has associated with it a contract curve in exchange space where it is possible to depict, for two individuals, various levels of satisfaction arising from the

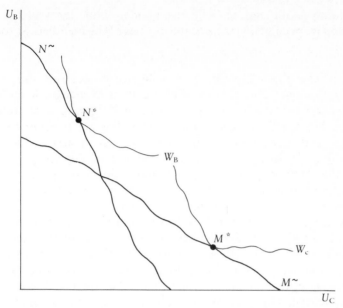

Figure 5.16   Mine Safety and Social Welfare for B and C

available quantities of coal and general safety conditions in the mines. Recall that one need not be a miner to have preferences for safety conditions in mines, just as one need not cavort in the great outdoors to have preferences about how wilderness areas should be protected and managed. Each of these two contract curves will map into (or yield) a utility possibilities frontier in utility space. I show two possibilities in figure 5.16. Curve $N^\sim$ is derived from output bundle N in figure 5.15, while curve $M^\sim$ is derived from bundle M. The two individuals in figure 5.16 have different preferences regarding the output of coal and the working conditions in mines. The preferences of Curmudgeon (U_C) reveal that coal availability and price matter much more than working conditions. On the other hand the preferences of Benevolent (U_B) indicate that rather more significance is attached to the conditions under which coal is mined. The point N^* in figure 5.16 corresponds to the combined utility levels shown as point N' in figure 5.15, while M^* corresponds to point M' in figure 5.15.

Judgments about social efficiency require that analysis be conducted against the backdrop of *some* social welfare function and its implicit social utility function. This is the business of the political process to determine what they shall be; recall that the social utility function of equation (5.13) is specified in terms of the bundle of goods and services (including public and/or collective goods), while the social welfare function is specified in terms of the utilities of the members of society. That is:

$$W = W(U_A, U_B, U_C, \ldots, U_n) \qquad (5.14)$$

The social welfare function is a collective choice rule that allows aggregation over the preferences of members in society. It should be understood to have a very special role in the problem of collective choice. Sen specifies four types of issues that are relevant to social choice: (1) the aggregation of individual *interests* to arrive at collective *decisions*; (2) the aggregation of individual *judgments* to arrive at collective *decisions*; (3) the aggregation of individual *interests* to arrive at *welfare judgments*; and (4) the aggregation of individual *judgments* to arrive at *welfare judgments* (Sen, 1982).

The use of a social welfare function as in figure 5.16 is concerned with the fourth problem – the aggregation of individual judgments to arrive at a collective welfare judgment. That is, the exact positioning of *the* social welfare function in figure 5.16 is a problem of deciding how to aggregate individuals' judgments of their own welfare into some collective rule. This requires that collective judgments be made on the strength and relevance of judgments made by the individuals in society – in this case Benevolent and Curmudgeon. The problem comes, obviously, in deciding whose interests will count in the aggregation of individuals' respective judgments about welfare. If the political process determines that the judgments of Benevolent are more relevant for collective choice (an indirect ratification of the interests of Benevolent) then the social welfare function is properly depicted by W_B in figure 5.16. Or, if it is decided that the judgments of Curmudgeon are more relevant for collective choice (again, an indirect ratification of the interests of Curmudgeon) then the appropriate social welfare function is depicted by W_C.

Regardless of which is chosen (and the choice can extend over an infinity of those not depicted in the figure), judgments regarding social efficiency – and ultimately social optimality – cannot be made until that choice has been taken. Once a social welfare function has been regarded as relevant, one can work back through all of the conventional welfare theory to derive the optimal allocation of factors of production, the optimal output bundle in society, and the optimal allocation of goods and services among individuals. But of course the problem is precisely one of knowing the appropriate social welfare function to inscribe in figure 5.16. The problem cannot be wished away by pretending that scientific objectivity is preserved if the economist computes what is "efficient" and leaves the political matters to others.

The redistribution of economic opportunity is seen, therefore, to be driven by the changing nature of attitudes and preferences in society as a whole. It is not something driven by the relentless pursuit of productive efficiency for the simple reason that for any given structure of institutions there are infinitely many productively efficient points along production possibilities frontiers; and there are infinitely many institutional possibilities as well. The only place to start is with some notion of the guiding vision behind the relevant social welfare function. When collective action is taken – and institutional transactions occur – in response to new social preferences then it is consistent with an altered vision of the relevant social welfare function. Institutional transactions that reallocate economic opportunity are represented by a realignment of new economic conditions to the newly articulated vision of whose interests count.

But there are instances in which collective action and institutional transactions occur quite at odds with any vision of the relevant social welfare function. There has been no new expression of preferences for different patterns of interaction and hence for different outcomes. In spite of this, certain interests will mobilize to undertake actions quite at odds with prevailing sentiments about whose interests count. I refer to this situation as one in which *institutional transactions redistribute economic advantage.*

D   Institutional Transactions that Redistribute Economic Advantage

The growing literature on rent-seeking behavior illustrates the manner in which scarce resources will be used to alter the product mix in society, but also to compete for the rents that are thereby created. The basic model of rent seeking comes from the work of Krueger (1974). Assume a situation in which labor is the only scarce factor available in some fixed magnitude (L^*). There is one good produced according to the production function $Y = aL$, where a is the average and marginal product of labor. A second good is imported at a fixed price P (in terms of Y). Individual consumers have identical tastes represented by a set of indifference curves that therefore reflect both individual and social preferences. The line FM in figure 5.17 is a consumption possibility frontier. Imports must be distributed and, if this were costless to accomplish, FM would accurately depict the full range of consumption possibilities along that locus. However, because the distribution of imports is not costless, the Krueger model depicts the cost of additional imports in terms of forgone domestic food production. Hence, the actual consumption possibility locus is shown as FM^*.

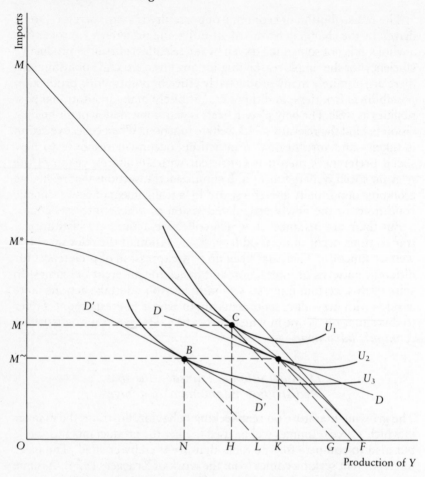

Figure 5.17 Import Restrictions and Rent Seeking

If community preferences are given by U_1 then social efficiency is found at point C. Free trade at C is optimal since the marginal rate of transformation between consumption of Y and imports is equal to the marginal rate of substitution in consumption. The price ratio given by FM indicates that OG is produced, imports are OM', consumption of Y is OH, and HG of Y is exported.

Now allow an import restriction to be imposed so that M' is reduced to $M^\sim$. As a result the domestic price of imports will rise (DD), as will the cost of their distribution. There is a welfare loss in moving from U_1 to U_2. Domestic production increases from OG to OJ,

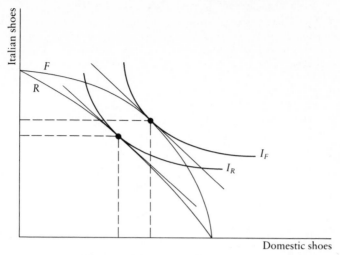

Figure 5.18 Import Restrictions

exports decline from *HG* to *KJ*, and consumption increases from *OH* to *OK*.

The restriction on imports gives economic value to those fortunate enough to have import licenses and so there evolves competition to acquire such licenses, or to protect licenses already held. This competition for licenses is the rent-seeking behavior that uses scarce resources to yield a new equilibrium at *B* – with even lower utility. A point such as *B* will be reached at the same level of imports (*OM* ˜) but there will be a smaller total production of *Y* (say, *OL*) arising from the devotion of resources to obtain valuable import rights. There will also be a reduced level of consumption of *Y* (*ON*), and less available for export (*NL*).

The rent arising from import restrictions would ordinarily be regarded as a redistribution from consumers to whomever was fortunate enough to receive it. However, the situation is more serious in light of the realization that some of the scarce labor resources will be allocated not to the production of *Y* but to the securing of licenses or shares of the restricted imports. The model can be recast in more familiar terms by referring back to the problem of cheaper Italian shoes being restricted from the market. There is a free-trade production possibilities frontier, and there is one that includes the allocation of resources toward the maintenance of import restrictions on Italian shoes. These are denoted as *F* and *R* in figure 5.18. The vertical axis labeled "Italian shoes" requires some explanation. That is, Italian shoes are clearly not

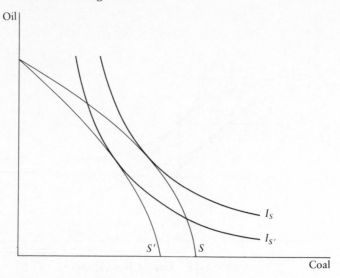

Figure 5.19   Redistribution of Economic Advantage

produced domestically and hence one might wonder about depicting a production possibilities frontier with the transformation of domestic shoes into Italian shoes. Recall that the production of Italian shoes is, in a sense, represented by the outflow of funds to Italy to purchase shoes and so represents a resource cost to the nation in terms of some other goods forgone. The rate at which Italian shoes can be transformed into domestic shoes is depicted as the rate at which these forgone goods could be transformed into domestic shoes.

An institutional transaction that results in the imposition of an import restriction alters the social production possibilities frontier from F to R, and results in a change in the relative prices of the two goods under consideration, and a corresponding loss in utility for society. The difference between institutional transactions that redistribute economic advantage and those that reallocate economic opportunity is to be found in the nature of the social utility function. In the mine safety problem there is a social utility function and so a structure of social indifference curves that revealed social efficiency to be consistent with greater safety conditions in mines (I_1 as opposed to I_0 in figure 5.15). In the matter of import restrictions on Italian shoes there is no social utility function (and corresponding social indifference curves) that reveals such restrictions to be socially desired and therefore social efficiency is not achieved with the restrictions; in figure 5.18, I_F and I_R belong to the same family of social indifference curves, whereas I_0 and I_1 in figure 5.15 are members of two different families.

The mine safety problem would become analogous to the shoe import problem if mine workers were able to achieve an outcome for which there is no argument in the social utility function. Imagine that laborers, through threat of a crippling strike, were able to extract work concessions to maintain total daily pay at its current level, but to reduce the work day from 8 hours to 6 hours. This could be depicted in a modified figure 5.14 to show a new (interior) production possibilities frontier (S') that would yield reduced production and a loss in social utility. This is shown in figure 5.19, where I_S and $I_{S'}$ (in contrast to the indifference curves in figure 5.14) belong to the same family of social indifference curves.

V   SUMMARY

I have argued here that there are four kinds of institutional transactions. The first concerns those instances in which institutional change is clearly in the interest of increasing net national income; the motivation and results are for improved productive efficiency. The increase in productive efficiency that results from such institutional transactions is not driven by changes in either the social utility function or the social welfare function. Rather, such changes are driven by changes in relative scarcities (prices) and not by changes in preferences, attitudes, or tastes. The second example concerns changes in the institutional environment that alter the distribution of income. This change in income will, over time, alter the allocation of resources in the economy through induced price effects, and the differential tastes and preferences of those with a higher level of disposal income as opposed to those from whom the income was taken (say, through higher marginal taxes on the rich). Institutional transactions that directly redistribute income are based on changes in the social welfare function rather than on changes in relative scarcities or changes in the utility of society's product mix.

The last two examples of institutional transactions represent important classes of collective action that have, heretofore, been regarded as similar in motivation and final result, and have been lumped together – along with those actions whose primary purpose is to directly redistribute income – as actions that are "merely redistributive." However, there are critical distinctions to be drawn between institutional transactions that redistribute economic advantage, and those that reallocate economic opportunity. The obvious question becomes one of how to distinguish these analytically; that is, how does the shoe import problem differ from the mine safety problem?

In the mine safety problem it was possible to depict two competing goods (coal and oil) under two different assumptions regarding safety conditions in coal mines; this is shown in figure 5.14. But attitudes about mine safety are a social issue, and therefore safety is not a direct substitute for coal as Italian shoes are a direct substitute (though at a lower price) for domestic shoes. We define a *policy objective* as something that appears in the utility function of the decision maker(s) as opposed to a *policy instrument* that will not appear there.

Attitudes about the way in which society is organized and operates – or rather how it *should* be organized and operate – give rise to collective efforts to redefine choice sets. In the case of western mining law, the community of miners undertook collective action to promote the evolution of institutional arrangements as *policy instruments* whose sole purpose was to reduce uncertainty and chaos in the mining of valuable ores. The precise structure of western mining law was not a policy objective; the policy objective was simply to allow the production of minerals at the lowest possible social cost. In the case of coal mining, where safety *is* an issue, then it (safety) enters into the objective function of the decision maker(s) by becoming a legitimate argument in a social utility function, and therefore the level of utility of coal miners becomes an argument in the social welfare function. As long as no one cares about mine safety, the welfare of miners *qua* miners is immaterial; they are just "labor" or they are just "consumers" along with all other members of society. Similar logic applies to recent concern for the handicapped, for the aged, for ethnic or racial minorities, or even for prisoners under cloud of the death sentence.

Slavery was arguably a productively efficient way to organize plantation agriculture in the southern United States in the early nineteenth century, but changing attitudes meant that it ceased to be socially efficient. Factories in the early phases of industrialization found that child labor was productively efficient. But, as attitudes about such practices changed it was no longer the case that social efficiency was served by such treatment of children, and laborers in general. With changes in working conditions it became more expensive to produce the same goods, but it is not correct to claim that the economy was less efficient than it had been previously. There was simply a new set of social indifference curves and hence a new socially efficient level of output. The economy moved to a new production possibilities frontier, optimality was determined by a new constellation of social indifference curves, and a new set of relative prices emerged out of the new equilibrium. A new socially efficient point had been reached reflecting the new social attitudes about working conditions, and so the new social indifference curves. Because it took the force of the state to bring about this new pattern of interaction and the attendant outcomes, it may appear to represent government "intervention." But the engine of change was a new collective sense – articulated through the political process – calling for new institutional arrangements (and so new choice sets) in factories and mines. While some might object that efficiency was sacrificed for the sake of redistribution in favor of labor and away from capital, economic theory cannot support that conclusion.

Economic opportunity was simply allocated differently from what it had been under the status quo, but the economy was as socially efficient as it had ever been. Institutional transactions that reallocate economic opportunity may arise either from changes in social utility relations, or from changes in social welfare considerations. If by the former, then changing preferences for safety, changing income effects, or a shift in attitudes are candidates. If by the latter, then the impetus comes from a change in the weight of authority (or political legitimacy) as between owners of capital and owners of labor.[9]

Finally, institutional transactions that redistribute economic advantage are not based on the specifications of a social welfare function, nor are they based on new forms of a social utility function. Rather, certain members of the polity are able to countermand prevailing conceptions of both social utility and social welfare in order to improve their relative position. The process of collective action and social choice allows dysfunctional institutional change when economic advantage is redistributed. Unlike the first three types of institutional transactions – each of which makes a positive contribution to social welfare – institutional transactions that redistribute economic advantage are strictly redistributive of welfare. Rent seeking, as a special case of redistributing economic advantage, further compounds the problem by reducing total social welfare.

The orthodox dichotomy between efficiency and distribution derives from an incomplete specification of the social utility function and the social welfare function. With respect to the former, the conventional approach often deals inadequately with any argument in the social utility function that is not expressed in terms of monetary income. In terms of the social welfare function, orthodoxy denies any knowledge of it at all, and invites the serious mistake of regarding an improvement in national income as an improvement in social welfare. By denying analytical knowledge of the social welfare function, the way is open to show that it is not necessary to pronounce on social optimality. In the best positivist tradition, the social welfare function is thought to pertain to value judgments and cannot, therefore, possibly be of much operational concern to those who believe that scientific objectivity demands the purging of such judgments from economic analysis. However, as indicated previously, this is a source of much confusion within economics.[10]

To admit the relevance of social utility functions and social welfare functions is not to undermine objective economic analysis, but is necessary to reach conclusions about aggregate social – as opposed to productive or price – efficiency. Indeed, explicit concern for the nature of the social welfare function enriches and expands analytical possibilities. The economist is now liberated from the narrow trap of regarding all institutional change as being in the interest of allocative efficiency, or "merely" redistributive. It is now possible to understand that: (1) some institutional transactions improve directly the monetized net social dividend; (2) some institutional transactions directly change the distribution of income; (3) some institutional transactions reallocate economic opportunity; and (4) some institutional transactions redistribute economic advantage. These institutional transactions will arise as autonomous responses to new economic conditions and opportunities, or they will arise because of an absence of autonomous change and so they will be imposed from without. The circumstances under which these types of institutional change will arise are critical to the understanding of institutions and of institutional change.

NOTES

1 The term "commodities" is used here to denote the full constellation of goods and services that exist in a society and which are the subject of conventional transactions in economic theory.

2 Of course if a miner is injured or killed the mine owner will always have the opportunity to console the widow with small (or even large) gifts. But this act of charity is precisely that and as long as it remains voluntary it is not regarded as a marginal factor cost to the owner.

3 There is a similar situation in the current arguments over the health aspects of smoking. In spite of what most regard as convincing evidence, the tobacco interests are adamant that the data are not conclusive. This "uncertainty" is then used to oppose institutional change regarding smoking in public places; the plea of the tobacco interests is that we must wait for better evidence before we infringe on the (presumptive) "rights" of smokers.

4 This is dismissed in theoretical conversations by asking that the reader assume perfect capital markets.

5 See Schmid (1987, pp. 214ff).

6 The reader well versed in welfare economics can easily skip this section.

7 The use of the term "claims" in prospecting is seen to be consistent with my usage in the context of institutional transactions. A miner's *claim* is an expectation that his/her *interest* in a particular geographic domain can be given effective protection via an *entitlement*.

8 The prior example was not driven by such concerns, although the structure of mineral entitlements will have an impact upon the ultimate distribution of income among miners.

9 I am grateful to Chris Nunn for assistance in clarifying this point, as well as the subsequent one about institutional transactions that redistribute economic advantage.

10 I will develop this argument more fully in chapter 8.

6
Interests, Institutions, and the Framing of Choice

The good old rule
Sufficeth them, the simple plan,
That they should take, who have the power,
And they should keep who can.
William Wordsworth, *Rob Roy's Grave*

The previous material has been concerned with clarifying the concept of institutional arrangements, institutional transactions, and institutional change. In that context a more careful consideration of the bundle of goods and services making up the social utility function, and a more concerted effort to discern the relevant social welfare function, were seen to be important. With this knowledge the economist will be able to identify four distinct types of institutional change.

Independent economic agents operate from within a choice domain (called choice sets) that is defined by extant rules and conventions – that is, by the institutional arrangements. These institutional arrangements will reflect preexisting preferences about the ways in which individuals wish to interact with one another as they go about their daily existence. It is from within these choice sets that utility-maximizing behavior, as ordinarily modeled, can be said to exist. Out of this structure of constrained choice will emerge particular patterns of interaction among independent economic agents (individuals, groups, firms, other organizations) that will give rise to particular outcomes: a certain level of investment, particular consumption patterns, a rate of unemployment, aggregate savings, a particular level of environmental quality, and the like.

These *outcomes*, the result of *patterns of interaction* arising from the prevailing *institutional arrangements*, will undoubtedly lead to considerations of the *performance* of the going concern we call the economy and society. By performance I mean more than simply the net national income as reckoned in monetary terms. By performance I mean the full gamut of indicators of well-being that individuals and groups marshal to convey their satisfaction with how things are going. This rather broad indication of performance may not satisfy those who find the greater comfort in per-capita income measures. Such monetized indicators are clearly part of some performance assessment, but they are not the whole of it. There will be some collective sense of how things are progressing in society. There will be concern with the loss of jobs in the manufacturing sector, there will be concern with regional disparities in economic growth and adjustment, there will be concern with excessive agricultural output, there will be concern with land-use tendencies in urban areas, and so on. All of these concerns reflect the outcomes from existing institutional arrangements and patterns of interaction. That is, these concerns reflect a new awareness that maximizing behavior from within existing choice sets is leading to social situations that are no longer viewed as benign. Perhaps exchange rates have made manufacturing non-competitive in a newly invigorated world economy; some regions, more dependent on manufacturing, will be more seriously affected; agricultural price supports may have stimulated excessive production; tax laws may encourage building on open spaces as opposed to revitalizing derelict areas in central cities.

The central issue here is one of individual interests, claims, and entitlements in the structure and functioning of the economy and society. Those who have an interest in a particular structure or functional characteristic will want to have that interest recognized as a legitimate claim, and then – ideally – given protection through entitlements. My concern here has been to recognize, to elaborate, and to give conceptual content to this situation rather than to celebrate or to denigrate it. To celebrate it is to hold that society ought to be whatever those in the position to have their interests given protection want it to be; to denigrate it is to hold some idealized version of the economy and the state where a Paretian Commissioner of All-Around Optimality offers faultless pronouncements on the propriety of each and every action. But to recognize it is to understand that policy analysis that is to be relevant must start with a clear understanding of the way in which the status quo defines the metric against which alternative institutional arrangements can be judged. In other words, it is to have a model of institutions and of institutional transactions that recognizes that the costs and benefits of the status quo – as well as of some alternative configuration of institutions – are defined in both their magnitude and their incidence by those very institutional arrangements that are under scrutiny at any moment. We thus need to be concerned with how the prevailing constellations of interests and institutions combine to create a *framing effect* on the problem of collective choice and institutional change.

Interests represent the extent to which individuals are impacted by particular outcomes and thus motivated to show concern for choices to be made. *Claims* represent their effective stake in a particular set of outcomes, while *entitlements* represent the nature of the institutional arrangements that will apply to their interests. The nature and character of entitlements will determine their claim in situations in which they have an interest. The entitlement structure also will determine how the decision process is viewed by those in a position to make choices. This understanding of the existing structure of entitlements is missing when public policy discussions begin with a search for proof of "market failure" before any collective action can be justified on economic grounds. The market failure metaphor allows the outcomes of the status quo to be accepted unless a more "efficient" alternative can be discovered; for to do anything inimical to efficiency is regarded as being in the grip of selfish pleaders and the special interests. Economic efficiency is regarded as being in the general interest, while all other actions are undertaken for narrow special interests.

I want now to turn to several illustrations of this issue. The concern will be to explain how the status quo structure of entitlements (property rights – either actual or presumptive) leads to particular definitions of the choice problem. Once the problem has been formulated (framed) in a particular way, conventional analysis will yield particular outcomes – in the name of economic efficiency – that are dominated by the prevailing institutional setup.

I   MISSING MARKETS, PRESENT-VALUED CLAIMS, AND DISCOUNTED INTERESTS

The status quo institutional setup indicates how choice problems are to be framed. If Alpha is free to act without regard for the interests of Beta, then Alpha is said to have *privilege* with respect to Beta, and Beta has *no rights* with respect to Alpha's actions. On the other hand if Alpha is constrained to act in a way that does not disregard Beta's interests then Alpha is said to have *duty* and Beta has a *right*. The earlier examples of entitlements for Alpha and Beta were cast in a timeless world. I will now introduce an intertemporal dimension to the problem of interests, institutions, and the calculation of economic efficiency.

Let Alpha represent those now living, while Beta represents those living in the future. If those living in the present (Alpha) are free to act in total disregard for the implications of their actions for those living in the future (Beta), then those living in the present have *privilege*, and those living in the future have *no rights*. The presumed (or actual) structure of entitlements is central to the problem of intertemporal choice since those living in the future are not here to speak for their interests, nor are they able to have their interests protected by entitlements. That is, the future stands fully exposed to the *privilege* of the present, and therefore has *no rights* with regard to its interests. The interests and claims of the present are reflected in prevailing entitlement structures, while the interests of future generations are discounted.

Consider two discrete groups of citizens, Alpha which is alive in both time periods, and Beta which is not now alive but will be alive ten years from now. Alpha, as part of its economic activity, discharges pollutants that will affect Beta in ten years. These pollutants, while detrimental to Beta, are not harmful to Alpha at that future period. Note that the harm which accrues to Beta does not occur until ten years have passed. The status quo institutional arrangements allow Alpha to do as it wishes with its pollutants. Notice that the institutional setup is one of *privilege* for Alpha and of *no right* for Beta. There is no uncertainty about whether or not these effects will be experienced by Beta, nor is the magnitude of these effects in doubt.

Imagine that an environmental authority suggests that Alpha should undertake corrective measures to protect Beta from damages from Alpha's current polluting activity, but Alpha is persuasive in convincing the authority that such corrective action is justified only if it is determined to be economically efficient. This position is accepted by the authority and the problem becomes one of determining the efficient action. Assume that the choice problem is to decide whether to have Alpha spend $300 on a device that will prevent Beta from incurring certain costs of a known magnitude ten years into the future. To frame the choice problem Alpha would suggest that it should weigh its costs ($300) against the present value of the damages to be experienced by Beta.

To determine those damages from Beta's perspective would require that the analyst regard $t = 10$ as $t = 0$ in a determination of the present value of Beta's costs should there be no corrective action by Alpha. That is, Beta will be interested in the present value of a future stream of losses that start in $t = 10$ ($t = 0$ to Beta) and continue into the future. Beta has a social marginal rate of time preference that permits the present value of its future losses to be calculated; the exact rate of time preference is not at issue here. Assume that the present value of Beta's costs directly attributable to the inaction of Alpha is $450. This $450 is the loss (in present-value terms) experienced ten years hence by Beta.

Note that Beta's exact marginal rate of time preference is not at issue here, nor is there any reason to suppose that it will be the same as that of Alpha. Since the environmental authority knows that the present value of the pollution damages to Beta in $t = 10$ is $450, it is a simple matter to calculate the present value of $450 not at $t = 10$, but at $t = 0$. If the social marginal rate of time preference for such actions is assumed to be 8 percent, then the present value of $450 is $208. The decision problem has been framed and it is now possible to determine the efficient choice. Recall that the certain cost to Alpha for decisive corrective action is $300, and the present value of the losses to be experienced (albeit by Beta) is but $208. There is little doubt but that the efficient course of action is not to install the $300 device. After all, if Alpha should be required to spend $300 it would create benefits (albeit for Beta) of only $208 in present-value terms. Beta, of course, would be inclined to point out that an expenditure of $300 by Alpha would save Beta $450 in damages.

The decision problem can be viewed with the aid of figure 6.1. The line WZ reflects the social opportunity cost of capital and, by assumption, the prevailing social marginal rate of time preference between consumption today ($t = 0$) and consumption ten years from now ($t = 10$). Assume that Alpha has at its disposal $1800 that can be used for consumption and for investment. Start at point W by inquiring into the possibilities for using investment funds today that will yield various returns in ten years. The line WZ depicts the return on those funds if invested in a ten-year 8 percent bank note. For instance, if $300 were invested in $t = 0$ it would yield, after ten years at 8 percent, $648. Notice that WZ defines financial opportunities in a perfect capital market where funds can be loaned and borrowed at the same rate (8 percent). This can be confirmed by noting that $648 has a discounted present value (when $i = 8$ percent) of $300. But there are other profitable uses of the $300 and these are traced out by the intertemporal production possibilities frontier MW. For instance, if Alpha invested $300 there, rather than in a bank note, it would yield approximately $1,080 after ten years; this is a gain of $432 over the return available in capital markets. Given the prevailing discount rate of 8 percent, it can be seen that the efficient point in terms of maximizing

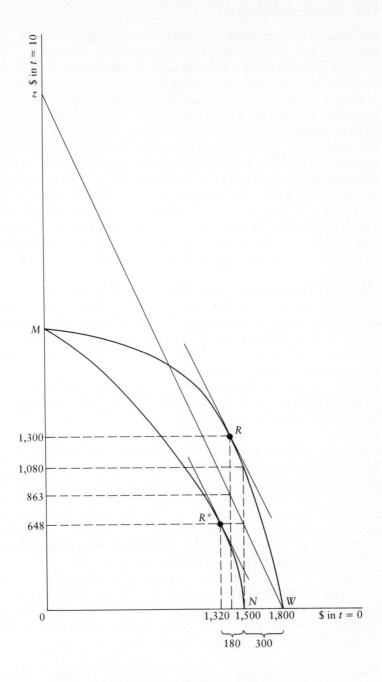

Figure 6.1 Privilege for Alpha, No Right for Beta

the value of consumption over the two periods is found at R. At R, where the rate of time preference (8 percent) is equal to the rate at which production today is transformed into production in $t = 10$, $400 would be invested. This would leave $1,400 available for consumption in $t = 0$ ($1,800 minus $400 used as investment funds), plus $1,300 available in $t = 10$, for a total intertemporal consumption of $2,700.

The prevailing institutional setup is one in which Alpha has *privilege* and Beta has *no right*. The environmental authority is considering a requirement that Alpha install a pollution control device. In reality, the environmental authority is pondering the efficiency implications of altering the institutional arrangements that define Alpha and Beta. Specifically, what is under consideration is the economic wisdom of a change in the entitlements such that Alpha would have *duty* toward Beta, and Beta would acquire *rights vis-à-vis* Alpha. The comparison of these two institutional arrangements might be cast as follows:

Option A   Alpha sustains its position of *privilege* with respect to Beta and thus is free to ignore the costs imposed on Beta. Alpha therefore spends $400 (point R) on productive investments that will yield $1,300 in $t = 10$. Coupled with the $1,400 remaining for consumption by Alpha in $t = 0$, note that Alpha enjoys $2,700 of intertemporal consumption benefits, while Beta suffers a loss of $450 in $t = 10$ arising from the inaction of Alpha in $t = 0$. Total intertemporal consumption benefits for the two parties come to $2,250 ($2,700 for Alpha, minus the $450 loss for Beta).

Option B   Alpha is made to have a *duty* toward Beta and thus invests $300 in a control device in $t = 0$ that will prevent $450 worth of damages to Beta in $t = 10$. The investment opportunities open to Alpha are now depicted by the MN curve reflecting an "off-the-top" commitment to prevent losses to Beta. Alpha would then seek to maximize intertemporal consumption benefits and would be efficient to move to point R^* where the interest line is just tangent to the intertemporal production possibilities frontier. This would imply investment of $180, present consumption of $1,320, and consumption in $t = 10$ of $648. Beta avoids a loss in $t = 10$ of $450 because Alpha invested in the control device in $t = 0$. Total intertemporal consumption benefits (valued at the time of consumption) for Alpha come to $1,968 ($1,320 plus $648), with zero loss for Beta.

There may be a tendency to view this as the familiar problem of efficiency for Alpha versus equity for Beta. If Alpha should have to invest $300 in the control device, note that current consumption would be $80 less than if it could ignore Beta's losses, and in $t = 10$ the income loss to Alpha is $652 ($1,300 versus $648). The total intertemporal consumption benefits to Alpha are reduced by $732 ($2,700 versus $1,968) if Alpha should be required to spend $300 to prevent losses to Beta. And, of course, if Alpha should spend $300 on the control device, Beta does not suffer the loss of $450 in $t = 10$. Alpha will be looking at the relative costs and benefits to it, and would be inclined to notice that an investment of $300 in the control device has a present value of but $208, and that its total intertemporal consumption benefits will fall by $732 should the control be undertaken to save only $450 to Beta. Given the entitlement structure of *privilege* for Alpha opposed to *no right* for Beta, Alpha might be excused for its considered indifference to the problems of Beta. We should not be surprised to find Alpha challenging the environmental authority for its "inefficient" proposal that pollution be controlled.

Consider further the alternative entitlement structure in which Beta's interest in this matter is converted from one of *no right* to a *right*, and Alpha is found to have *duty* as opposed to *privilege*. How might such a change in entitlements occur? One possible explanation would be collective action resulting in something we might call a Clean Air Act under which Alpha is made responsible for the damages that it would otherwise impose on Beta. With Alpha now having no option about whether or not to regard the interests of Beta, it is possible that other actions by Alpha might be more efficient.

Specifically, Alpha might search for actions that would enhance its intertemporal consumption possibilities compared to the mandated installation of pollution control devices (option B from above). Consider two additional options. Alpha, rather than investing in the control device to preclude the $450 loss to Beta, could proceed with the optimal investment strategy at R along MW, and then agree to compensate Beta in $t = 10$ for the $450 in damages created by Alpha's failure to install a corrective device in $t = 0$. Call this option C. Or, Alpha could invest in a ten-year note at 8 percent and agree to assign this yield to Beta at maturity such that the losses ($450) borne by Beta because Alpha does not invest in the $300 control device could be exactly compensated. That is, a $208 note today has a value of $450 in $t = 10$. Should Alpha choose this option it would require that we modify figure 6.1 somewhat. Specifically, Alpha would face a new intertemporal production possibilities frontier (MN') in figure 6.2 along which it could make the efficient investment choice. Notice that at point R^* it would be efficient for Alpha to invest $172, leaving

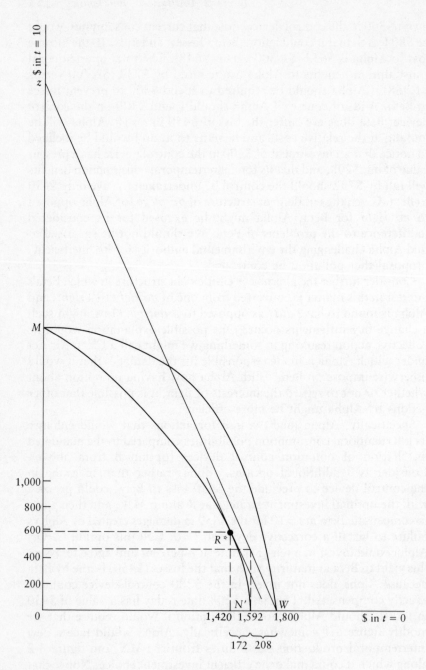

Figure 6.2 Duty for Alpha, Right for Beta

$1,420 for consumption in $t = 0$, and yielding $580 for consumption in $t = 10$. Call this option D.

Under the new entitlement structure of *duty* for Alpha, the decision problem now consists of option B from before, plus two new options:

Option B Alpha invests $300 in a control device in $t = 0$ that will prevent $450 worth of damages to Beta in $t = 10$. The investment opportunities open to Alpha are now depicted by the *MN* curve reflecting an "off-the-top" commitment to prevent losses to Beta. Alpha would then seek to maximize intertemporal consumption benefits and would be efficient to move to point R^* where the interest line is just tangent to the intertemporal production possibilities frontier. This would imply investment of $180, present consumption of $1,320, and consumption in $t = 10$ of $648. Beta suffers no loss in $t = 10$ because Alpha invested in the control device in $t = 0$. Total intertemporal consumption benefits (valued at the time of consumption) come to $1,968 for Alpha, with zero loss for Beta.

Option C Alpha does not invest in the control device. Rather, Alpha agrees to transfer $450 to Beta in $t = 10$ to compensate for the damages that Alpha's inaction in $t = 0$ holds for Beta. As in option A, Alpha spends the efficient amount on a productive investment ($400) that will yield $1,300 in $t = 10$. Coupled with the $1,400 available for consumption in $t = 0$, Alpha enjoys $2,250 of intertemporal consumption benefits ($2,700 minus the $450 compensation to Beta). Beta is exactly compensated for its losses in $t = 10$.

Option D Alpha purchases a ten-year 8 percent note for $208 that will yield $450 for Beta in $t = 10$. Alpha then makes an efficient investment decision, devoting an additional $172 to that end. This leaves Alpha with $1,420 for consumption in $t = 0$, and yields $580 for consumption in $t = 10$. Beta is exactly compensated for its losses in $t = 10$ by the note, and Alpha has an intertemporal consumption benefit of $2,000 ($1,420 in $t = 0$ and $580 in $t = 10$)

These options are summarized in table 6.1.

When the problem is framed this way, intertemporal efficiency is served if Alpha is allowed to pursue option C rather than being forced to adopt option B, and Beta is left as well off as if Alpha had invested in the $300 control device (option B). *Duty* for Alpha and *right* for Beta does not mean that the former has an obligation to improve the wealth position of Beta; it means only that the interests of Beta must

Table 6.1 **Intertemporal Consumption under Different Entitlements**
($i = 8$ percent)

Entitlement	Option	Alpha	Beta	Aggregate
Privilege for Alpha, no right for Beta	A (ignore Beta's damages)	2,700	−450	2,250
Duty for Alpha, right for Beta	B (control)	1,968	0	1,968
Duty for Alpha, right for Beta	C (compensation)	2,250	0	2,250
Duty for Alpha, right for Beta	D (note)	2,000	0	2,000

be given protection. Both options C and D protect those interests, and leave Alpha better off than if option B had been required by the pollution authority. But option C improves the position of Alpha over option D; aggregate consumption benefits for Alpha and Beta are equal between options A and C. However, Beta's losses under option A are compensated by Alpha under option C and hence option C may seem the "fairer" policy.

The institutional arrangements play a critical role in framing of the choice problem. The efficient solution under *privilege* for Alpha is for Alpha to ignore the damages that will be imposed on Beta. Under the new institutional structure of *duty* for Alpha there are several possibilities for proper consideration of the interests of Beta, and the efficiency implications differ across the alternatives.

Under the status quo entitlement structure of *privilege* for Alpha and *no right* for Beta it appears inefficient to pursue action that would prevent losses of $450 being imposed on Beta; Alpha would compute a total reduction in intertemporal consumption benefits of $732 ($80 of that coming in $t = 0$, and the remaining $652 in $t = 10$) and would see that Beta would gain $450. But consider the position of Beta. The status quo would mean that no action on the part of Alpha would cause a certain loss of $450 for Beta; action on the part of Alpha to mitigate these losses means a gain of $450 for Beta compared to its position if Alpha did nothing. Does this make Beta richer? Yes, if the entitlement structure giving Alpha *privilege* to Beta's *no right* is accepted as the proper one. No, if the proper entitlement structure is one giving Alpha *duty* to Beta's *right*. That is, the institutional structure not only determines how decisions are framed and choices made, but also determines how one shall assess the impacts of those choices. If Beta is regarded as having *no right* to have its losses covered by Alpha then one might be tempted to view the problem as one of Alpha having to sacrifice present and future income in order to make Beta better off. On the other hand, if Beta is regarded as having a *right* not to incur losses at the hands of Alpha, then Alpha will be viewed as doing what is correct – giving up ill-gotten income – in order not to make Beta worse off. But *better off* and *worse off* are emotive terms and have no analytical meaning in isolation from the assumed structure of entitlements.

It is sometimes suggested that the type of intertemporal problem explored here would not arise if the social rate of discount were zero rather than some positive number. Imagine that the rate of discount were assumed to be zero, a situation in which $1 today is worth exactly $1 ten years from now. In this instance, the intertemporal production possibilities frontier depicting investment and consumption tradeoffs would remain unchanged (MW). However, the line WZ would now rotate around the point W toward the southwest. The efficient solution is option C, and so it can be seen that the assumed social rate of discount (by which the $450 of damages gets reduced to $208) is immaterial to the policy choice. Both option C and option D dominate option B, the only one that could benefit from an assumed zero rate of discount. It is, instead, the new institutional arrangement of *duty* for Alpha and *right* for Beta that dominates the policy choice.

Under either assumption of discount rates, the institutional structure of *privilege* for Alpha and *no right* for Beta makes Alpha better off at the expense of Beta. A forced control strategy for Alpha is inferior to other institutional arrangements under any discount rate.

To argue, as some have, that the solution to the intertemporal problem is found in a zero discount rate would seem to be rather too simplistic. Instead, the story about Alpha and Beta should be understood to suggest that efficiency must be seen in its fullest manifestation, and *this requires that there be no missing markets*. An entitlement structure of *privilege* for Alpha and *no right* for Beta means that there is no recognition of Beta's interests in a particular situation and hence no effort need be made by Alpha to contract with Beta. It is not in the interest of efficiency to cast the decision problem as a simple calculation of whether or not to invest in the $300 protective device. True social efficiency requires that all parties with an interest in the outcome have an opportunity to have those interests considered. That consideration includes not only the interests of the future, but the alternative actions open to the present that will protect the interests of the future. Intertemporal choice that considers present-valued claims, but discounted interests, does not serve the cause of efficiency.

This issue can be understood in the larger context of intertemporal justice where one expects that the present (Alpha) will take actions *vis-à-vis* the future (Beta) that reflect, were their respective temporal positions reversed, actions that Beta would be inclined to take *vis-à-vis* Alpha. Rather than one of making Beta better off at the expense of Alpha, the issue is properly seen as one of selecting an institutional structure to mediate intertemporal choice that all participants would agree to from behind a Rawlsian veil of ignorance.[1] There:

> No one knows his place in society, his class position or social status; nor does he know his fortune in the distribution of natural assets and abilities, his intelligence and strength, and the like. Nor, again, does anyone know his conception of the good, the particulars of his rational plan of life, or even the special features of his psychology such as his aversion to risk or liability to optimism or pessimism. More than this, I assume that the parties do not know the particular circumstances of their own society. That is, they do not know its economic or political situation, or the level of civilization and culture it has been able to achieve. The persons in the original position have no information as to which generation they belong. (Rawls 1971, p. 137)

The implications for economists should be obvious. The *efficient choice is dominated by the presumed institutional structure*. The policy question is one of which institutional structure would be selected if Alpha and Beta had no prior basis for knowing which party would hold precedence in time over the other. It seems reasonable that unanimous assent would be forthcoming only for a structure of entitlements that bestowed *duty* on the early generation, and *right* on the later; it seems unreasonable to suppose that unanimous agreement would be given to an institutional structure that gave the earlier party *privilege*, to the later's *no right*. For what incentive would either have to vote for such an entitlement structure if they could not be certain that they would be first in time? This assumes, of course, risk aversion on the part of the individuals under consideration. When the extent of – and the implications from – environmental damages are uncertain, it may not be far wrong to assume that individuals are risk averse. If long-term survival is at stake the assumption of risk aversion becomes more tenable.

II ENTITLEMENTS, RISK, AND CHOICES

The previous discussion concerned a choice problem in which the presumed institutional structure was central to the computation of the efficient policy decision. The issue to be addressed here moves away somewhat from an explicit computation of consumption benefits, but it is still concerned with making choices under alternative presumptions of *privilege* for one party and *no rights* for another. I also will introduce uncertainty over the possible damages from the current actions of Alpha.

Continuing with the example of air pollution, it is possible to identify at least six different aspects of uncertainty. The first dimension of uncertainty would pertain to the identification of the sources of particular pollutants. The second would pertain to the conveyance process and hence the ultimate destination of particular emissions. The third aspect of uncertainty pertains to the actual physical impacts at the point of destination. The fourth aspect of uncertainty concerns the human valuation of (or reaction to) the realized impacts at the point of destination of the emissions. The fifth dimension of uncertainty concerns the extent to which a particular policy response will have an impact on emissions, conveyance, ultimate physical impacts, and finally the human reaction (the putative benefits of the policy) to those changes. And, the sixth dimension concerns the actual cost level and the incidence of those costs that are the result of the policy response.

These six dimensions of the air pollution problem define the boundaries of the uncertainty that plagues policy formulation. This uncertainty creates the opportunity for errors in policy choice and so frequently is used to justify doing nothing. Those favored by the status quo of *privilege* (and the resultant *no right* for the cost bearers) will suggest that not enough is known to justify such a "drastic" policy as requiring the elimination (or the reduction) of pollution emissions. Those well served by the status quo will suggest that it is better to continue to fund research to determine whether or not a policy of full (or partial) restriction on emissions would be appropriate. But those bearing costs (or, in the intergenerational problem, those who speak for Beta) will argue that to do nothing about current pollution is, in fact, to decide to continue a policy of ignoring their interests and hence to sanctify a *de facto* entitlement structure of *privilege* for the emitters, and *no right* for others. The presumptive rights of the status quo define a particular decision environment and require that any action be judged against that bench mark. Invariably the choice is cast as one of acting now or waiting until more (and presumably better) information is available. That this biases action in favor of the status quo ought to be obvious – for it is always easy to protest that we do not yet know enough to be certain that a policy response would improve the situation.[2]

A properly comprehensive benefit–cost analysis of policy choices would include the probabilities attached to alternative outcomes of pursuing a few distinct policy options. For instance, in the current debates over acid rain policy the options are usually cast in terms of percentage reductions in SO_2 (or NO_x). With that information one may then speculate about the possible impacts on future damages from these alternatives. The concern in such policy is to provide decision makers with an array of choices and to urge adoption of that action with the highest expected value.

One complication is that public decision makers may not regard losses and gains symmetrically and therefore the presumptive entitlement structure takes on considerable importance. That is, the *expected value* decision maker will choose the action that produces the greatest expected payoff, while the decision maker concerned to *minimize maximum regret* will choose the action that promises the smallest expected opportunity loss. Under conventional treatments of risk analysis the expected payoff is simply the obverse of the expected opportunity loss. However this is a symmetry of theory that may contradict empirical reality.

Specifically, recent developments in the theory of risk analysis provide an opportunity to illustrate the importance of status quo institutional arrangements in problems where uncertainty is present (Kahneman and Tversky 1979; Tversky and Kahneman 1981). In prospect theory one partitions the decision problem into two parts: (1) framing the actions, outcomes, and contingencies; and (2) evaluating the choices to be made. Experimental evidence indicates that people do not behave as expected utility theory predicts that they will. In an illustration of the *certainty effect*, Kahneman and Tversky found that 80 percent of their respondents preferred a sure gain of 3,000 units to the following choice: a 4,000-unit gain with probability of 0.8 or a zero gain with probability of 0.2. The expected value of the sure thing is 3,000 while the expected value of the gamble is 3,200. Yet the sure thing was the dominant choice. When concerned with losses as opposed to gains they found the opposite effect. That is, a sure loss of 3,000 units was preferred by only 8 percent of the respondents, while the following gamble was preferred by 92 percent: a 4,000-unit loss with probability 0.8, or a zero loss with probability of 0.2. In the positive domain the certainty effect contributes to risk aversion so that a sure gain is taken rather than a larger, but probable, gain. In the negative domain the certainty effect leads to risk-seeking preferences for a probable loss over a smaller – but certain – loss.

This distinction between the positive and negative domains is relevant because, unlike conventional investment analysis, many instances of collective action (the Alpha and Beta problem) require that expenditures be undertaken (by Alpha) to protect against probable losses (to Beta). It is important to understand that expected payoffs from productive investments differ from expected losses from failure to make defensive investments – even if the problem is cast in terms of a single generation (that is, Alpha taking action that affects only Alpha). Consider the choices studied by Kahneman and Tversky. To keep the problem tractable, assume that the policy maker is presented with a fairly simple choice problem:

A   Do nothing about acid rain and suffer certain losses in habitat valued at 3,000; or
B   Install engineering devices that precipitate out acid precursors. If this action is taken there are two possible outcomes:
   1   There is an 80 percent probability that the devices will not work and we will lose the cost of the devices plus the habitat for a total loss of 4,000; or
   2   There is a 20 percent probability that the devices will work and net losses, after paying for the devices, will be zero.

Here we have a decision problem very much like the one studied by Kahneman and Tversky. The value of the gamble in the Kahneman and Tversky experiment indicated that 92 percent of the respondents preferred option B (control acid rain) to option A (do nothing about acid rain). Expected utility theory predicts that the respondents would prefer option A (do nothing about acid rain) since its loss has the lowest expected value. In fact, their respondents were risk seeking in the domain of losses in the hopes of hitting the 20 percent chance of no loss at all. In the above choices there is a sure loss if nothing is done, and a fairly high probability of a loss if action were taken.

In another experiment Kahneman and Tversky offered the following choices regarding possible losses:

A   A 45 percent chance of a 6,000-unit loss, and a 55 percent chance of zero loss; or

B   A 90 percent chance of a 3,000-unit loss, and a 10 percent chance of zero loss.

In both instances the value of the gamble is the same (an expected loss of 2,700) and yet their respondents favored option A by 92 percent to 8 percent. If we again imagine this to be an acid rain problem, it is not hard to see that option A (some control strategy that still has only a near 50-50 chance of reducing losses) might be preferred even though its expected value is identical to the do-nothing option (B). Risk aversion and risk seeking have been found to have different dimensions when choices involving gains are compared with choices involving losses. Tversky and Kahneman refer to *loss aversion* as the situation in which there is a discrepancy "between the amount of money people are willing to pay for a good and the compensation they demand to give it up." (1987, p. 74)[3] The hypothesis here is that these differences reflect underlying perceptions regarding presumed rights.

Public decision makers will often seem to be taking actions that will minimize losses as opposed to actions that will maximize gains; for this they are often thought to be irrational. Yet it may well be that those in a position to make collective decisions are willing to gamble to avoid certain losses, but are risk averse in the domain of gains, preferring a certain gain to a chance at a much larger one. The minimax regret decision criterion from expected utility theory addresses the difference between the payoff from the correct decision and the payoff from the actual decision. Because of the presence of irreversibilities in many choices, and the social stigma of being thought to make "wrong" choices, it is reasonable to suppose that many policy makers – just as with most participants in the Kahneman and Tversky experiments – reject the formal equality of the expected value of gains and losses. This would make them more amenable to a strategy that seems to minimize their maximum regret.

While under conventional assumptions that seems equivalent to choosing so as to maximize expected benefits, prospect theory suggests otherwise. Perhaps risk-averse choices in the face of certain gains reflect a particular attitude of *rights* toward the expected gains. If that is so, then decision makers may see no reason to engage in probabilistic games that may enhance those gains, but which may also reduce the gains to zero. On the other hand, when decision makers are faced with certain losses, it may be that a notion of *no right* is present where some other party has *privilege*; in such instances the decision maker will not sit idly by without undertaking actions to attempt to reduce those certain losses – even with the remote prospect of even greater losses.

The different perceptions of gains and losses, and the fact that much collective action is concerned with *defensive* actions (pollution control devices, regulation of new drugs, seat-belt laws, laws that prohibit smoking in public places), seem important for how we analyze collective choice situations. But the essential issue here is that the entitlement structure that is presumed to prevail will influence the framing of the choice problem and also the evaluation of the efficiency of alternative policy options. An entitlement structure that seems to accord a position of *privilege* so that individuals may freely engage in certain behaviors (pollute, use whatever drugs they can afford, be maimed in a car crash, smoke wherever they choose) will clearly color the way in which the decision problem is cast and evaluated.

III ENTITLEMENTS AND EFFICIENCY: REALLOCATING ECONOMIC OPPORTUNITY

The two previous examples concerned problems in which efficiency calculations and preferred choices were dominated by the presumed institutional setup. In the problem of present-valued claims and discounted interests, Alpha was seen to have an entitlement of *privilege* while Beta had *no rights*. A change in the status quo entitlement structure to one of *duty* for Alpha and *right* for Beta was seen to offer several new interpretations of the classic efficiency problem in policy analysis. Specifically, the new institutional arrangement did not automatically imply that the installation of a pollution control device was necessarily the most effective way for Alpha to regard the interests of Beta. It also was demonstrated that gains and losses are viewed differently in situations of uncertainty; certain gains may seem to suggest a *right* to a benefit stream while certain losses may seem to suggest that others are exercising *privilege* in the face of the decision maker's *no right*.

It is possible to assess the impact of alternative institutional arrangements on the more familiar externality problem when uncertainty and the intertemporal dimension are missing. As before, however, the discussion will illustrate the effect of alternative rights structures on judgments regarding efficiency. Specifically, I will now make explicit the role that alternative institutional arrangements play in the efficient solution to policy disputes. In the process, I will also illustrate the concept of *reallocating economic opportunity*.

Assume a very simple situation of two contiguous economic actors, Alpha and Beta, engaged in two distinct economic activities, yet ones in which the former (Alpha) imposes uncompensated costs on the latter (Beta). Imagine that Alpha is a coal-fired electricity generating plant, and that Beta is a firm that receives electronic transmissions of data which it then processes in its computers for resale to subscribers. Alpha imposes a technological externality on Beta as opposed to a pecuniary externality. Whether or not this technological externality is Pareto relevant or Pareto irrelevant is yet to be determined. Following Marchand and Russell (1973), assume that these two activities have non-separable cost functions, that Alpha produces q_1, that Beta produces q_2, and that Beta imposes no costs on Alpha. The cost functions of the two are given as:[4]

$$A(q_1) \tag{6.1}$$
$$B(q_1, q_2) \tag{6.2}$$

where it is noted that Beta's costs are a function of its own output, but also of the output of Alpha. The cost functions have the following properties:[5]

$$A_1 > 0 \tag{6.3}$$
$$B_1 > 0 \tag{6.4}$$
$$B_2 > 0 \tag{6.5}$$
$$A(0) = 0 \tag{6.6}$$
$$B(q_1, 0) = 0 \tag{6.7}$$
$$B(0, q_2) > 0 \tag{6.8}$$

The status quo institutional arrangement is one in which Alpha has *privilege* in its imposition of costs on Beta (who has *no right* with respect to those costs). The decision problem for Alpha can be shown as:

$$\max_{q_1} p_1 q_1 - A(q_1) \tag{6.9}$$

subject to $q_1 \geqslant 0$

and that for Beta as:

$$\max_{q_2} p_2 q_2 - B(q_1, q_2) \tag{6.10}$$

subject to $q_2 \geqslant 0$

The two firms will make output decisions by finding the levels of output ($\hat{q}_1$ and $\hat{q}_2$) for which price equals marginal cost. That is, where

$$p_1 = A_1(\hat{q}_1) \qquad\qquad (6.11)$$
$$p_2 = B_2(\hat{q}_1, \hat{q}_2) \qquad\qquad (6.12)$$

Notice that Beta is in the unhappy position of constantly needing to modify its output (q_2) to retain economic efficiency in response to variation in Alpha's output. That is, Beta must adjust its production levels after considering the output level of Alpha. The traditional solution to this form of externality is to internalize the variability. That is, to seek the optimal output level of the two activities as if they were being produced by a unified firm. A single owner would manage Alpha and Beta in such a manner as to pick the economically efficient level of output recognizing the costs that Alpha imposes on Beta. The implications of the externality would be optimally regarded by the sole owner. This newly adjusted level of output from the two divisions of the unified firm provides the bench mark against which the extent of market failure would be judged. The unified firm then has the decision problem to:

$$\max_{q_1,\, q_2} \quad p_1 q_1 + p_2 q - A(q_1) - B(q_1, q_2) \qquad\qquad (6.13)$$

subject to $q_1 \geqslant 0$, $q_2 \geqslant 0$

The manager of the unified firm would now be seen to choose output levels (q_i^* and q_2^*) of the two divisions (A and B) such that:

$$p_1 = A_1(q_1^*) + B_1(q_1^*, q_2^*) \qquad\qquad (6.14)$$
$$p_2 = B_2(q_1^*, q_2^*) \qquad\qquad (6.15)$$

Marchand and Russell use the second-order conditions to prove that under the status quo (two separate firms) Alpha produces too much of q_1, and Beta produces too little of q_2. That is:

$$\hat{q}_1 > q_1^* \qquad\qquad (6.16)$$
$$\hat{q}_2 < q_2^* \qquad\qquad (6.17)$$

Marchand and Russell note that the Coasian contribution was to point out that with zero transaction costs it is not proper to formulate the objective function for Alpha as it is in equation (6.9), nor is Beta's objective function properly depicted by equation (6.10). The Coasian position is that the two firms would be aware of the effects that Alpha has on Beta and would undertake negotiations to mitigate the interdependence. To put it somewhat differently, the status quo (two-firm) situation depicted in equations (6.9) to (6.12) cannot properly be compared with the unified firm of equations (6.13) to (6.15). Hence, the comparisons of equations (6.16) and (6.17) are inappropriate for policy conclusions, and are irrelevant for judgments about output levels and the need for corrective action.

In the status quo of permissive institutions where Alpha can impose external costs on Beta, Alpha must recognize the possibility of payments coming from Beta as it (Beta) attempts to reduce the magnitude of costs that it is made to incur. Moreover, Beta would be quite indifferent whether it must be made to bear an unwanted cost at the mercy of Alpha, or instead must pay Alpha to reduce its imposition of external costs on Beta. In this way, Alpha's true cost function must reflect the income it is forgoing when it chooses a particular level of output. Similarly, Beta's cost function must reflect this possible payment to Alpha.

If Alpha produces its individually optimal output level $(\hat{q}_1)$ then it must reckon as part of its costs the forgone income that could be forthcoming from Beta to produce at a level less than $\hat{q}_1$. The maximum possible payment from Beta is given by:

$$S = [B(\hat{q}_1, q_2) - B(q_1, q_2)] \tag{6.18}$$

For Alpha, its real revenue is therefore given by:

$$p_1 \hat{q}_1 - [B(\hat{q}_1, q_2) - B(q_1, q_2)] \tag{6.19}$$

By producing its privately optimal level of output, its gross revenue $(p_1 \hat{q}_1)$ precludes the possible payment (6.18) coming from Beta. It is necessary to reformulate Alpha's decision problem under the status quo institutional arrangement that gives Alpha the presumptive right (*privilege* in my terminology) to impose unwanted costs on Beta, and in the realization that Beta has an economic incentive to pay Alpha to reduce the incidence of such costs. Under this new concept of the status quo, where transaction costs are assumed to be zero and bargaining between the two interdependent parties is therefore easy, Alpha's decision problem is seen to be:

$$\max_{q_1} p_1 q_1 - A(q_1) + [B(\hat{q}_1, q_2) - B(q_1, q_2)] \tag{6.20}$$

subject to $q_1 \geqslant 0$

For Beta the decision problem is:

$$\max_{q_2} p_2 q_2 - B(q_1, q_2) - [B(\hat{q}_1, q_2) - B(q_1, q_2)] \tag{6.21}$$

subject to $q_2 \geqslant 0$

Alpha and Beta would now select optimal output levels reflecting these new maximization problems. The first-order conditions for each would yield output decisions that have Alpha selecting an output level to satisfy:

$$p_1 = A_1(q_1'') + B_1(q_1'', q_2'') \qquad (6.22)$$

and Beta would choose an output level to satisfy:

$$p_2 = B_2(\hat{q}_1, q_2'') \qquad (6.23)$$

The Marchand and Russell model illustrates that the classical Coase solution – that the outcome will not matter as long as transaction costs are zero – depends upon the assumption that the cost function of Beta is additively separable in its arguments (q_1 and q_2).[6] If this is not the case, even with zero transaction costs, the reformulated maximization problem of Alpha and Beta as given by equations (6.20) and (6.21) will lead to output decisions that differ from those of the unified firm, and of the status quo. That is,

$$\hat{q}_1 > q_1^* < q_1'' \qquad (6.24)$$
$$\hat{q}_2 < q_2^* > q_2'' \qquad (6.25)$$

In the status quo, whether or not bargaining between the two parties is permitted, the firm (Alpha) producing technological externalities is seen to produce more output than is socially optimal, and the firm that must contend with those unwanted costs (Beta) will produce an output that is below the social optimum. The proper question from an economic perspective is why Beta must pay Alpha to be rid of these unwanted costs. Coase argued that the status quo assignment of rights in such cases did not matter because of the possibility for bargaining as illustrated in the Marchand and Russell model. This will be seen not to be true. Returning to the matter of the status quo, Beta might be assumed to suggest that it has a *right* to be free of the costs imposed by Alpha, and that the mere fact that Alpha has been doing this for as long as both can recall hardly makes it correct to continue.[7]

That is, Beta would propose that the relevant maximization problem is to start from a status quo in which Alpha had a *duty* not to impose unwanted costs on Beta; such *duty* for Alpha constitutes the *right* for Beta to be free of these costs. Rather than impose a rigid prohibition on Alpha's offending actions, this new institutional structure implies that Beta's *right* is protected such that Alpha must pay Beta to be allowed to contravene the existing right held by Beta.[8] This payment is the financial liability of Alpha for the costs it imposes on Beta and is reckoned as:

$$L = B(q_1, q_2) - B(0, q_2) \qquad (6.26)$$

This suggests that Alpha would be financially liable to Beta for the difference in Beta's costs arising from Alpha's actual output (q_1). The maximization problem for Alpha is now seen to be given by:

$$\max_{q_1} p_1 q_1 - A(q_1) - [B(q_1, q_2) - B(0, q_2)] \qquad (6.27)$$

subject to $q_1 \geqslant 0$

and for Beta the maximization problem is given by:

$$\max_{q_2} p_2 q_2 - B(q_1, q_2) + [B(q_1, q_2) - B(0, q_2)] \qquad (6.28)$$

subject to $q_2 \geqslant 0$

Now Alpha will select an output level that satisfies the following first-order conditions:

$$p_1 = A_1(q_1') + B_1(q_1', q_2') \qquad (6.29)$$

For Beta the optimal output level will be found where:

$$p_2 = B_2(0, q_2') \qquad (6.30)$$

The second-order conditions from Marchand and Russell indicate that this modified institutional structure will result in an output mix in which Alpha produces too little compared to the unified firm, and that Beta produces too much. That is:

$$q_1' < q_1^* < q_1'' < \hat{q}_1 \qquad (6.31)$$
$$q_2' > q_2^* > q_2'' > \hat{q}_2 \qquad (6.32)$$

A status quo entitlement of *privilege* for Alpha and *no right* for Beta leads to excessive output of q_1 and too little output of q_2 compared to the levels that would be produced by a unified firm that was able to internalize the original externality. If the situation is then embellished to allow for the possibility of bargaining by the two firms starting from the status quo of *privilege* and *no right*, note that the respective outputs will continue to differ from the optimally integrated unified firm: Alpha still producing too much q_1, and Beta still producing too little q_2. This will arise in spite of payments from Beta to Alpha to reflect the possibility of the latter receiving financial inducements not to impose unwanted costs on the former.

When the entitlement structure is altered to one of a *right* for Beta (to be free of unwanted costs imposed by Alpha), and a *duty* for Alpha (not to impose costs on Beta), then it is Alpha that must incorporate the necessary payment to Beta to be allowed to contravene Beta's rights to be free of unwanted costs. Here, Alpha is led to produce too little of q_1, and Beta is led to produce too much of q_2 – where the norm against which these comparisons are made remains the profit-maximizing output levels of the mythical unified firm.

It can be seen, therefore, that even under the ideal – and unrealistic – conditions of zero transaction costs, the presence of a non-separable cost function for Beta means that free and willing bargaining between the two firms will lead to an output bundle (q_1 and q_2) that is socially inefficient, regardless of how the status quo institutional setup defines the starting point – that is, whether there is *privilege* for Alpha and *no right* for Beta, or a *right* for Beta and a *duty* for Alpha. The Coase position is that even though Alpha is producing offensive by-products from its activity – whether electrical interference with Beta, or air pollution in the form of coal dust – the externality is simply a matter of the proximity of these two incompatible activities. He would suggest that while Alpha imposes costs on Beta in the form of either electrical interference or coal dust, Beta imposes costs on Alpha by its presence that forces Alpha to take account of these aspects of its productive activities.

It can be admitted that if the status quo entitlement structure is one of *right* for Beta and *duty* for Alpha, then the latter will be forced to produce less than the efficient level of q_1 (as defined by the norm of the mythical unified firm), and that Beta will be induced to produce more than the level of q_2 defined as ideal by the mythical firm. This can be considered in terms of figure 6.3. In a world of zero transaction costs, the world that Coase was attempting to model, all four output possibilities would be found along the same production possibilities frontier in figure 6.3. The conditions imposed by equations (6.31) and (6.32) require that the relations among the four output bundles be as depicted there. With zero transaction costs the unified firm – and the bargaining possibilities for Alpha and Beta – promise no productivity advantages over the status quo.

If the assumption of zero transaction costs is relaxed then the status quo situation of technological externalities would be depicted by an interior production possibilities frontier. The unified firm would then reflect a productively superior situation as shown in figure 6.4. Under the assumption of positive transaction costs, consider the two production possibilities frontiers, one depicting the status quo institutional arrangement of two distinct firms (Alpha and Beta), and the other depicting the new institutional arrangement of one unified firm with two divisions (call them Alpha and Beta). The status quo output bundle ($\hat{q}$) is found on the former production possibilities frontier, while the more efficient bundle (q^*) is found on the latter

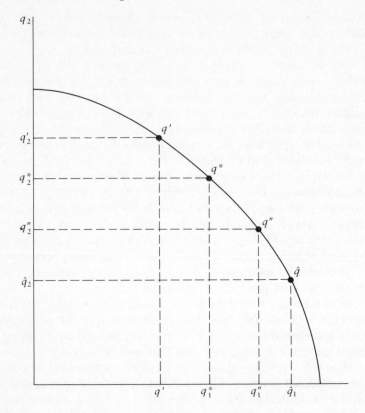

Figure 6.3   Production Possibilities Frontier Assuming Zero Transaction Costs

frontier. The question is, however, what should be assumed about the other two output bundles q' and q''? The Coasian position is that the status quo is not the correct basis for analysis since it does not reflect the existing opportunities for bargaining between Alpha and Beta. And if bargaining has not been pursued by the two protagonists, it might be supposed that the status quo output bundle has been realized. Modeling the unified firm, however, indicates the most efficient possibilities and yields the superior production possibilities frontier. The question then becomes one of determining whether or not the output bundle q^* represents the socially optimal output bundle. Worded somewhat differently, should the output bundle from the mythical unified firm – with the externality optimally internalized – be regarded as the policy objective to be pursued?

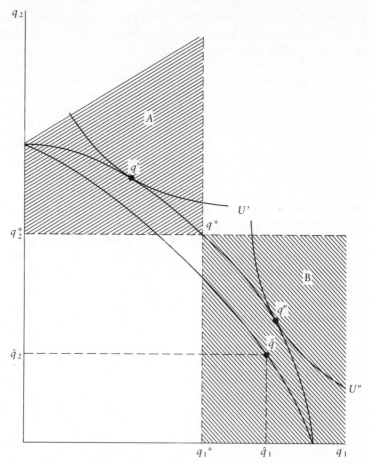

Figure 6.4 Production Possibilities Frontiers with Positive Transaction Costs

The bundle q^* and its production possibilities frontier only becomes a candidate for policy recommendations if it can be proved that there is not some higher frontier on which one might find the other two output possibilities q' and q''. Recall from (6.31) and (6.32) that output bundle q' is one in which $q'_1 < q^*_1$, and $q'_2 > q^*_2$. This means that the bundle q' can exist only in region A of figure 6.4. It is also known by conditions (6.31) and (6.32) that $q''_1 > q^*_1$, and that $q''_2 < q^*_2$, which together require that the bundle q'' can exist only in region B of figure 6.4. To meet these two conditions it will be necessary for the production possibilities frontier(s) on which the bundles q' and q'' reside to pass through the point q^*. Since non-convexities and other manner of ill-behaved production possibilities frontiers are here excluded, it follows by necessity that: (1) both bundles q' and q'' lie on the same production possibility frontier; (2) said frontier meets the original two frontiers at the axes (since if the other firm's output were zero there would be no external effects); (3) the frontiers do not cross; and (4) this frontier passes through the point q^*. Note from figure 6.4 that there is but one frontier which meets these conditions, and that is the one on which point q^* is found.

Several conclusions are in order. First, Coase maintained that the outcome would be the same with respect to efficiency regardless of who started with the property right. In this sense, even with non-separability of cost functions, note that this requires agreement as to what is meant by "outcome." It is true that the output bundles q' and q'' are both as productively efficient as is that from the unified firm (q^*); they both are on the superior production possibilities frontier. But it is one thing to conclude that either is productively efficient, and quite another to say that the bundle of goods and services available in society is unaffected by the status quo assignment of *rights* and *duties*, or *privilege* and *no rights*. For it is clear that output bundle q', one which results from a *duty* for Alpha and a *right* for Beta, is different from output bundle q'' resulting from *privilege* for Alpha and *no right* for Beta. And, obviously these two candidate bundles differ from that of the mythical unified firm.

The mythical unified firm provides one bench mark, but it does not represent the socially optimal outcome of a situation in which two economic agents interact as depicted here. That is, the output bundle of the unified firm lies on the same production possibilities frontier as do the other two bundles, and in that sense productive efficiency is met by all three possibilities. This is the necessary condition for social efficiency, but it is not sufficient. For note in figure 6.4 that q' and q'' represent two very different bundles of q_1 and q_2, and hence two very different situations in terms of the visitation of costs or corrective action. The status quo may also be defined, with the output bundle $\hat{q}$, as one in which *Alpha enjoyed economic advantage over Beta*. That is, the status quo situation of *privilege* for Alpha and *no right* for Beta was not only productively inefficient, it led to the wrong output of q_1 and q_2 (social inefficiency), and to a situation in which Alpha held *unsanctioned* economic advantage over Beta. I emphasize *unsanctioned* because the status quo institutional setup is often a structure by default rather than one of explicit consideration and agreement. Overcoming this situation of undue economic advantage for Alpha moved society to the optimal production possibilities frontier, thereby attaining productive efficiency. Finding the optimal point along that new frontier constitutes the *reallocation of economic opportunity* that leads to social efficiency.

As in the matter of safety in coal mines, the real issue here is the *reallocation* of economic opportunity as between Alpha and Beta. To regard this reallocation as one of *income distribution* is to trivialize the policy issues being addressed here. It is more than income redistribution to observe that q' and q'' differ substantially in terms of the quantities of goods and services available in society, the employment of resources to produce those goods, and the factor payments flowing to those resources. To say that it is merely a matter of distribution is to miss the fact that there is a considerable difference between productive efficiency (existing anywhere along the exterior production possibilities frontier) and social efficiency. It is seen to matter a great deal whether there will be an abundance of q_1 and not much q_2 (bundle q'') or the converse (bundle q').

The sufficient condition for the determination of social efficiency is to learn something of the social indifference curves pertinent to this problem. That is, are they depicted by U'' or by U' in figure 6.4? By pursuing productive efficiency it is possible to move from the status quo bundle ($\hat{q}$) to a new and superior production possibilities frontier. But productive efficiency alone does not deal with the question of social efficiency, where the problem is one of reallocating economic opportunity along the socially efficient frontier on which q', q'', and q^* reside. Much public policy is precisely about selecting an output bundle along that frontier.

Since the unified firm is an analytical fiction, it cannot be relied upon to determine the optimal output bundle for society; its role is necessarily restricted to that of indicating the pertinent production possibilities frontier. But the second step, the reallocation of economic opportunity, is required to reach a point of social efficiency as opposed to productive efficiency. Social efficiency, found along the new production possibilities frontier, will result in the appropriate structure of choice sets (production sets) for Alpha and Beta. That is, social efficiency will define a new domain for both Alpha and Beta within which they are free to choose their production plans. And that is why I call this problem one of *reallocating economic opportunity*.

IV   LANGUAGE AND CONCEPTS: PRODUCTIVITY AND EFFICIENCY

I have previously expressed concern for situations in which individuals are not clear regarding the important distinction between policy objectives and policy instruments. When that distinction is clear, it is possible to proceed to undertake policy analysis with the intent of understanding whether a policy is to improve productive efficiency, to change the distribution of income, to reallocate economic opportunity (and improve social efficiency), or to redistribute economic advantage. The problem setting for this discussion will be that of land reform, wherein governments in the developing countries expropriate large estates of the wealthy and distribute small parcels to a number of landless laborers. There has grown up around this policy issue a considerable literature attempting to discern whether or not large farms are more productive than small farms, or conversely. That is, if large farms are more productive then the economy is paying an important penalty to engage in this manner of land reform in the name of equity. On the other hand, if small farms are more productive than large farms then the country is doing what is efficient, and perhaps attaining an equity goal as well.[9] But this particular formulation, as familiar as it is, fails to understand the important distinction between productive efficiency and social efficiency.

Start by assuming that the same types of products would be grown on the land regardless of whether it is in the hands of a few large landowners or is instead divided among the masses.[10] The question is, starting at point q (on *PPF*) in figure 6.5, will a land reform program

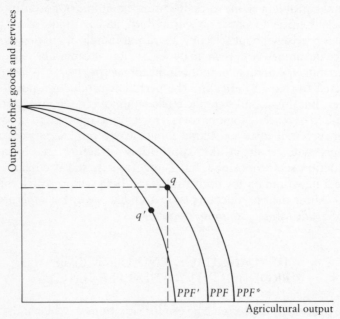

Figure 6.5   Production Possibilities of Land Reform

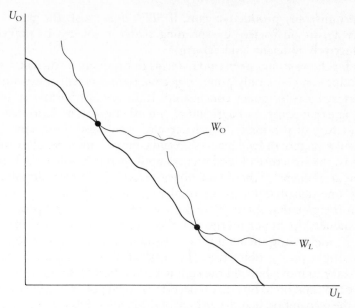

Figure 6.6   Two Possible Formulations of a Social Welfare Function

lead to *PPF'* or to *PPF**? Point *q* represents the status quo bundle of outputs, and *PPF'* might be regarded with two possibilities in mind. First, it may represent the new production possibilities resulting from a costless change to a new institutional structure that reflects expropriation of the large estates and their redistribution to the landless. Or, it may represent the new production possibilities as the landowners spend scarce financial resources to prevent expropriation. Under the first possibility it might be concluded that a redistribution of land reduces productive efficiency. Under the second possibility we see the gentry attempting to preserve a status quo structure of economic advantage. In more contemporary terms, a landed group engages in rent-seeking behavior. This use of scarce resources to preserve economic advantage detracts from the overall production of both agriculture and other goods and services. There would be a new output bundle of, say, *q'* .

Now consider the two possibilities presented by *PPF**. If *PPF** *does not* exist, the redistribution of land is irrelevant to agricultural production (this implies constant returns to scale), and productive efficiency is served by not redistributing land. Efforts by the gentry to preclude a redistribution of land are doubly counter-productive; scarce resources are devoted to the prevention of a move that would not promise any productive gain. If *PPF* does* exist, the gentry can inflict a cost on society by spending scarce resources to prevent a productively efficient land reform.

So far the story has been told in terms of productive efficiency only. If production is the only policy objective then this will constitute the necessary basis for policy conclusions. If the policy objective concerns only aggregate output of agriculture and other goods and services then this picture of productive efficiency also yields social efficiency; the particular pattern of land ownership and control is immaterial to policy. That is, the structure of land ownership is merely a policy instrument in the attainment of the policy objective and the correct distribution is the one that maximizes the total value of production in society.

But imagine that there are two policy objectives – total production *and* ownership opportunities for the landless. When one observes nations addressing the land reform issue it is clearly a manifestation of multiple policy objectives. To analyze this situation it will be necessary to move beyond the simple production picture presented in figure 6.5, and on to one that reflects these dual policy objectives. Start with the recognition that the welfare of the landless laborers has become a legitimate policy concern, and policy objectives must be recast in terms of this new concern. Consider figure 6.6, in which the relevant social welfare function is seen to have two possible formulations: one in which the interests of the landless are given expression (W_L), and another in which the interests of the landless are relatively insignificant compared with those of the landowners (W_O).

The implication of these dual policy objectives can be explored by considering figure 6.7. Assume, for instance, that *PPF** in figure 6.5 does not exist – that is, aggregate productive efficiency in society will not be enhanced by redistribution of land. If such a program were to proceed, agricultural output would be reduced and (possibly) leave the production of other goods and services unchanged. While this looks like a classic instance of decreased welfare as the economy moves to *PPF′*, this conclusion has no basis in theory. Specifically, U and U' belong to two different families of social utility functions, derived from two distinct social welfare functions (W_O and W_L). That is,

$$U = U(A, O) \qquad\qquad (6.33)$$
$$U' = U'(A, O, L) \qquad\qquad (6.34)$$

where A reflects agricultural output, O reflects the output of other goods and services, and L reflects ownership opportunities for the landless. That is, point q is socially efficient under U, while q' is socially efficient under U'. It might be thought that the potential compensation test

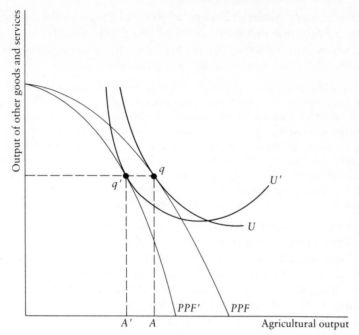

Figure 6.7   Reallocating Economic Opportunity

would fail here and reveal that q' is inefficient when compared to q'. But recall that the status quo is an institutional structure in which the landless must offer bids to current landowners if the new institutional arrangement is to be put in place. Contrast this with a status quo in which the landless suddenly have *rights* to land and others have *duty* to observe those rights. Here the reservation price of the landless becomes relevant to any Pareto test, and it could be seen that the Pareto-optimal outcome is, in fact, dominated by the status quo from which one party or the other had to make a bid.

Judgments of social efficiency require more than the location of an output bundle on a production possibilities frontier; such location insures only productive efficiency. Social efficiency demands concordance of marginal rates of transformation along a production possibilities frontier and marginal rates of substitution along a social indifference curve that reflects all relevant social objectives. Under a multiple-objective situation that includes both production and land-ownership opportunities, q' in figure 6.7 is a socially efficient output bundle, and q is irrelevant.

A recent investigation of land policy in Israel illustrates the distinction between a resource allocation that improves productive efficiency, one that reallocates economic opportunity, and one that is concerned only with the distribution of income. To quote the authors:

> This study compares the production and distributional consequences of three hypothetical land allocation rules to the equal land allocation rule actually used on Israeli *moshav*. A *moshav* . . . is a cooperative village consisting of small, equal-sized family farms which share agricultural, financial, and marketing services. . . . The settlements were made with each family plot as near to equal in land, water, and other resources as possible. This equal allocation and restrictions on land sale or rental have prevented both scale economies and the farming of the land by the best qualified farmers. (Berck and Levy 1986, p. 605)

The authors then considered three alternative land policies: (1) a value-maximizing policy of distributing land to the current farmers, a policy that "approximates the market outcome when labor is immobile" (p. 605); (2) a policy of allocating land based on a number of aspects of human capital that are regarded as non-discriminatory (that is, taking account of differential farming skills, but ignoring ethnic origin) under the assumption of immobile labor; and (3) a value-maximizing policy that allows for labor mobility. "These policies are compared to the equal distribution currently in effect. We seek to discover if the equality inherent in the current system is bought at a reasonable price in terms of forgone value of output." (p. 606) The conventional way in which this problem would be cast would be to ask whether or not the equality of land allocation comes at the expense of economic efficiency. Indeed, Berck and Levy conclude:

> Our land allocation simulation indicated that the losses from allocating land on *moshavim* are low; and, in terms of inequality, the costs of doing otherwise are high. The efficient land allocation value added, which is 7.476% higher than the output resulting from equal land allocation, comes only at the cost of reducing the income of the poorest farmers by 36% and doubling the overall income inequality. The less drastic . . . policy of allocating land according to schooling but not according to nativity or ethnicity still has modest output gains and still substantial impoverishment of the poorest and worsening of the income inequality. Intersector mobility of the farmers does not greatly change these results. Therefore, more efficient distribution of land is not an attractive policy. (p. 613)

My concern with this form of analysis is not in the modeling or in the formulation of the empirical work. It is, rather, a problem in concepts and language, and it is a problem that one finds repeatedly in public policy analysis.[11] It is maintained by the authors that the "efficient land allocation value added . . . comes only at the cost of reducing the income of the poorest farmers by 36% and doubling the overall income inequality." (p. 613) This is a conceptually flawed argument for the simple reason that there is no one "efficient land allocation value added" but rather an *efficient land allocation value added for each possible institutional arrangement being considered.* At the beginning of their paper Berck and Levy say that their objective is to compare the "production and distributional consequences of three hypothetical land allocation rules to the equal land allocation rule actually used." (p. 605) However, by the end of the study the authors state that the "efficient land allocation" carries with it a higher value added, but a serious loss in income equality.

What should have been reported is that the land allocation policy that results in the greatest value added (production) is the one that has serious implications for equality.[12] This is very different from being told that equality comes at the expense of efficiency. This subtle difference is critical for the simple reason that most policy makers feel differently about a sacrifice in *production* as opposed to a sacrifice in *efficiency.* To be inefficient is to be doing less well than what is thought to be possible, and it often has a connotation that gives the impression of permanence. But merely to be producing a little less conjures up far different sentiments about the "costs" of equality and economic opportunity than does the recognition that such policies are costly in terms of forgone efficiency. Such is the unfortunate and incorrect use of the concept of efficiency in economics; increased production is almost uniformly taken to mean increased efficiency.[13]

In terms of figure 6.7, the Israel land study seems to indicate that if equality of land holdings should no longer be a policy objective, then agricultural output would shift from point q' to q. But to conclude thereby that q is the efficient output, and that q' is not, is to make a serious conceptual error for the way in which policy choices are defined and evaluated. *Both* q and q' are socially efficient ways to accomplish two different policy objectives. Social efficiency is not being sacrificed or enhanced under either policy; one policy yields more production, the other yields a different constellation of economic opportunity, of income distribution, and of agricultural output. The *moshav* policy in Israel is one of *reallocating economic opportunity* and there is *no social efficiency cost to be paid in so doing.* There is, to be sure, a small (7.5 percent) loss in total value added in agriculture, but this is a production loss, not an efficiency loss.

V   SUMMARY

The usual practice among economists when concerned with public policy issues is to start with the concept of the market and to ask whether or not there is evidence of market failure. The test for market failure rests on evidence that gainers from institutional transactions could potentially compensate losers from a change and still leave an economic surplus. The extension of this approach is to see all institutional change either as improving economic efficiency, or as redistributing income. In intertemporal concerns there is often worry about the dominance of the present over the future, a discussion that will usually focus on the proper discount rate whereby future benefits and costs might be made commensurate with current costs and benefits. This concern for the discount rate is the wrong question to ask for it assumes that the present generation has *privilege* and the future has *no right*. Social efficiency demands that there be no missing markets; an institutional structure that gives the present *privilege* with respect to actions that hold implications for the future (therefore leaving future generations with *no rights*) is precisely a situation of missing markets. Social efficiency can be achieved only by comparing actions under both possible structures of entitlement: *privilege* for the present as compared to *duty* for the present; *no rights* for the future as compared to *rights* for the future.

When uncertainty is introduced it was seen that the formal symmetry of expected utility theory is negated by recent empirical work in prospect theory. In this work there seems to be clear evidence that the framing of the question has profound implications for choices made – assuming no change in underlying preferences. Those in a position to make choices feel differently about undertaking actions to modify certain gains than about undertaking actions to modify certain losses. And the status quo structure of institutional arrangements is at the core of how collective choices are framed, and thus acted upon.

In the single-period pollution problem it was seen that the Coasian result of symmetry of outcomes is a very special case. The mythical unified firm provides only the production possibilities frontier along which the resulting outcomes will be determined as a function of the prevailing institutional arrangements. These institutional arrangements will dominate the situation in terms of output of the two interdependent firms.

The conventional view that equity and efficiency are traded off is seen to be overly simplistic, and conceptually flawed. Production (and productive efficiency) may be linked with a land allocation program that is more egalitarian in nature, but any particular structure of land ownership is associated with a socially efficient output bundle where all productive factors are optimally allocated. Social efficiency is a concept that recognizes pertinent social objectives, social indifference curves, and relative prices; productive efficiency recognizes only increments to the monetized value of the outputs that are found along a production possibilities frontier.

As long as the output of goods and services is found along a production possibilities frontier, it can be said that the economy is organized in a productively efficient manner. However, it is the exact position on the frontier that will determine whether or not the outcome is considered to be socially efficient. The top-level optimum is found where marginal rates of transformation in production are exactly equal to marginal rates of substitution in consumption, under the assumption that relative prices will sustain this equality.

NOTES

1   This assumes that individuals are not risk seeking.
2   There is growing interest in understanding "choice under ambiguity." Specifically: "There are important psychological differences in the way people experience the uncertainty inherent in gambling devices as compared with those faced in everyday life. In gambling devices, the nature of uncertainty is explicit since there is a well-defined sampling space and sampling procedure. In contrast, when assessing uncertainty in real world tasks, the precision of the gambling analogy can be misleading . . . beliefs about uncertain events are typically loosely held and ill defined. Moreover, feelings of uncertainty are not limited to random influences that affect outcomes from a well-defined process (e.g. the proportions of different colored balls in an urn) but can extend to uncertainty about the underlying data generating process itself. In short, ambiguity or uncertainty about uncertainties is a pervasive element of much real world decision making." (Einhorn and Hogarth 1987, p. 43)
3   Also see the work by Bishop and Heberlein (1979) and Knetsch and Sinden (1984).
4   It should be noticed here that the external costs visited on Beta are a function of Alpha's output rather than Alpha's inputs. This requires one of two assumptions: (1) that the offending item for Beta is indeed q_1 rather than one of the inputs used by Alpha in the production of q_1; or (2) that the offending item for Beta is in fact one or more of Alpha's inputs, but there exists a direct and unalterable functional relationship between those one or more inputs and q_1 such that q_1 is a precise proxy variable

for the offending input(s). An example in which q_1 is the offending item can be found in which Alpha's generation and transmission of electricity causes interference with Beta's reception of radio signals and data processing. An example in which one of Alpha's inputs is the offending item for Beta can be imagined where Alpha's burning of coal to generate the electricity gives rise to a situation in which the coal dust and smoke foul Beta's computers.

5   A_1 represents the partial derivative of A with respect to q_1; it is the marginal cost of firm Alpha. Likewise for B_1 and B_2.

6   Additively separable in its arguments requires the following to be true: the cost function $C(q_1, q_2)$ is separable, that is $C(q_1, q_2) = C^1(q_1) + C^2(q_2)$, if and only if $q_1 = F(x, q_2)$ is separable; that is, if and only if $q_1 = F^1(x) + F^2(q_2)$ where x is an input vector for the production of q_1.

7   To avoid the problems associated with worrying about which activity, Alpha or Beta, was there first, assume that both began operation at precisely the same moment. The courts will, of course, be interested to know which activity was already established and which activity came second. If Alpha were there first then Beta might be found guilty of "going to the nuisance." If Beta were there first then its claim to a "right" to be free of the interference will obviously carry more weight. The interest here is to explore the solution to the externality that would enhance economic efficiency, regardless of which activity was first in time. See *Spur Industries* v. *Del Webb* (1972) for an example of how the courts deal with such problems.

8   This is analogous with the illustration of intertemporal externalities discussed in section I of this chapter.

9   The literature on this subject, though large, does not seem to allow a clear answer on this matter of relative productivity. For a review and synthesis of the debate in the Indian context see Verma and Bromley (1987).

10   This assumption is patently false as we know from the land-use practices of the Latin American *haciendas vis-à-vis* the crops that peasants grow. However, the assumption does not alter the basic story or the conclusions to be reached, although it may accentuate the differences between the two institutional arrangements under consideration.

11   Because this problem of language and concepts is frequent in the literature, it may seem that I am being unfairly critical of the Berck-Levy study. This is unfortunate since I regard the study to be very well done, and pertinent to policy discussions about land policy in agriculture. I use the study because it so clearly illustrates the problem that arises when great care is not taken with language and concepts.

12   Al Schmid reminds me that this may not be strictly true if the different rights structure leads to output changes that alter relative prices.

13   This practice is most pronounced in the benefit–cost literature where some people talk of "efficiency benefits" and "distribution benefits." See also the reference to the North model of institutional change in chapter 2.

7
Property Rights and Institutional Change

The law locks up the man or woman
Who steals the goose from off the common;
But leaves the greater villain loose
Who steals the common from the goose.[1]

Edward Potts Cheyney,
An Introduction to the Industrial and
Social History of England

The contentious nature of institutional transactions has already been addressed in the sense that those who find the status quo to their particular liking, or who despair of change, will seek to have their interest better protected by calling it a "right." Similarly those who may wish for institutional change will suggest that they have a "right" to some new institutional structure that is more to their liking. The language of rights is closely related to concepts of property, and property is essentially about the security of future income streams. One important class of institutional arrangements is that of *property institutions*. Some property institutions pertain to physical objects of value such as an automobile, a house, a Dali original, or a violin. Other property institutions pertain to streams of benefits such as job security, continued access to a stream of revenue from a natural resource, or the future income from one's creative talents (patent and copyright).

The purpose in this chapter will be to explore the concept of property institutions. I will be concerned with the elements of ownership, I will elaborate both the philosophy and practice of property, and I will develop the idea and essence of property relations as entitlements.

I   CONCEPTS OF PROPERTY IN ECONOMICS

The traditional connotation of property is that of a piece of land or a dwelling. Often the term is applied to some asset of value that is being retained for economic gain. But this popular usage of the term is at odds with the historical meaning of property. More importantly, this connotation is not very helpful in an analytical sense. One early reference to property in economic writing is found in Scott Gordon's 1954 article on the high-seas fishery entitled "The economic theory of a common property resource," an article that did much to give prominence to the term "common property." Gordon's terminology soon began to appear in other writings on the fishery, as well as with respect to other natural resources. The now-famous article by Garrett Hardin (1968) finally brought the term "commons" to the attention of a much wider audience, and rendered it virtually synonymous with resource depletion. Indeed, the term "common property" has taken on the central responsibility for the exhaustion of fish stocks, the poverty of fishermen, the overcapitalization of fishing fleets, air pollution, the world's burgeoning population, the overdraft of ground water, overgrazing, excessive pumping from oil pools, and – more recently – the depletion of hunting and gathering territories among primitive peoples. The conventional economic literature on property relations has tended to identify three general types of property: (1) private property; (2) state property; and (3) common (or communal) property. For instance Demsetz argues that:

> By communal ownership, I shall mean a right which can be exercised by all members of the community. Frequently the rights to till and to hunt the land have been communally owned. The right to walk a city sidewalk is communally owned. Communal ownership means that the community denies to the state or to individual citizens the right to interfere with any person's exercise of communally owned rights. Private ownership implies that the community recognizes the right of the owner to exclude others from exercising the owner's private right. State ownership implies that the state may exclude anyone from the use of a right as long as the state follows accepted political procedures for determining who may not use state-owned property. (1967, p. 354)

This three-part conception of property has been instrumental in the creation of what might be called the conventional wisdom of property rights. With respect to many natural resources the discussion invariably is reduced to a choice between communal property and private property. The irony of the situation warrants some comment. When resource destruction is observed in settings of joint ownership and control it is the institutional arrangement (joint responsibility) that is immediately said to be at fault. When resource destruction is observed in settings of private ownership and control – and there are many examples indeed – it is not the institutional arrangement (private property) that is to blame but the excessively high rate of time preference of the owner, or imperfect capital markets, or incomplete contingent-claims markets, or some other imperfection in the larger economic system. The logic of this approach seems to be: since everyone *knows*, as a matter of faith, that private owners take care of their assets in the best interest of society at large, it goes without saying that the fault must be seen to lie elsewhere. Few economists find much benefit in property arrangements other than private property; the quotes from both Demsetz and Posner in chapter 2 capture the conventional view well.

But the wisdom of private property has been seen to lie in the fact that it is the only property structure that brings the scope of decision-making authority into coincidence with the very essence of a market economy – the individual autonomous decision maker. Small wonder, then, that individual (private) property is found so conducive to an efficiency framework that venerates the free choice of the individual.[2] The concern here will be with concepts of property as entitlements, and property as it relates to the notion of ownership. This latter discussion is necessary since many commentators use the terms *property* and *ownership* quite indiscriminately, and often synonymously. Consider first the issue of ownership.

II   THE ESSENCE OF OWNERSHIP

Those who use the terms *property* or *property rights* will rarely be specific about the content of those terms as it bears on analysis of the constituents of ownership. That is, some tend to talk of property, and of ownership, and of ownership of property as if these terms were widely understood, when in fact quite the opposite tends to be the case. Honoré has given the basis of ownership by listing eleven characteristics that are said to be present in full, or liberal, ownership. These are listed and briefly discussed below (Honoré 1961).

A   *The Right to Possess*

Possession, or exclusive physical control, is said to lie at the center of the notion of ownership. Any legal system must accord the right to be put in control of something valuable, and must also assure that such control cannot be terminated arbitrarily. In the absence of this, there is no ownership. And, in the absence of ownership of valuable assets it is impossible to have a functioning economic system. This does not mean private ownership is necessary; it only requires that some form of recognized ownership exist.

B   *The Right to Use*

The term "use" can have a broad or a narrow interpretation, with the more strict notion pertaining to the owner's personal use and enjoyment of something. The fact that certain uses are restricted does not diminish the content of ownership, though it reduces the range of choice open to the owner.

C   *The Right to Manage*

This aspect of ownership includes several ancillary rights such as the right to admit others to one's land, the power to permit others to use one's things, and to set the limits of such permission. That is, contracting with others over the benefit stream which arises from the valuable asset is the essence of management.

D   *The Right to the Income*

As pointed out by Honoré, the right to income has always loomed rather significant in any discussion of rights of ownership; especially is this so as the importance of income versus capital becomes more pronounced.

E   *The Right to the Capital*

This right comprehends the power to alienate the valuable item, or to consume it, or to destroy (waste) it. As such, this introduces important intertemporal issues into ownership.

F   *The Right to Security*

The issue here is the owner's expectation that ownership runs into perpetuity assuming solvency and behavior consistent with accepted social norms. This is immunity from arbitrary appropriation; the concern with eminent domain versus the police power is pertinent here.

There is a fine line, however, for Honoré argues that a general policy of expropriation – even with full compensation – would be devastating to the concept of ownership.

This matter of security requires some elaboration. Eminent domain is an attempt to provide security over the income stream arising from a valuable asset in the sense that if that asset is required by the state for public benefit, the costs of the acquisition will not be borne by the unlucky individual whose asset is required, but will instead be spread over the entire polity (e.g. it will be socialized). But there is no desire to provide similar security to those who are creating a public harm; here the police power of the state is used to prevent antisocial acts.

G   *Transmissibility*

No one can enjoy something after death, but an interest in an asset that is transmissible to a successor is more valuable than one that stops at death. To the extent that transmissibility is restricted then one's property is diminished.

H   *Absence of Term*

Along with security, this comprises the owner's interest in something we might refer to as "duration." Different legal systems convey different interests over time. The interests of the owner are best served by a determinable time horizon, where longer is more valuable than shorter. The absence of term means that full ownership runs into perpetuity.

I   *The Prohibition of Harmful Use*

Externality problems are characterized by the use of something owned to cause harm for others. Ownership does not include the ability to harm others and the exercise of the police power of the state mentioned above is a reflection of this prohibition.

J   *Liability to Execution*

Full ownership involves the liability of the owner's interest to be used to settle debts. In the absence of such provisions, property would become a vehicle for defrauding creditors, and national income would suffer accordingly as those with liquid capital would be wary of loaning it to those with assets lacking this proviso.

K   The Right to Residuary Character

Here one has the existence of social rules to govern situations in which ownership rights lapse; there must be rules for deciding what to do when, for whatever reason, the preexisting ownership rights are no longer relevant.

By way of summary it should be noted that none of these eleven is a necessary constituent of ownership as such, since individuals will be recognized to own something in a restricted sense where one or more of the conditions is not met. Yet the more complete is the presence of these, the more thorough can we regard one's ownership of something valuable. Similarly the more thorough the ownership interests, the more valuable they are.

III   THE PHILOSOPHICAL CASE FOR PRIVATE PROPERTY

The arguments over concepts of property will often focus on land as the major item of dispute. Many physical objects are avowedly personal in nature, divisible, and used primarily for consumption as opposed to production. But land, with all of the historical significance that it carries, is a productive asset of great economic and political significance. Prominent in the debates over the preferred structure of property institutions is the advantage that flows from the ability to exclude others from a piece of land. Implicit here is that exclusive individual property is necessary as an inducement to labor. As capitalist modes of production became prominent, labor changed from a chattel to a marketable good that could be exchanged. Land too became commoditized at about this same time. Since each person now had property (a claim) in the exchange (market) value of his or her own labor, property as exclusivity was reinforced. If a person mixed property in the form of labor power with property in the form of land, did it not follow that the product was also property? Also, is it not obvious that such exclusivity to this product was required, else there would be insufficient inducement to undertake the arduous mixing of one's labor?

It is no accident that this notion is also central to Locke's concept of property. Bentham too was impressed with the security of enjoyment of the fruits of one's labors, as were Mill and Green. Mill wrote:

> The institution of property, when limited to its essential elements consists in the recognition, in each person, of a right to the exclusive disposal

of what he or she have produced by their own exertions, or received either by gift or by fair agreement, without force or fraud, from those who produced it. The foundation of the whole is the right of producers to what they themselves have produced. (Schlatter 1951, p. 249)

This logic provides the scientific rationale for exactly the kinds of property required by nascent capitalism. This is what Macpherson means by *justificatory theory*; it is theory derived to justify a seemingly advantageous social practice. Macpherson writes:

The concept of property as nothing but an exclusive, alienable, individual right not only in material things but even in one's own productive capacities was thus a creation of capitalist society: it was only needed, and only brought forth, when the formal equality of the market superseded the formal inequality of pre-capitalist society. (1973, p. 130)

But in a world of scarcity this inalienable right to exclude others is also the right to deny access to the very means of existence (land and capital assets). In the abstract who can be against the right of an individual to reap where they have sown? For as reminded earlier by Demsetz and Posner, what incentive will there be to plant corn if anyone can pick the fruits of that effort with impunity? But what is true in the abstract is not necessarily acceptable in the larger picture of daily life. If the world still consisted of a large number of independent farmers and artisans then property as exclusivity is seen to serve its original purpose. But when, as in some countries, 80 percent of the cultivable land is owned by 10 percent of the population, the ethical appeal of exclusivity is seriously undermined by widespread poverty and the absence for many of access to capital in the form of land. In a world of truly atomistic producers, exclusion to encourage the mixing of labor with land (capital) is compelling. In the world as it is today, exclusion to deny Alpha the opportunity to mix his labor with Beta's land (or capital), for Alpha owns no land (or capital), is to deny Alpha access to something of great importance.

Beta's right to exclude Alpha seems proper from Beta's perspective, but how does it look from Alpha's perspective? Private property as celebrated by those who believe in pervasive markets and decentralized choice is compelling since it is the perspective of the owner that is being considered. But how does the non-owner feel? Is private property only beneficial for those fortunate enough to own assets of some current economic value? Tawney draws a distinction between active property and passive property. He writes:

The characteristic fact, which differentiates most modern property from that of the pre-industrial age, and which turns against it the very reasoning by which formerly it was supported, is that in modern economic conditions ownership is not active but passive, that to most of those who own property today it is not a means of work but an instrument for the acquisition of gain or the exercise of power, and that there is no guarantee that gain bears any relation to service, or power to responsibility. (1978, p. 140)

And, he continues:

Property has no more insidious enemies than those . . . who, by defending all forms of it as equally valued, involve the institution in the discredit attaching to its extravagances. In reality, . . . the greater part of modern property, whether, like mineral rights and urban ground rents, it is merely a form of private taxation which the law allows certain persons to levy on the industry of others, or whether, like property in capital, it consists of rights to payment for instruments which the capitalist cannot himself use but puts at the disposal of those who can, has as its essential feature that it confers upon its owners income unaccompanied by personal service. (p. 143)

To Tawney, the ethical justification of exclusive property is missing. If the benefits of such property are to be found in exclusion, then he insists that the costs of such property are also to be found in exclusion.

The detailed examination of the rationale for private property will require the recognition of three possible levels at which one must deal in discussing private property rights. These are considered by Becker (1977) to be levels of justification for the exclusive private control of valuable objects. At the *general* level, the question is one of why there should be any private property rights at all. The second question would then concern why there should be a *specific* sort of property right – say private property in land. Finally, Becker notes that the issue is one of why a *particular* person (or entity) ought to have particular property rights in a particular object of value. There are three levels, therefore, at which one must address the justification of private property.

Next, it is necessary to specify the essential elements in an analysis of any type of rights, of which ten have been recognized. First, the right holder must be specified. Second, it is necessary to specify the right regarder; these are individuals or entities that must pay heed to the rights held by the right holder. Right regarders have a duty to observe rights, on pain of criminal or civil action being brought against them. Third, one must be clear about the general nature of the relation between the right holder and the right regarder. These were introduced earlier as legal relations between Alpha and Beta, and they will be elaborated upon later in this chapter. The fourth specification represents the content of the right and indicates what is being protected or given by the right. For instance, Alpha owes Beta $10,000 on January 5, 1999. The fifth element is a specification of the conditions under which a right-claim may be considered to be sound.[3] Drawing on the three levels of justification of rights, this element constitutes the general justifying conditions (the things that justify any right-claim), specific conditions justifying the type of right-claim at issue, and the particular justifying conditions for the particular right-claim at issue.

The sixth element is a detailed account of the conditions under which reasonable people would agree that a right has been violated. There are two components here: (1) the conditions under which a right regarder has failed to fulfill the right-claim; and (2) the conditions under which a particular right can be overridden. Under the first it is necessary to know that the accused party has indeed undertaken a certain act that contravenes a party's rights – such as driving her automobile across one's lawn. Under the second, larger moral principles are invoked to admit that some rights will be ignored under some circumstances. That is, Alpha's presumed right must be found to have general moral support; Alpha's right of privacy does not include the right to prevent a police search if the police have reasonable evidence that Alpha is harboring stolen goods. The seventh element specifies the conditions under which the violation of a right is excusable. For instance, the woman who drove across Beta's lawn may have been taking evasive action to avoid hitting a child in the road. The eighth element is the specification of appropriate remedies – letting the punishment fit the crime. The issue here is the need for – and the mix of – measures of compensatory as well as retaliatory justice. And of course in cases of the loss of life and limb, compensation is either too late for the victim and hence irrelevant, or it is usually a poor substitute for what has been lost. The ninth element is a specification of the means to be used for extracting the remedies. Tenth, and finally, it is necessary to have a specification of the agent(s) empowered to extract the remedies.

With this background it is now possible to explore the five major arguments in favor of the concept of private control over valuable objects. These are: (1) first occupancy; (2) the labor theory; (3) the utility theory; (4) political liberty; and (5) moral enhancement.

A First Occupancy

The phrase "first in time, first in right" applies in most social settings from queues at airline ticket counters to general admission seats at a theatre. The extension of this principle from ephemeral and recurring events to those that hold into perpetuity is bound to cause no little difficulty. Why, after all, should the first Portuguese sailor to land on the northeast coast of what is now Brazil have the right to claim that land into perpetuity for his sovereign? What of the indigenous people already there? What rights do they have?[4]

The arguments for private and exclusive rights from first occupancy fail to answer the general question as to why there should be private property rights at all. The claims that can be made for a first-occupancy argument are severe indeed. First occupancy does not define clearly how much of what is being claimed can be occupied. That is, does the temporary occupation of a landing site on Brazil – or the moon for that matter – automatically qualify the landing party to claim everything? And what is everything? As far as the eye can see? All contiguous land? All that not claimed by others? Rousseau has argued: "On such a showing . . . the Catholic King need only take possession, from his apartment, of the whole universe, merely making a subsequent reservation about what was already in the possession of [others]." . . . (1959, pp. 20–1)

Occupancy, according to Becker (1977), is hardly sufficient; it must be for the purpose of appropriation. This derives from his view that occupation must not be merely intentional but must be purposeful. If one occupies land to cultivate it but does not, then the claim of the first occupant is empty. When the Europeans first landed in the Americas their mere occupation seemed sufficient at the time – given prevailing social norms – to claim a right. When they came and began to encounter previous occupants (the native Americans) it was probably easy to rationalize the taking of the land since the previous occupants did not seem to be using the land as the Europeans understood the term *use*; to the new settlers, use meant to cultivate it and grow crops.

In the absence of actual use the first occupant may simply be claiming a right so as to exclude all future claimants; this may seem, to some, rather indefensible as a general justification for private property. The problem is, of course, that one individual could appropriate for perpetuity a vast portion of the landed estate. It is necessary, therefore, to understand the difference between possession, and the *right* to possess. In the animal world one sees possession – of a carcass, of a burrow, of a territory – without any social recognition of the right to possess; possession is enforced by power and not by a general recognition that other non-possessors have a duty to respect the right of the possessor.[5]

The argument from first occupancy, then, fails to provide a general justification for private property rights in valuable objects. That is, it fails to answer the question as to why there ought to be any private property rights in such assets. As for the particular justification, first occupancy provides a clear criterion once the correctness of using the first-occupancy principle has been established. Once a society has determined that valuable assets should be owned by someone, a good place for the law to start is to ask: "Well, who was there first?" One would then need to examine the legal and moral implications of the original appropriation, and of subsequent transfers. But to assume that "first in time" is "first in right" down through the ages is to impart great social and economic significance to events of great luck and serendipity, or the providence of having been born earlier than most of the others in the world.

B Labor

The rationale here is that individuals are entitled to hold as property whatever they produce by their own initiative, intelligence, risk taking, and labors. Enunciated within the context of the natural rights movement of the seventeenth century it seems almost self-evident (Becker 1977). But it is too dependent upon the notion of natural rights to serve as a universal principle. In Greek political theory, for instance, the right to the fruits of one's labor is hardly mentioned. The proponents of the labor theory of property acquisition rarely discuss the basis of such an argument as its general justification. Rather, one finds specific instances being used to justify the general argument for all-around privatization of natural assets; if the farmer cannot be assured of reaping where he has sown he will not sow – and we will all be the poorer. But, except for Locke, few writers take seriously the notion that labor can indefinitely entitle anyone to anything. As Nozick (1974) notes, one might just as easily argue that by mixing one's labor with the land you simply lose your labor rather than gaining the land.

Perhaps the strongest argument against the labor theory of property acquisition can be found in the case of children. Most would agree that individuals have property in their own body – that is to say, they alone control what is to be done to their person, subject to the larger proviso that they have not harmed others and hence become charged with some criminal act. But it is logically inconsistent to argue that individuals have property in their own person, and then to say that one acquires property in some object by mixing one's labor with that object. For what object has more labor mixed with it than one's children? Is it credible that children become the property of their parents by virtue of all of the labor that the latter expend in the course of bringing them to adulthood? Do children only recover their property in themselves when their parents are deceased? Or when their parents decide to transfer it to them? What if their parents decide to transfer the "property" to someone else?

One is left with the notion that sometimes labor can be used to establish that one is owed possession or use or management of an object by virtue of having labored on it. Becker (1977) would call this a *recipient claim right*. An example of a recipient claim right can be found in the statement "every pregnant woman has the right to an abortion if her health is in jeopardy." But to say that she has a right to this service is not to say that any particular doctor is duty bound to provide that service if he or she is morally opposed to abortions. That is, there is a claim right but also an unspecifiable duty that says no particular party is bound to make good on the right.

The labor theory holds that laborers are entitled to property in the very things they produce, and where these are inseparable from the raw materials worked on, they are entitled to property in the things worked on. But this clearly will not do for the whole class of employees, or for the large class of people who perform services for others. "Once it is acknowledged that some labor is expected to yield property rights in the very things labored on, while other labor is not, the root idea of the labor theory must be seen as a poor choice for a fundamental principle." (Becker 1977, p. 47)

One final possibility is that laboring on something constitutes what Becker calls *psychological appropriation*. And for this consider the matter of *just deserts*. First, note that desert is a two-edged sword: if a benefit is due by virtue of having added value through working on something, then a cost is to be paid whenever value is subtracted; if a farmer adds value by growing a good crop the deserts due must be offset by the costs that will accrue to others because of the erosion that occurred as a result of cultivating the land. It is doubtful that this is quite what the labor advocates had in mind. To follow Becker:

> This results in an argument for a tax on entrepreneurs whose activities deplete the community's stock of unowned resources or limit the opportunity of others without their consent; and it results in an argument for compensation to any persons who suffer a demonstrable net personal loss. The size of such penalties may in effect cancel the benefit entirely, of course. (Becker 1977, p. 51)

This would seem to imply that when individuals "deserve" a benefit for their labor, and when nothing but property in the things produced will do, then, other conditions satisfied, the individual deserves property. But if substitutes will do equally well then they should be offered instead. But this is hardly a compelling case for the notion that only property in the thing labored on is an acceptable desert. As such, the labor theory of property acquisition is considerably weakened.

C Utility

There are several grounds on which it is possible to argue from utility that private appropriation of valuable things is justified. First, in order to carry out simple tasks each of us must own and possess certain tools and artifacts. If, each morning, I should need to argue with my children over whether the blue toothbrush is mine, chaos would be the normal state of affairs. If the carpenter or the painter had every day to arrange for some tools to use, the social dividend would surely suffer. Secondly, there is the familiar argument that private appropriation is necessary to ensure proper care of the thing owned. As will be elaborated later, this argument confuses the absence of individual ownership rights with the absence of individual duties of care; as long as the latter is present and enforced then non-private property is well cared for. The summer pastures of the Swiss Alps, and public libraries, are examples of non-private property; neither seems to be savaged by this ownership structure. Finally, Hegel argued that private acquisition was essential to the expression of the human personality. If one accepts these arguments, then there is a case for general private rights in some objects; which things, and how those rights are to be structured, are begged by the general justification.

D Political Liberty

The general justification for private rights in property from political liberty arguments focuses on the innate characteristics of humans that have them acquiring, accumulating, controlling, using, and modifying valuable objects; to deny this urge is to violate fundamental precepts of human expression and therefore liberty. Liberties that are not dependent on the existence of conventions or social institutions are referred to as *natural liberties* and they are regarded as being prior to the state. In the Hobbesian state of nature each individual has complete natural liberty. In such a setting no individual has a claim right against any other individual.

Becker (1977) argues that any system of political liberty that can provide a general justification of private property rights must have several features. First, it must distinguish political liberty from material liberty; that is the liberty to do something (political liberty) must be more than merely the physical (material) liberty or ability to act in a certain way. Political liberties must be rights that entail the absence of claim rights in others that one may not do the thing in question. Second, if political liberty is to provide a general justification for private property it must encompass material as well as formal liberty – that is it must encompass the physical ability to do something with the legal recognition of that ability. Finally, since the existence of any material liberty requires one's continued existence, any system of political liberties must at least include the right to survive long enough to carry out the act in question. These are the minimal conditions if a political liberty argument is to be made in defense of private property.

But by justifying private property, the argument from political liberty also places some restrictions on the general justification, as well as on the specific justification. For instance whenever a resource that is critical for survival is scarce, is non-renewable, or is exhaustible by appropriation or misuse, complete exclusive ownership – that is privatization – will not be compatible with the general justification of private property on liberty grounds. And, Becker adds:

> Further, wherever a thing can be used to interfere with another's liberty to survive, ownership rights will have to be restricted – specifically use rights and management rights. More extensive systems of liberty – for example, ones which guarantee a'l or some the right to some degree of personal fulfillment or self-realization – will place even further restrictions on ownership. (Becker 1977, p. 78)

Note the irony here. One often finds an argument that thoroughgoing private property will fully guarantee individual liberties. Yet, if that privatization results in the denial of the means of survival for a portion of the population one would think it easy to argue that their most basic liberty, survival, had been denied. When the private ownership of land is concentrated in the hands of a fraction of the population, and others are reduced to daily wages at starvation levels – if they can gain employment at all – one would think that the contradictions would elicit some comment.

E   Moral Character

The final argument for a system of private property rights contains two lines of argument: (1) who in society should possess the rights; and (2) the effects of such rights on the citizenry as a whole. The first theme, regarding who should have property, has three components:

1 If property is justified at a general level, then those rights should belong to members of society who will use the benefits to a good effect. That is, property should go to those who will use it in socially beneficial ways.

2 Private rights in property should belong to those who will manage the asset well. This differs slightly from the first moral argument, speaking to the management of the thing as opposed to the role of the thing and its management in the larger arena of society.

3 Property should belong to those who are virtuous.

The second main theme is that private rights are necessary to the development of good moral character.

Neither of the two themes can be used to justify the existence of private property. However, the first, with its moral suggestions regarding who should have such rights if they are deemed appropriate, finds some general acceptance in many societies. There is, understandably, less concern that property rights should reside with those who are virtuous, than there is with the idea that property rights should reside with those who will use those rights to good effect, and who will wisely manage the object owned.

The empirical evidence of both good and bad moral character emanating from societies in which the full gamut of property rights is in place should be sufficient to pay little continuing attention to the claim that private property is a necessary ingredient in the development of moral character.

F   *Summary*

There are four general justifications for the existence of private rights in valuable objects – two justifications from the labor argument, one from utility, and one from liberty. Once coordinated into a coherent picture of general justification, any restrictions will have to come from the specific or the particular justifications.

From the labor theory, note that when labor service is beyond what is morally required to be done for others, when it produces something that would not exist except for that labor, and when exclusion from labor's product will not cause losses to others, then it seems wrong for producers not to exclude others from enjoying the fruits of their labors. And, whenever giving producers ownership rights in the fruits of their labor is a justifiable way of excluding others under the conditions spelled out immediately above, then such ownership rights are justifiable. The second labor argument is that when labor is beyond what is morally required to be done for others, then labor demands some reward for socially permissible efforts; conversely labor deserves disbenefits for any harms that it creates.

The argument from utility is that people need to acquire, possess, use, and consume certain things in order to achieve some general level of happiness. Insecurity in the possession and use of these objects makes said achievement very difficult and expensive. Therefore some level of security in certain utilitarian objects is justified.

Finally, the argument from political liberty has it that individuals will naturally try to accumulate and control certain physical objects, and to deny others unrestricted access to them. To prohibit such acquisition would deny something that is very fundamental to perceptions of individual liberty. But political liberties are protected only if all acquisitive behavior is regulated by a general system of property. Hence, private rights in certain objects are justifiable.

The implications of this for the economist concerned about institutional change, property relations, and economic processes are several. One can start in the eighteenth century with its general acceptance of the natural rights theory of property; that is, with the idea that rights to control property individually were logically prior to institutional arrangements created by human society. Liberalism in the eighteenth century accepted the natural-rights approach, but by the nineteenth century liberals were more likely to find comfort in the utilitarianism of Bentham, though Hume, as early as 1739, had articulated the same concept (Schlatter 1951). Hume argued that the rights to private property rested on the acceptance of those rights deriving from individual self-interest. In a world of thoroughgoing abundance there would be no need for laws of property, for obvious reasons. But in this world, where scarcity is prevalent, practical persons soon realized the obvious advantage and necessity of the distinction between "mine and thine."

Hume rejected the idea that contributed labor could serve to justify private property. At most, invested labor leads to an association of ideas out of which the concept of property is born (Schlatter 1951). But demolishing the arguments of the natural rights philosophers did not mean that he rejected their ultimate conclusion; his view was simply that they had failed to give full recognition to the practicality of private appropriation.

That Hume should come, by a different path, to the same end as John Locke is not surprising; they were both defending the same social system, they were both admirers of that economic society which Adam Smith was to describe so persuasively, they agreed that the protection of free, individual property was the chief end of the state. The Utilitarians from the beginning had no quarrel with the aims of the natural rights theorists. (Schlatter 1951, p. 242)

And John Stuart Mill, in his *Principles of Political Economy*, provided the ultimate unification of the natural rights and utilitarian views on property, as seen in his quote about private property earlier in the chapter. But Mill seems to have recognized the difficulties inherent in attempting to forge a link between natural rights and utilitarian concepts of property.

He himself accepted the logical conclusion that landed property could not be justified by this theory unless the proprietor were also the cultivator. He recognized that large transfers of property by inheritance might result in divorcing ownership from labour. (p. 250)

According to Schlatter, subsequent economists were unwilling to accept the reforms that Mill suggested were necessary if property was to be justified on the usual utilitarian grounds.[6] They began, instead, to justify the prevailing system of property on the narrow utilitarian grounds that it led to the greatest output. "By substituting 'production' for 'happiness' they were able to maintain the general arguments based on utility and yet discard the natural right concept of the proper relation between work and ownership." (p. 251) So the prevailing rationalizations of private property were modified by such influential economists as Marshall and Taussig to avoid the obvious conclusion that much modern property was unjustified. And, as Schlatter points out, "The fact that influential socialist thinkers had adopted the natural rights theory and used it as an argument for socialism helps to explain why the defenders of capitalism abandoned that theory." (p. 252)

The philosophical debates over property, which go back to antiquity, are thus seen to have been much influenced by the political and economic conditions – and tensions – prevalent at the time. Learned men and women rarely spend much energy debating and rationalizing abstract and possibly irrelevant social arrangements. Concepts of property serve both *to explain* the logic of a contemporary socioeconomic system, and *to justify* that system. In turn, that particular system is then used *to justify* the prevailing concept of property upon which it is said to be based. A causal linkage is formed in the mind – and in theory – to support the notion that the concept of property is necessary to the status quo, and the status quo is equally necessary to the concept of property.

This process has the unfortunate practical result of locking the two together in such a way that any modifications around the edge of either is seen as a direct threat to the other. A market economy (which is said to be the engine of all wealth) is thought to be impossible without thoroughgoing private property, and private property (which is said to be the foundation of political liberty) is thought to be impossible without a market economy. The philosophical debates about the proper form of property institutions have done more to justify or demolish – in sweeping form – private property than to help address *particular* or *specific* instances in which property relations are seen to lead to antisocial outcomes. If one has a grand theory that justifies private property at the *general* level (in the Becker sense), then a *particular* or *specific* problem can pose a serious logical and political nightmare.

How can one deal with the specific or the particular when to do so is to challenge the very essence of the more encompassing general belief? The utilitarians have provided an opening. By basing the justification for private property on its contribution not to *happiness* but to *production*, the contemporary economist can assess the economic contributions of existing property structures quite within the prevailing economic orthodoxy, and without challenging dominant social beliefs. That is, utilitarian precepts can be used to modify property relations where particular or specific economic conditions warrant, without at the same time becoming mired down in protracted debates about political liberty or natural rights.

IV   THE PRACTICE OF PROPERTY

The previous material presented several philosophical arguments regarding private property, and the issue now turns to a discussion of the practice of property. The interest here will be in the way in which property relations function in everyday life. The earlier concern tended to focus on ownership of (or property in) physical objects such as land. A more enduring interest is in property relations as they pertain to social conventions and rules among economic agents, with respect not only to objects but also to future benefit streams that depend upon things other than physical objects.

Property arrangements are social relations among members of a collectivity with respect to an array of items of social worth. Property arrangements are not dichotomous; they link not merely a person to an object, but rather a person to an object against other persons. This triad calls attention to the social content of property institutions. Hallowell

(1943) suggests three sets of variables with which to comprehend property relations: (1) the nature and kinds of rights that are exercised, and their correlative duties and obligations; (2) the individuals or groups in whom these rights and duties are vested, and those who play the correlative roles in the collectivity; and (3) the objects of social value over which these property relations pertain. These correspond to Becker's specific and particular aspects of justification.

Earlier, the four fundamental legal relations that define one's rights, duties, privileges, and no rights were discussed. More specificity with respect to individuals and groups with respect to certain objects of value will now be introduced. To proceed, consider the term *ownership*. To most modern observers the word "ownership" is clear; it means the full rights left to an individual after certain governmental restrictions and reservations are taken into account. Individuals surely own land, although its market value is a function of the covenants placed on it by previous owners or the community at large. But there is little doubt that subject to this caveat, the individual controls the land and access to it, and is free to do with the income stream as seen fit. There are generally no corollary obligations to let first cousins grow vegetables on the southeast part, nor is there any restriction on how the income produced from the land is to be divided. The owner is free to keep it all, or to give it away. Of course relatives may be given access to a piece of it for a garden, and other income earned from the land may be given to any number of other persons. But both of these acts are grants or gifts rather than obligations or duties. Ownership implies sovereignty of the owner – subject to the ubiquitous reservations of the state.

Another confusion arises over the term *property*. As indicated above, property is a claim that individuals within a polity can count on having enforced in their behalf. Ely notes that "Property is the right, and not the object over which the right extends." (1914, p. 108) But it is the *expectation* that matters – an expectation sanctioned by the collectivity, and enforced by the collectivity. Problems arise because access to land is vastly different from a secure claim on the benefits which that land can produce. Property is a claim on something of value, whereas the ability to use one's trawler to cruise the high seas in search of fish is no claim on anything at all; it is simply the exercise of material liberty. Similarly, the physical and economic ability to develop an oil well is far different from a claim on a particular quantity of oil. When that claim exists – when there are expectations – then one has *property*. When access is available – but there is no claim on an income stream that the collectivity will protect – there is no property, there is only access.

Demsetz has recognized this crucial distinction, and he argues as follows: property rights "convey the right to harm oneself or others . . . It is clear then that property rights specify how persons may be benefited and harmed, and therefore, who must pay whom to modify the actions taken by persons." (1967, p. 347) Under conditions of open access there is no accepted system for claims settlement, and hence individuals are uncertain as to how they may or may not benefit or be harmed. Since each individual in the group of fishermen (or ranchers, or those interested in pumping oil or groundwater) has the opportunity (via open access) to make use of the scarce resource, the benefits from its use are *ex ante* undefined. This must be the case since the gains to one individual are a function of the number of others who also make use of the resource, as well as the intensity of their use.

It is important to remember that benefits of use of a scarce resource arise from that which is gained *ex post*. The mere opportunity to gain will result in an actual gain only when the actions of others are such that some potential gain is available in light of these other actors. Since there is no secure claim in a situation of open access, it is logically inconsistent to define these resource situations as property (or common property). While one will often see the cliché "everybody's property is nobody's property," nothing could be more incorrect. What ought to be said is that "everybody's access is nobody's property." There is no property in an open-access situation. This distinction is important in light of the many instances of common property resource use where depletion is absent, and poverty is not the order of the day. Ciriacy-Wantrup and Bishop (1975) have commented on the important distinction between common property and open access, and more will be said momentarily on these differences.

Consider now an issue only touched upon earlier – the distinctions in property relations among three types of rights that may be exercised with respect to an object of economic value. That is, consider the distinction among who may use the object, who controls the object, and who benefits from the object. To clarify these distinctions somewhat, consider an example of a canoe in a primitive society. It is not uncommon to find rather elaborate institutional arrangements surrounding an object such as a canoe. For instance, it is not uncommon for one individual to construct the canoe and exercise seemingly dominant control over it. To outsiders it may appear that this individual indeed owns the canoe. Yet the full accounting of the rights and duties bound up in a canoe would reveal that things are not so simple. This one person may indeed nominally control the canoe in that he decides when it is to go on fishing voyages, and where it will go. But he may have little control over who may use the canoe, or whether he is to go along on every trip. Additionally, if the canoe is the only one for a group of some size then he surely is not the only one to benefit from its use; the group at large will benefit. It is important to recognize a difference between who has a right to use something, who has a right to the stream of benefits from something, and who controls the access to something. This multiple dimension of the property relation is essential to a clear understanding of property as a social institution. I list as follows the essence of entitlements in four types of property regime:

State property   Individuals have a *duty* to observe use / access rules determined by a controlling / managing agency. Agencies have a *right* to determine use / access rules.

Private property   Individuals have a *right* to undertake socially acceptable uses, and have a *duty* to refrain from socially unacceptable uses. Others (called "non-owners") have a *duty* to refrain from preventing socially acceptable uses, and have a *right* to expect only socially acceptable uses will occur.

Common property   The management group (the "owners") has a *right* to exclude non-members, and non-members have a *duty* to abide by exclusion. Individual members of the management group (the "co-owners") have both *rights* and *duties* with respect to use rates and maintenance of the thing owned.

Non-property   There is no defined group of users or "owners" and so the benefit stream is available to anyone. Individuals have both *privilege* and *no right* with respect to use rates and maintenance of the asset. The asset is an "open-access resource."

Hence there are at least four general types of property relations in any society: open access (no property), common property, state property, and private property. It warrants reemphasis that property is not a person and an object. Rather, property is triadic – a person and an object against all other persons. This object may be something physical such as a canoe or a house, but it also may be something such as a stock in trade, or a social position of some value. "Property rights describe the relationship of one person to another with respect to a resource or any line of action." (Schmid 1987, p. 5) This *person/object against other persons* does not mean that property is only individualistic. The triad is also person(s)/object against other persons where these other persons may be those considered outside of the polity ("them").

But this triad emphasizes that property is primarily a social – not an individual – relation. It also tends to emphasize that the core of property is not the physical objects but the rights, the expectations, the duties, and the obligations that must exist in any collectivity before property can exist. Ely offered the following insight regarding property: "The essence of property is in the relations among men arising out of their relations to things." (1914, p. 96)

Firth notes:

> It must be realized in considering the problem of the control of man over material goods that such terms as "property" and "ownership" which are employed to indicate a certain set of relationships in our own society, do not necessarily preserve the same connotation when applied to a native community. The essential factors in the situation – the individual, the goods, and the other members of his community – remain unchanged, but the set of concepts by which these are related has been formed against a different cultural background. (1929, pp. 330–1)

To elaborate on this idea that language and concepts are, ultimately, dominated by context, Hallowell adds:

> Property, considered as a social institution, not only implies the exercise of rights and duties with respect to objects of value by the individuals of a given society; it also embraces the specific social sanctions which reinforce the behavior that makes the institution a going concern. (1943, p. 130)

The problem of concepts and language is captured in the concern among anthropologists between the *emic* and the *etic*. To quote Marvin Harris:

> Emic operations have as their hallmark the elevation of the native informant to the status of ultimate judge of the adequacy of the observer's descriptions and analyses . . . Etic operations have as their hallmark the elevation of the observers to the status of ultimate judges of the categories and concepts used in descriptions and analyses. (1979, p. 32)

V PROPERTY ENTITLEMENTS

Property is more than institutional arrangements defining who may use an object of value, who controls the use of that object, and who may receive the benefits from that object. *Property is also the legal ability to impose costs on others.* In the language used here, property arrangements indicate who has *privilege* and who has *no rights*; this was one of the legal relationships that permitted individuals to ignore certain costs imposed on others. The absence of clear property arrangements in solar rays means that my neighbor can impose costs on me in terms of allowing her shade trees to invade my access to the sun. The ambiguity in rights was not important until solar rays became scarce to me. At that moment the actual rights became important since the rights structure indicates who must pay to have their interest protected against the costs imposed by the other party. These costs are known as externalities. While the subject of externalities will be treated below, the idea of interference will be introduced in the context of property relations as entitlements. The importance of interference in the context of collective choice should be self-evident; much of the concern is with mediating the existence of certain kinds of interference – whether it is a smoky factory, soil erosion, or an obnoxious neighbor.

In earlier times, property arrangements were integrative in nature, with the primary purpose being to weave individuals together in a network of mutual expectations and obligations. Since the Industrial Revolution a constellation of property arrangements supportive of atomistic choices has evolved, largely because such arrangements seem essential to democracy and ubiquitous markets. Such individualism requires property arrangements that are also individualistic in nature. This is where the notion arises – at least among those who consider the market to be a necessary ingredient to freedom – that private property is socially superior to other forms of property arrangements.

As integrative property arrangements gave way to atomistic property arrangements the nature of interdependence among individuals also changed. When common property prevails – as, for example, in the Swiss Alps – the interdependence is mediated through the group decision process. This political forum is the nexus of interdependence; it is the place where conflicts over scarce resources are heard and settled. It is an interdependence that is both recognized and confronted. The users are the group over which costs and benefits are distributed – that is, costs and benefits of joint use are internalized to the group. Where there is ubiquitous private property, as well as ambiguities about the exact nature of property arrangements in certain instances, these interdependencies are not mediated in this fashion by the direct participants in the use of the resources, but instead are external to the decision calculus of any one economic agent; hence the term *externalities*. Mutual interference will always arise when scarcity is present – for if one thing is done Alpha gains, while if another thing is done Beta gains.

The nature of interdependence and interference among economic agents can be highlighted by drawing a more careful distinction among the various types of entitlements within the fundamental legal (Hohfeldian) relationships. There the concept of rights and duties was manifest both in practice and in the law. Consider two people – Alpha and Beta – who are represented by the rights/duties and privileges/no-rights correlates. Alpha has rights and Beta has duties, but what sorts of rights and duties are these? That is, how are these correlates given effect in everyday life? This can be illuminated by considering various ways in which Alpha and Beta might interfere with one another. Such interference could take the form of allowing trees to block the other's access to the sun, building a high-rise apartment in the line of the other's view of the lake, or dumping industrial wastes into a river which then kill the fish sought by others.

Consider first the rights/duties correlate. The rights that Alpha has are of several possible varieties. The first type is the right which says that Beta may not interfere with Alpha without the latter's consent. This is the purest type of right/duty correlate, and the one most obvious when mention is made of the concept of a right and a duty. An example of this type of relationship would be the situation in which Beta could not harvest broccoli from Alpha's garden without the latter's permission. Classify this type of right as the protection of Alpha by a property rule, or say that Alpha's rights are protected by a property rule. Similarly, Beta's duties are proscribed by a property rule protecting Alpha.[7]

The essence of rights protected by property rules is that the party wishing to contravene those rights must initiate the bargaining process, and must bear the bulk of the transaction costs related to that process. In this instance it is Beta who must approach Alpha prior to any interference with the latter's rights. This is the essence of protection by a property rule.

Now consider a second way in which Alpha might have rights protected. Assume it is possible for Beta to proceed to interfere with the rights of Alpha, but such interference is done with the knowledge that compensation will be required *ex post* – the exact magnitude to be determined by a (presumably) neutral third party. An example is found here with respect to certain types of damages that are difficult to anticipate before the fact; oil spills from tankers on the high seas are a classic case. A coastal nation is protected from oil spills by a liability rule that requires compensation from the ship owner after the fact. It would make little sense to have these rights protected by a property rule since this would require *ex ante* bargaining, when the full magnitude of the interference – that is the full magnitude of the damages from the spill – cannot be known until after a spill. The ship owner (Beta) has duties while the coastal nation (Alpha) has rights. These rights are protected by a liability rule.

Another example of protection for Alpha by a liability rule is that of compensation for wildlife damage on a farmer's fields. In this instance the state department responsible for wildlife management acts as agent for hunters, and pays damages to farmers who make claims for crop losses by, say, deer. Here, the farmers (Alpha) have an entitlement protected by a liability rule. Again, the impossibility of determining *a priori* what the necessary payment will be precludes protection of Alpha by a property rule. Alpha still has rights, but they are protected by a liability rule rather than a property rule. The final manner in which Alpha's rights might be given protection is that of an inalienability rule. Here Beta may not interfere with Alpha under any circumstances; there is no price at which Alpha would agree to the interference. The example that comes to mind under the inalienability rule is the right to be free from dangerous toxic chemicals in domestic water supplies. The outright prohibition of certain chemicals would mean that Alpha is protected by an inalienability rule.

Hence, within the rights/duties correlate there are three different ways in which Alpha may be protected, and thus there are three ways in which Beta might be bound by duties. When Alpha is protected by a property rule Beta has no choice but to approach Alpha to attempt to bargain. When Alpha is protected by a liability rule Beta may proceed to act with the possibility that by so doing she will interfere with Alpha, but must be prepared to pay compensation set by a third party. Finally, when Alpha is protected by an inalienability rule there is no price that would permit Beta to interfere with Alpha; bargaining either *ex ante* or *ex post* is precluded.

Now consider the second set of correlates, those pertaining to privilege and no rights. Recall that privilege is a situation in which Alpha may undertake actions that may be quite detrimental to Beta, but need hold no particular concern for the feelings of Beta about such interference. Here we have a situation in which Alpha may interfere with Beta and can be stopped only if Beta buys off Alpha. In this instance Alpha is the interfering party, while Beta is the receiving party; it is Beta upon whom costs are being imposed by Alpha's actions, yet it is Beta who must initiate ameliorative action to prevent the harm from being imposed. Mitigative action would consist of Beta buying out Alpha. In this case Alpha's privilege is protected by a property rule against Beta's no right. To return to the earlier example concerning solar collectors, in the absence of a right to solar rays the only way

I can influence the way in which my neighbor chooses to manage her trees is to buy her off. Since I have no rights it costs me money to have my interests represented. When I do not have the law on my side, my desires can only be given effect if I spend money.

The second property relation (entitlement) under the privilege/no-rights correlate is that where Beta may stop the interference by Alpha, but in doing so must be prepared to compensate Alpha after the fact by an amount to be determined by a neutral third party. Alpha still has privilege over Beta – that is, Alpha may still impose costs on Beta. If Beta wants those costs terminated then it will be necessary to pay some compensation. As in the rights/duties correlate, this second form of protection for Alpha is one of a liability rule. Also, as above, the compensation is to be determined by a third party rather than as a process in which Alpha and Beta become engaged in bargaining. Property rules imply injunction and prior bargaining where both parties must agree to a price or there will be no change in the status quo. Liability rules imply efforts to redress grievances after the fact – with the settlement (the compensation) not being subject to the relative strength and wealth of the antagonists but rather set by the neutral eye of a third party (usually the state). These static legal correlates are depicted in table 7.1

The relations in table 7.1 are static in that they describe, at any moment, the extant entitlement structure. In a dynamic setting, the

Table 7.1   The Three Types of Entitlements under Right/Duty and Privilege/No-Right

Alpha	Beta
Right	*Duty*
Alpha has a right protected by a property rule	Beta has duty against Alpha's protection by a property rule
Alpha has a right protected by a liability rule	Beta has duty against Alpha's protection by a liability rule
Alpha has a right protected by an inalienability rule	Beta has duty against Alpha's protection by an inalienability rule
Privilege	*No Right*
Alpha has privilege protected by a property rule	Beta has no right against Alpha's protection by a property rule
Alpha has privilege protected by a liability rule	Beta has no right against Alpha's protection by a liability rule
Alpha has privilege protected by an inalienability rule	Beta has no right against Alpha's protection by an inalienability rule

the particular form of entitlements found within the two separate correlates is a function of the way in which power is exercised by Alpha as against the liability of Beta. Notice that liability here is in reference to a position of being legally vulnerable to the desires of Alpha to create a new legal relationship. The liability rule just discussed in connection with property rules and inalienability rules represents a form of legal compulsion to be held financially liable for one's actions. There is an important distinction between Beta having financial liability toward Alpha because Alpha is protected by a *liability rule*, and Beta being legally vulnerable (having liability in the Hohfeld scheme) to the whims of Alpha to exercise legal power.

When Alpha exercises power there are several ways in which that might run *vis-à-vis* Beta. The three kinds of entitlements found under the rights/duties correlate, and the three types of entitlements found under the privilege/no-rights correlates, are six possibilities. The final set of legal correlates – immunity and no power – is covered by the inalienability rule. That is, Alpha is immune to the actions of Beta to create a new legal relationship that will bind Alpha. Alpha enjoys inalienable protection against the interpositions of Beta.

I now return to the proposition advanced earlier that property institutions legitimize the imposition of costs on others. That is, property relations – or the structure of status quo entitlements – *indicate which costs must be considered by the various decision-making units in a society.* In the early days of the Industrial Revolution workers had very limited property in their labor power, and so it was cheap for early capitalists to ignore the costs to those workers suffering injury in the workplace; it was, of course, not unnoticed as an inconvenience to the families of the injured workers, but the workers had *no rights*, and the capitalists had *privilege*. A similar story could be told, as seen earlier, about early coal miners where mine safety could be ignored by the owners of the mines. Once it became more expensive for the owners to ignore mine safety – that is, once the workers had some property in their future income stream – then it became more costly for owners to be so cavalier about safety. It was then that a benefit-cost calculation by the owner would reveal that it suddenly would "pay" to invest in mine safety. The workers were able to convert their *no rights* situation to one of *rights* and the mine owners were moved from a position of *privilege* to one of *duty*. Not only did institutional arrangements change, but economic opportunity was redefined.

It should not be assumed from this that the privilege/no-rights correlate is the only one in which costs are imposed on ungrateful victims. A binding labor contract – or slavery for that matter – are instances where the rights/duties correlate holds and yet those with duty may still be bearing some large unwanted costs. Similarly with the immunity/no-power correlate; when civil rights are not universally extended many citizens have no power against the immunity of their daily antagonists. The essence of protection by right, privilege, power, and immunity – and the more specific protection by property rules, liability rules, or inalienability rules – is that one can disregard certain costs. Property arrangements define which of these costs might legally be ignored, and property legitimizes those costs that are so visited on others. It is the confrontation between those causing such costs and those on whom they fall that is at the heart of the conflict over social arrangements in general – and economic problems in particular. When people complain about "government interference" what they really mean is that some costs which they were formerly able to ignore must now be internalized. *One person's government interference is another's government protection.*

This inability to continue to ignore certain costs is obviously uncomfortable to people who have often grown quite comfortable – literally as well as figuratively – with the status quo. Is it any wonder that they complain? When the state began to regulate the workplace and to outlaw child labor the factory owners complained about government "interference". But if government had not acted in the interests of the children it is unlikely that this inaction would be regarded as government interference in the lives of the children as it left them to the whims of factory owners. When governments sanction those who are currently able to ignore certain costs visited on others, few consider this protection to constitute government "interference" with those now bearing such costs. On the other hand when governments seek to protect those currently being visited with costs – those with duties, no right, liability, or no power – that action is invariably referred to as government "interference." Put another way, when the right (presumptive or actual), privilege, power or immunity of certain economic agents is threatened, then government quickly becomes the enemy.

Factories had the presumptive right to treat children as their owners saw fit, and to discharge their effluent into the nearest river. Mine owners had the presumptive right to disregard the safety of those sent below. Milk vendors had the presumptive right to adulterate their product with water.[8] Farmers had the presumptive right to allow their cows' manure to wash into the stream. Meat packers had the presumptive right to sell any product on which they might make a profit – regardless of the health implications for those who might eat the product. All of these presumptive rights have been challenged and found not to have been a right at all but merely a practice. But this consideration of accepted practice, and its subsequent rejection, did not occur without complaints and struggle by those inconvenienced by the need suddenly to absorb costs that were formerly imposed on others.

I have shown how the four legal relations attributable to Hohfeld can be further categorized into property rules, liability rules, and inalienability rules. The obvious question becomes: which type of situation calls for which type of rule? One obvious place to start is with the nature of the transaction costs implied by each form of entitlement. Under a property rule it is necessary for the parties to negotiate prior to the action and to arrive at some bargain. Under a liability rule it is understood that actions with unwanted external implications are going to occur, and compensation for the inconvenience follows the action.

For the property rule to be effective it must be possible for the parties to the interference to meet prior to the offending action. When many individuals have an interest in the situation this is usually impossible. Thus, a liability rule would be more practical in that the interfering party could proceed, but with the knowledge that a subsequent payment would be necessary. Environmental legislation modifies the structure of entitlements for pollution emissions into streams, lakes, and rivers by changing the institutional arrangements from privilege protected by a property rule for those who dump, to a right for recipients that is protected by either a property rule, a liability rule, or an inalienable entitlement for toxic substances. The issuance of permits for effluent discharges, with a graduated fee paid by the dumping party, is neither an effluent tax so often advocated in the literature, nor compensation in the sense implied in the above discussion of the liability rules. Yet, it does represent a shift from the former situation in which dischargers enjoyed privilege.

It also is important to recognize that the tendencies for interference will differ as between the two types of entitlements. Since the property rule requires a prior arrangement, if my lake view is protected by a liability rule, my neighbor will have a greater incentive to build a fence in my line of sight than if I am protected by a property rule. Even assuming that the required compensation from the neighbor under a liability rule exactly matches the bargained price under a property rule, the latter entitlement requires that the neighbor must approach me first and begin the (possibly) tedious bargaining process. The level of transaction costs for the neighbor is much greater under a property rule than under a liability rule; hence interference is hypothesized to be greater under the latter. This difference in transaction costs arises since, under the liability rule, it is I (the "injured" party) who must initiate action that will result in compensation; I must actively initiate the compensation process, even though I did not initiate the action for which compensation is to be paid. Under an entitlement by which I am protected not by a liability rule but by a property rule, the active party must initiate the action to seek my approval.

Another matter concerns entitlements in use and transfer compared to entitlements in litigation. For example, an owner of a piece of land is protected by a property rule in use and transfer of that land, but by a liability rule in the case of condemnation through eminent domain (an entitlement in litigation). But if a neighbor persisted in dumping garbage on that individual's land, there might be injunctive relief from the courts that would validate and enforce the individual protection by a property rule in litigation.

The distinction between a liability rule and a property rule can be very helpful in understanding a critical element in the famous cattle-corn conflict developed by Coase. In his analysis – and in much of the literature that followed – one can conclude that the assignment of property rights between the corn farmer and the cattle rancher is immaterial with respect to resource allocation. If the cattle rancher is liable (in Coase's terminology), then the rancher proceeds to add steers, knowing that damages will be assessed and must be paid to the corn farmer; this would need to be arrived at by an independent assessor acting with the force of law. The corn farmer is protected by a liability rule. However, if the corn farmer is liable (in Coase's terminology; he has *no rights* in my terminology) then the farmer must approach the rancher and pay not to have steers added. The rancher is protected by a property rule. If the corn farmer is protected by a property rule (a case not discussed by Coase or others), then the rancher would need to approach the corn farmer and arrange a bargain. This type of entitlement prevails in most places where ranchers purchase forage from others; it is called a market.

The interesting issue here is the mixing of types of entitlements when Coase says, in one case, that the rancher is liable, and in the other that the corn farmer is liable. This latter situation is a curious circumstance since the corn farmer must pay the rancher not to add steers that will graze the farmer's land; if expressed in terms of me paying someone not to drive his car across my yard the novelty of it is more obvious. Before leaving cattle and corn it should be pointed out that because Coase focused on producer–producer relationships he was able to conclude – by assuming zero transaction costs and no income effects – that the same level of cattle and corn production obtains regardless of the liability rules. The corn farmer is said to be indifferent as to whether total receipts are solely from the sale of corn or are a mixture of corn revenue and damage payments by the cattle rancher. If liability runs the other way, the cattle rancher is said to be indifferent between total receipts from the sale of cattle or total receipts mixed with cattle sales and payments from the corn farmer for cattle not raised.

But moving from a world of idealized producer–producer conflicts to one of producer–consumer conflicts – or of consumer–consumer conflicts – renders the neutrality much less credible (Mishan 1974; Randall 1972, 1974). No longer are the parties to the interference indifferent as to whether their receipts come from the corn or cattle market or from their neighbor. In a way that was not so before, income becomes a constraint on behavior and the resulting bargain. In the producer–producer situation, income is not a constraint since both are merely trying to maximize net revenue. But when the situation involves shifting property rules and liability rules between producers and consumers – or between two consumers – not only do income effects become important, but also current endowments and entitlements dominate the outcome. If the pulp producers have privilege protected by a property or a liability rule then those who favor oxygen (and hence fish) in the rivers and pine scent in the air must pay to attain these amenities. On the other hand, if those who favor amenities have rights protected by a property rule or a liability rule, then it is the pulp producers who must incur the costs. Depending upon the structure of entitlements, natural resources can be utilized either by producers to lower the cost of manufactured goods, or by consumers to enhance the quality of life. Under one form of entitlement consumers of amenities must pay to return the natural resources to their natural state, while under the other form of entitlement it is the producers (and ultimately the consumers of their products) who must pay to alter the natural environment. In one case there is the willingness to pay for something now held by someone else (the right to dump by producers, or the right to a cleaner environment by consumers); in the other case there is the reservation price necessary to induce one to sell that which is currently protected by a property rule.

Finally, consider the concept of interference. If odors from a cattle feed lot pollute the neighborhood some might consider this to be an interference. But if the feed lot is precluded from polluting, the owner would define that injunction as interference. To the economist the obvious answer is to balance, on efficiency grounds, the interference (harm). But is this always the best solution? If a benefit–cost assessment is undertaken for the purpose of determining the greater harm, there is danger of introducing a market-monetary bias that will seriously discount non-market and non-monetary aspects of the situation. An apartment building that blocks a scenic vista has monetary attributes that will give it enhanced credibility against the non-monetized pleasure of a beautiful sunrise. The fetid air that attends the economic activity generated by a kraft-process paper mill is not likely to receive the same weight in the collective decision process as the market value of the paper that leaves the plant.

It is one thing to say that, in a perfectly certain world, the decision should be made by balancing the harm. However, where uncertainty enters, and where important yet non-monetary effects are relevant, a serious bias can be introduced into the outcome. As many others have noted, particularly Mishan, the production of goods tends to be favored over the preservation of amenities.[9]

VI   SUMMARY

The matter of property and changes in property arrangements can best be addressed by making reference to new costs and/or benefits that arise because existing property arrangements are no longer able to guide individual behavior in a desired manner. As indicated in chapter 2, Demsetz puts it as follows:

> Changes in knowledge result in changes in production functions, market values, and aspirations. New techniques, new ways of doing the same things, and doing new things – all invoke harmful and beneficial effects to which society has not been accustomed . . . the emergence of new property rights takes place in response to the desires of the interacting persons for adjustment to new benefit–cost possibilities . . . property rights develop to internalize externalities when the gains of internalization become larger than the cost of internalization. (1967, p. 350)

If one does not read into this description a preference for any particular form of property arrangements then it seems to offer a useful starting point. Society is organized according to collectively derived institutional arrangements – of which property arrangements are an important subset – which define individual rights, duties, obligations, and exposures. When new things become scarce, when tastes and preferences change, or when relative prices change, it follows immediately that the old rules will no longer suffice. New attitudes about pollution mean that former ways of disposing of industrial by-products are no longer socially acceptable. The rapidly rising price of petroleum fuels means that previous institutions concerning ownership of solar rays are no longer suited to the new situation. There should be little trouble in accepting the Demsetz notion that the engine of change in property arrangements is as described.

But it tells little if anything about the progression of property arrangements, nor does it address the obvious question of the suitability of the property institutions prior to change. Implicit in the Demsetz scenario is the presumption that property rights were appropriate before the new conditions emerged, and that once they change all will be well once again. As for the progression of property arrangements, that issue can be addressed rather quickly. Because property arrangements are not costless to define, to agree upon, to enact, and to enforce, it is safe to assume that they will increase in specificity as the relative values at stake increase. This does not mean that property arrangements will necessarily move in the direction of private property. It only means that as objects become more valuable it will pay to invest a greater amount of time, effort, and financial resources in their delineation and assignment.

Consider an example from pastoral Africa. The Somalia herders have an elaborate and specific property structure with respect to water supplies, but a more flexible property arrangement with respect to land and forage. It is water that is the limiting factor – it is the scarce commodity – and so it is with respect to water that one finds ownership carefully defined. With the rise of external markets for livestock among Somalia pastoralists it became profitable to invest in deep wells and modern pumps. This action caused a fundamental shift in what was scarce in the pastoral economy. While carefully defined ownership of the wells was not abandoned, it now became important to control (to "own") the increasingly scarce grass. Hence, under pressure of a new scarcity, there was a greater attention to the definition of property arrangements in forage and land. Under the former situation when the water dried up the herds would move on; as a consequence there was usually little damage to the grass even though it was unowned in the conventional western sense of that term. It was an open-access resource, but it did not matter since the availability of water set the effective limit on grazing pressure. Once new investments in deep-well pumps removed water as the limiting factor it suddenly mattered who controlled the grass (Swift 1977).

Or consider the extension of exclusive economic zones for fishing access. As certain nations experienced decreased catches with their existing fleets it became of great significance who had access to natural resources that were formerly assumed to be inexhaustible. The extension to 200 miles created a larger zone of common property for each coastal nation as opposed to the former open-access situation. Once the fishing zone was declared to be the common property of a particular coastal state, that nation was then able to define the particular institutional arrangements that would give its citizens access to the resource (Bromley 1977). Similar concerns are behind the continuing effort to define property arrangements in the high seas; the rising value of manganese deposits on the ocean floor triggered that process of institutional change and now keeps the search moving for a modified international order.

Existing institutional arrangements, and so property relations, are challenged by new tastes and preferences, as well as by new relative costs and benefits working through prices or perceptions of scarcity. The rise of concern for environmental quality is an example of how changes in tastes and preferences have brought about a fundamental change in institutional arrangements over natural resources. Changing attitudes about wetlands, about clean air, and about the natural environment in general have led to a number of legislative and judicial actions that alter the prevailing institutional arrangements (including property rights) over natural resources. Presumptive property rights were challenged in the courts, and in the legislative halls. This process is never finished, either in the industrialized nations, or in the developing countries – where it is just beginning to become a major factor in natural resource use. Serious concern for the rate of deforestation in Southeast Asia and the Amazonian Basin seems certain to continue.

Recognition that changes in tastes and preferences can play a critical role in a country's property institutions is found in the relocation of certain noxious chemical plants to the developing countries – especially to Brazil. When it became too cumbersome to obtain permission to operate in Japan, Western Europe or the United States some of these firms relocated to countries where tastes differ. It is surely only a matter of time until attitudes in these recipient countries change to an extent that the new firms may no longer be welcome. However, in the meantime, property arrangements seem conducive to the disposal of noxious – and possibly highly toxic – compounds into the environment. The obvious incentive for economists is that of changing relative prices. This can show up on the consumption side, or on the production side. The rapidly rising cost of home heating oil, natural gas and electricity suddenly changed the relative cost of insulation *vis-à-vis* the purchase of these energy sources. This brought pressure on local, state, and federal governments to modify existing institutions to more accurately reflect the new situation. An investment credit for the installation of solar collectors is one example, as is the tax deduction for the purchase of insulation. These are new institutions. Similarly, as mentioned previously, the concern for rights to solar rays has suddenly become an important issue.

On the production side, new relative prices cause firms to search for ways to economize in the use of certain resources. These changes also hold implications for property rights. To return to the Somalia grazing example, the new higher value of livestock sold to the export market was one of the incentives for the increased investment in wells and then the fencing of grazing lands. Both consumers and producers respond to supply uncertainties by searching for ways to modify certain institutional arrangements, including fundamental property relations.

In summary, property arrangements change in response to both market and extra-market pressures. The market pressures come by way of price changes, supply difficulties, and the expression of new tastes and preferences on the part of consumers. The extra-market pressures come by way of demands brought in the political arena in response to new tastes and preferences, new relative prices, and supply problems. The mix between market and extra-market will depend on the costs and potential gains available from each route.

NOTES

1   In June of 1826 two men, who between them owned three-quarters of the land around the village of Foxton, Cambridgeshire, England petitioned Parliament for the "Enclosure of the Common Fields." Upon passage ancient boundaries were eliminated, fields were consolidated, roads were moved and refined, and the two major landowners who instigated it all ended up with large plots of land equalling their original share of the total area. There were no more common fields or common rights. A remote plot of 6.25 acres was placed under the jurisdiction of the village overseers and churchwardens. "This land being situated in a remote corner of the parish, a good mile and a half from the nearest cottage, they saw fit to let . . . to the cottagers as allotments at an annual rent of five shillings, and no doubt felt aggrieved at the lack of gratitude on the part of the cottagers who had to walk three miles to fetch some potatoes for dinner." (Parker 1975, p. 211) From a situation in which the vast majority of the villagers were engaged in farming, twenty years after enclosure there were only 11 still so engaged (out of approximately 50 families). The dispossession was complete; at neighboring Barrington the poor were explicitly forbidden to keep livestock – including geese – on the village common. Enclosure had indeed stolen the common from the goose.

2   Recognizing, of course, that externalities will sometimes mean that atomistic choice is no guarantee of economic efficiency and of social optimality.
3   A right-claim is an effort by a right holder to have that right given effect.
4   I am reminded of the apocryphal dialogue between a city fellow and a Wyoming rancher who was shocked to find the interloper building a cabin on a remote corner of the rancher's vast estate:

> Rancher: This is my land, what are you doing here?
> City man: I am building a cabin. Who says it is your land?
> Rancher: I do.
> City man: How did you get the land?
> Rancher: My father left it to me.
> City man: How did your father get the land?
> Rancher: His father left it to him.
> City man: And how did your grandfather get the land?
> Rancher: He fought the Indians for it.
> City man: Fine, I'll fight you for it.

5   The opening quote to chapter 6 derives from a confused perception that, as in the animal kingdom, possession constitutes property. The emphasis here is precisely the opposite; property is a social phenomenon among humans precisely because it transcends mere physical possession.
6   By this time the organization of the working classes and the development of socialist theory had proceeded to the point that Mill was open to the idea of abolishing the private ownership of the means of production so as to secure to each worker the fruits of his labors. See Schlatter (1951, pp. 250ff).
7   For an elaboration of these ideas see Bromley (1978) or Calabresi and Melamed (1972).
8   The practice of food adulteration was both widespread and reasonably clever: chalk, carbonates of magnesium and ammonia, *nux vomica* (a poison), and alum were used to reduce the flour content of bread; sulfate of iron was added to tea; and copper and lead carbonate were mixed into sugar (Burnett 1966).
9   Mishan likens this matter to the problem with horse and rabbit stew. Just as the monetized (or market-valued) outputs will dominate over the non-monetized (or non-market-valued) outputs in a benefit–cost analysis, one who eats horse and rabbit stew in the hope of tasting rabbit meat will be disappointed.

Part III

Institutions and Policy Analysis

8

Theory Science and Policy Science: Beyond Positivism

> The concept of Pareto optimality and the associated concept of PPIs (potential Pareto improvements) *should* not be confused with theorems of positive economics. If this implies that economists must give up the notion that there are purely technical, value-free efficiency arguments for certain economic changes, and indeed that the very terms "efficient" and "inefficient" are terms of normative and not positive economics, so much the better; immense confusion has been sown by the pretense that we can pronounce "scientifically" on matters of "efficiency" without committing ourselves to any value judgments.
>
> Blaug, *The Method of Economics*

The economist concerned with making a contribution to policy science faces an awkward problem. There remains a persistent belief that adherence to efficiency, variously defined, constitutes the necessary condition for an objective and value-free approach to policy science. This means, among other things, that policy analysis that is not strictly efficiency driven runs the risk of being regarded as unworthy of serious economic notice. The market is seen as a mechanism for aggregating preferences, for signalling values in exchange, for allowing the greatest possible range in human initiative, and for channeling human energies into the proper directions. There can be little mystery to the appeal of thoroughgoing markets on both ideological grounds, as well as on grounds of the generation of material wealth. That is not being debated here, nor are the productive benefits of volitional market processes being denied.

The concern is, rather, with an analytical metaphor that sees two general organizing concepts in economics – the market, and market failure. Much intellectual activity is, and has been, devoted to these two ideas. Those who believe markets to be good will have a number of arguments as to why markets should be allowed to function in a rather wide domain, with but little "interference" from government. Here, evidence of "market failure" is regarded as a necessary condition to justify any change from the status quo, and then only if it is possible to prove that an alternative institutional arrangement could make an unmistakable improvement over the current situation.

Other economists will find more analytical interest in those policy issues where markets (or the status quo) lead to outcomes that are regarded by a large fraction of the citizenry to be quite undesirable; human poverty, environmental degradation, and working conditions in factories and mines are possible examples. The intellectual tradition has been for each group to rally round these stylized concepts of markets and market failure. While both will recognize market failure as a potential source of interest, they will differ in their attitude regarding the analyst's role.

For those who believe in the rather efficacious properties of markets, this concern for other aspects of a market economy will be frowned upon and will be regarded as being concerned with mere distributional matters – often thought to be outside of the core of legitimate activity for the economist who wishes to be thought an objective scientist. The intellectual heritage of economics is very much concerned with the necessity of being thought objective analysts of economic processes and outcomes. Those who find rather more social value in market processes have drawn upon a philosophy of science – a research program – to forge a link between the autonomy of market processes and the objective economist as unbiased observer and neutral technician who offers value-free advice. The overdrawn dichotomy that results from this metaphor of markets and market failure casts most collective decision situations into too restrictive a choice, and one that offers too much at each of its two poles. The obvious problems with calling in the state to redress problems with market processes have now been recognized as government failure, or non-market failure (Wolf 1979). And yet to expect the state always to do better than "the market" is not only asking a great deal, but is proposing an inappropriate template against which to judge performance. After all, if markets do not perform well in a given situation, is it valid then to judge non-market processes by market performance indicators?

The choice is not between the market and the government; it is, rather, one of choosing alternative institutional arrangements to guide and to sanction individual initiative in socially desirable directions.

There are policy objectives relating to the setting up (and the maintenance) of the legal foundations of the economy, and there are policy objectives concerning the desired aims of government policy. While the desired objectives are specified in the second situation, they are left for the evolved framework or economic order to generate in the former. The German terms for the two are *Ordnungspolitik* and *Prozesspolitik* – policies concerning the economic or constitutional framework, and policies concerning economic processes. Hutchison notes that the early economists were primarily concerned with *Ordnungspolitik*; Adam Smith and others were concerned with establishing and maintaining a constitutional framework in accordance with a competitive market mechanism. That is, they were concerned with what I here call *institutional arrangements*. Even the nineteenth-century efforts to modify the hours and conditions of factory labor were examples of *Ordnungspolitik*. Hutchison suggests that it was not until the rise of modern macroeconomic policies in the early 1900s that "extensive and systematic *Prozesspolitik* began to develop." (1964, p. 126)

In western society, where there is *a priori* political support for market-like processes, the social and economic processes and outcomes of that framework are thought to be, for the most part, beyond question. If economic efficiency is the result of the chosen world view then the general citizenry is regarded as being concerned with economic efficiency. If they are not, then some economists are not above saying that "they should be." This belief in an objective truth rule may often stand in the way of more meaningful economic analysis of collective choice. For instance Dahlman notes the role of property rights as

> determining income or wealth distribution, on the one hand, and also serving as signals for behavior, thereby guiding incentives, on the other. If we accept the view that institutions are really nothing but specific collections of attenuated property rights, then it follows that institutions are also tied up with both income distribution and incentive formation. (1980, p. 213)

He notes that this creates two kinds of problems for the economist. The first is that the question of

> the relative efficiency of various institutions now becomes dependent upon our ability to rank various income distributions. For if every set of institutions is associated with a certain distribution of income, and if we wish to ascertain which set of institutions is the most efficient with respect to transaction costs, then we are also, implicitly or explicitly, comparing various distributions of benefits associated with particular

institutions . . . This is an issue inextricably tied up with ethical judgements, moral considerations, and questions of personal and political value systems, and so outside the purview of science proper. If this is the case, then it will also follow that a full analysis of institutional efficiency is a problem more for a polity than for academics. (p. 214)

The second complication identified by Dahlman in such analysis is that

if institutions are associated with certain distributions of benefits, then a change of institutional structure will imply a change in the distribution of those benefits, except in those few cases when new institutions also yield an increase in income that is sufficient to avoid any effective redistributions. This provides one clue to why institutional change can be expected to be both traumatic and discrete rather than continuous. It will be traumatic because those who stand to lose from the change to new institutions will often not give in easily. It will be discrete rather than continuous because it will come about only if the gains from the institutional change are large enough to overcome resistance from those who might lose from a change and in addition increase real income. The implication is that it will be very difficult to formulate conditions for when, from a purely conceptual standpoint, a change of institutions is efficient or not. (p. 214)

Dahlman concludes by arguing that even though economists might admit to a strong element of economic efficiency in the functioning of various economic institutions, there are several

random elements that will effectively make it impossible for us ever to construct a theory of institutions and institutional change that relies exclusively on standard choice theory and its optimality and efficiency theorems. These random elements are associated partly with transaction costs and the individual-specific component of such costs, partly with the nature of technological progress that can never be completely foreseen and the effects this has for judging the performance of existing institutions. (pp. 215–16)

Dahlman argues that the implications of these conclusions imply rather less universality in approach than that to which many economists have grown accustomed. The analyst must, in most instances, be content with particularism in the sense that specific situations are looked at in comparison to a rather restricted range of alternatives. He notes

The price that must be paid for putting transaction costs in the constraints and making property rights and institutions endogenous choice variables is that at least some of the widely accepted results of economic theory can no longer automatically be presumed defensible.

We have hinted on several occasions earlier that this will include the notion of efficiency in accepted economic doctrine. With efficiency is normally understood the Pareto optimum of the competitive equilibrium. However, if we accept the definition of transaction costs proposed . . . as well as the realization that transaction costs are individual-specific, rather than market-general, then we must conclude that in the presence of transaction costs there is no such thing as a unique competitive equilibrium . . . this means that any propositions of welfare theory, insofar as they rely on the competitive equilibrium as a point of reference, become totally untenable in property rights analysis. (pp. 217–18)

One comes, it would seem, to a situation that is best described as agnosticism with respect to an objective and universally held truth rule. Economic efficiency must be defined for each particular collective choice problem in terms of transaction costs unique to that setting, the incidence of those costs, and the policy objectives being pursued by those pertinent to the situation at hand. By doing that the economist will be able to focus on the concept of social efficiency, and thus to differentiate policies that redistribute (or reaffirm) economic advantage from those that reallocate (or confirm) economic opportunity. While this particularism may seem troublesome, it would seem to be the only research program that can be supported by the fact situation of collective choice, and by the conceptual machinery of economic theory. There is, it seems, a need to move beyond the false objectivity of logical positivism, and to address directly the two roles of the economist as: (1) contributor to the development of theory; and (2) contributor to the public dialogue about what it is best, in any particular choice situation, to do. This modified research program for economists must be regarded against the prevailing methodological orthodoxy. I will, therefore, discuss – from a methodological perspective – the diminished legitimacy of logical positivism and its offspring logical empiricism. This will be seen to have implications for those who believe that economic theory can lay claim to an objective truth rule.[1]

I BEYOND POSITIVISM: POLICY SCIENCE AND THEORY SCIENCE

The distinction between positive and normative economics, between "scientific" economics and practical advice on economic policy questions, is now 150 years old, going back to the writings of Nassau Senior and John Stuart Mill. Somewhere in the latter half of the nineteenth century, this familiar distinction in economics became entangled, and almost identified with, a distinction among philosophical positivists between "is" and "ought," between facts and values, between supposedly objective, declarative statements about the world and prescriptive evaluations of states of the world. Positive economics was now said to be about facts and normative economics about values. (Blaug 1980, p. 129)

The protracted debates on economic method, to which T. W. Hutchison, Lionel Robbins, Milton Friedman, Ernest Nagel, Fritz Machlup, Mark Blaug, and Paul Samuelson have been the primary contributors, concern the proper way in which one ought to build theory. The concern is with epistemology (the theory of knowledge). Hutchison, who taught in Bonn in the late 1930s following his graduate studies at Cambridge, became an early proponent of positivism in economics.[2] Because of his affinity with the Vienna Circle, he was much influenced by efforts to purge science of metaphysical debates that seemed to lead nowhere. The philosophers of the Vienna group refined logical positivism, while three individuals in particular contributed to its prominence – Ernst Mach, Bertrand Russell, and Ludwig Wittgenstein, the latter two having also been at Cambridge.

While John Neville Keynes, Senior, and Mill advocated positivism, its acceptance among economists coincided with its rejection among philosophers of science who were moving towards a position favorable to the more modest logical empiricism. In logical positivism the relationships are

> represented formally by axiomatic hypothetico-deductive structures known as theories. In their formal state, such structures have no empirical import, which can only be achieved when certain of the symbols in the hypothetico-deductive system are given an empirical interpretation via correspondence rules. (Caldwell 1982, p. 31)

In addition to differences in the extent of required testing of separate statements in the theory, the goal of science to the logical empiricists became not just description and induction, but more importantly one of explanation. The logical consistency of the claim for explanation in science is that explanation and prediction (which had always been accepted by the logical positivists) are the same things separated only by time. To quote Caldwell with respect to the new view of logical empiricism:

> On that account, science is a cumulative and rational affair. Its goal is explanation, which is rigorously defined. Its theories are axiomatic systems, parts of which make reference to observable phenomena . . .
> It is a substantially weaker offspring, when compared to its hardy logical positivist forbearers, but it is also a more logically cohesive, formally pleasing, and judicious account of the scientific process. (p. 32)

The logical empiricists, as the new-wave positivists, focused on confirmation and falsifiability as a means for accepting hypotheses, a position that was successfully attacked for failing to deal with Hume's problem of induction,[3] and for introducing various paradoxes of confirmation that could not be resolved. The ultimate demise of logical positivism and logical empiricism carried an additional and steeper price however, namely the realization that "no single, unified approach has arisen in response to the failures of positivist philosophy of science." (p. 68) Caldwell points out that the current approach among philosophers of science is to question whether a "static set of procedural rules for, say, the appraisal of theories or for the definition of appropriate theoretical structure has ever been or should ever be followed by scientists in their attempts to gain knowledge." (p. 69) Thomas Kuhn, the leading philosopher in the "growth-of-knowledge" tradition of science states this problem as a matter of faith:

> A decision between alternative ways of practicing science is called for, and in the circumstances that decision must be based less on past achievement than on future promise. The man who embraces a new paradigm at an early stage must often do so in defiance of the evidence provided by problem-solving. He must, that is, have faith that the new paradigm will succeed with the many large problems that confront it, knowing only that the older paradigm has failed with a few. A decision of that kind can only be made on faith. (1975, pp. 157–8)

As if the idea of picking a research method on faith were not bad enough, a leading philosopher of science – Paul Feyerabend – argues that the meanings of both observational and theoretical terms are dependent upon the theory in which they are embedded. Since facts are theory dependent, the empirical content of scientific knowledge can best be increased by increasing the number of inconsistent theories:

> You can be a good empiricist only if you are prepared to work with many alternative theories rather than with a single point of view and "experience." This plurality of theories must not be regarded as a preliminary stage of knowledge which will at some time in the future be replaced by the One True Theory. Theoretical pluralism is assumed to be an essential feature of all knowledge that claims to be objective . . . Such a plurality allows for a much sharper criticism of accepted ideas than does the comparison with a domain of "facts" which are supposed to sit there independently of theoretical considerations. (1975, pp. 320–1)

In the end, Caldwell points out that the very success of the positivists was also their undoing. That is, positivists became dogmatic in their refusal to allow:

> any subjective, qualitative elements to enter into their rational reconstructions of science. That refusal artificially limited their analyses

and created gaps in their descriptions of science . . . They believed that
theories and explanations in science were uniform, and always (if
legitimate) translatable into a specified axiomatic form – and missed
the rich and complex diversity of patterns of explanation and theorizing
in science. (1982, p. 90)

Just as philosophers of science were developing an agnostic position
as regards the existence of one true scientific method, Milton Friedman
published his famous *Essays in Positive Economics* with the first chapter
entitled "The methodology of positive economics." In spite of
terminology, Caldwell insists that Friedman is not a positivist at all,
but is instead a *methodological instrumentalist*. Friedman's positivism
comes from his desire to advocate a "positive" as opposed to a
"normative" economics. To Friedman the ultimate goal of a positive
science is the development of a theory or hypothesis that yields valid
and meaningful predictions about phenomena. "The only relevant test
of the *validity* of a hypothesis is comparison of its predictions with
experience." (1953, p. 9) Friedman is a methodological instrumentalist
because he cares only how well a theory will predict, and is not
concerned about the truth content of its assumptions and basic premises.
Theory is like any other instrument; it must be judged according to
its usefulness, with predictive accuracy being the sole criterion of
success.[4] The fact that Friedman is not a positivist did not prevent him
from adopting fragments of a philosophical position (logical positivism)
that had been discredited for approximately two decades; philosophers
since the early 1940s were in general agreement that a theory must
have truth value, and that the goal of science was not prediction but
explanation.

Paul Samuelson accepted part of the positivist program, and in the
early 1950s was also claiming that economics should be content with
discovering "operationally meaningful theorems" and that there is no
explanation in science, but only description. Caldwell shows how
Stanley Wong, by attacking Samuelson on methodological grounds,
was able to undermine revealed preference theory. That is, Samuelson
first claimed to be constructing a new theory of consumer behavior
which:

dispenses with the need to refer to utility (ordinal or cardinal) and
preferences. He later switches to the claim that revealed preference theory
provides an operational method for the construction of an indifference
map for an individual. In his final commentary on the subject, Samuelson
asserts that his theory is the observational equivalent of ordinal utility
theory. As Wong easily shows, these goals are inconsistent. (Caldwell
1982, p. 197)

The messages to be drawn from this brief history are several. The dominant implications are that: (1) philosophers now reject positivism in all of its manifestations (including logical empiricism); and (2) the idea that there is but one true method for science is under serious challenge. The rejection of positivism implies, among other things, that it is no longer possible to maintain the view that there are only two kinds of scientific propositions: (1) those that are formal, as in logic or mathematics; and (2) those that are factual, or require empirical correspondence. The positivists had maintained that these two classes of propositions – which were called analytic and synthetic, respectively – were the only ones admissible in a science; all other statements expressed mere "emotional stances" or general "attitudes toward life." (Caldwell 1982, p. 13).

The loss of overarching credibility for positivism would seem to be serious for those who have grown familiar and comfortable with the idea that the scientific enterprise can be objective and value free. But to deny the existence of an objective truth rule in science is different from denying that individual scientists can operate in an exemplary, serious, and well-intentioned manner as they go about the business of science. The implications of this will vary somewhat, depending upon the nature of activity being pursued. In economics, it seems reasonable to consider this realization within two broad classes of research. I will call the first of these *theory science* to reflect the idea that individuals engaged here regard theory as their dominant interest, and I will call the second of these *policy science* to reflect the idea that individuals engaged here regard the world of choices and decisions as their dominant interest. I do not wish to leave the impression that an economist does either one or the other; indeed many of the most influential economists do both very well. But the distinction is indicative of the general divisions of labor within the discipline, one concerned primarily with improving the theoretical underpinnings of the discipline, the other concerned primarily with applying that received wisdom to important social problems.

Those engaged in theory science work back and forth between the real world and received theoretical wisdom. Some are more concerned with one direction than the other, but the essence of this activity is to pursue a closer correspondence between the postulates and conclusions of orthodoxy and its ability to characterize the world. Some economists are less interested than others in modifying or adding to theory, but most are still concerned with this problem of correspondence between the real world and the mental abstraction of it (a model or theory). The problems of individual objectivity and replicability are central here since it is important that "the world" be perceived and interpreted in such a way that independent researchers might duplicate each other's work. Of course economists will choose different segments of reality to study, but the work is ultimately prescriptive in that one is prescribing modifications in theory (received wisdom or orthodoxy) to ensure that it more closely accord with reality.

Methodological instrumentalism is no more useful than is positivism, since the structural validity and truth content of the model (theory) of the real world is the desideratum; mere correlation is not sufficient. That is, if people refuse to purchase a particular product for some psychic reasons,[5] then to model consumer demand as a function of price and income will not result in a very good model of consumer behavior. Those doing theory science want to be as neutral and as unpremeditated as possible in order that the growth of a science that only gains its ultimate legitimacy from how well it corresponds to human reality will, indeed, reflect that reality. *Theory science in economics is about discovering what existing theory needs in order that it might more accurately model human interactions.* The objectivity of the scientist lies in the extent to which independent investigators can reach similar conclusions about the correspondence of theory and reality.

By way of contrast, *policy science in economics is about discovering what individuals and groups want (or need) such that they might more easily fulfill their goals and objectives.* It should be clear that the methodological implications are quite different as between theory science and policy science. The theory scientist wants to adopt a research program – and a philosophy of science – that will maximize the probability that the end product (a theory) is the best possible abstract representation of what goes on in daily life – including causality as opposed to mere correlation. The policy scientist, on the other hand, wants to adopt a research program – and a philosophy of science – that will maximize the probability that the policy recommendation to result from the exercise corresponds exactly to what the individuals affected by the policy problem want to achieve.

This view of policy science is a departure from policy science as currently practiced within economics. The intellectual tradition is dominated by the notion that the task of the economist is to indicate what ought to be done in the name of economic efficiency and Pareto optimality. In many applications conventional policy science does not even have the redeeming value of being conditionally normative; it essentially determines what ought to be done (to be efficient, where efficiency in this context means maximize increments to net national income) regardless of how closely that may accord with the wishes of those affected. Hicks has commented on this stance by the economist who is allowed, or even encouraged, to argue that if he

> has shown that a particular course of action is to be recommended, *for economic reasons*, he has done his job . . . if he limits his functions in that manner, he does not rise to his responsibilities. It is impossible to make "economic" proposals that do not have "non-economic" aspects, as the Welfarist would call them; when the economist makes a recommendation, he is responsible for it in the round; all aspects of that recommendation, whether he chooses to label them economic or not, are his concern. (1959, p. x–xi)

In theory science, the economist is being both normative and positive. That is, the economist engaged in theory science is attempting to observe and describe reality in an unbiased manner (being positive) and then to prescribe how theory *ought to be* structured (being normative) in order to reflect that observed reality. In policy science the economist is being positive, but only *conditionally normative*. That is, in policy science the economist must first ask (or determine) the goals and objectives of those affected by a policy – an activity that requires the greatest possible level of objectivity – and then objectively draw on theory to propose which avenues will maximize the chances of attaining those objectives.

Objectivity in policy science is concerned with independent researchers reaching similar conclusions with respect to what the target population says it wants to accomplish. It is *not* the science – nor the conclusions – that are objective but rather the economist who stands between theory and the individual(s) who must make a decision with economic content and implications. This critical difference between the objectivity of the *scientist* and the *science* has been muddled in much of the literature on research philosophy in economics. Glenn Johnson comments on this unfortunate confusion by noting that:

> Two kinds of objectivity can be distinguished – the objectivity of *propositions or concepts* and objectivity of *investigators*. A *proposition or concept can be regarded as objective* in a particular context if it has been subjected to and has not failed tests of coherence, correspondence, and clarity sufficient for the purposes at hand . . . A *researcher or investigator can be defined as objective* in a particular context if he is willing to subject his statements to tests of coherence, correspondence, and clarity sufficient for the purposes at hand and to abide by the results. (1986, p. 51)

Of course the policy scientist is dependent upon the success of the theory scientist – for the very essence of policy science is the received orthodoxy that is the domain of theory science; and, as indicated earlier, the good policy scientist is also very likely to be engaged in theory science as well. But the policy scientist is not an apologist, or an advocate, for the dictates of theory science. That is, the objective policy scientist should be the last to denigrate those objectives of the citizenry that do not happen to accord with the economist's view that people should do what is "efficient." After all, if economics is serious about the sanctity and autonomy of the individual then it does seem somewhat inconsistent to disregard the wishes of those affected by collective choice as unscientific and to advocate, instead, the Pareto rule. Simply put, it is logically inconsistent to venerate individual preferences as expressed through volitional choice in markets, but to denigrate and to discount individual preferences as expressed through collective action. The economist as policy scientist is concerned with problem solving and helping to do what is desired by those affected by the particular event under consideration, not with advocating what is said to be right by the postulates of welfare economics.

This proposed view of policy science should not be confused with the triumph of process over substance, for that is exactly what it is not. The policy process is still *end-result oriented* in the terminology of Lawrence Tribe (1972). But the end results pursued are not necessarily (or restricted to) present-valued net benefits to the exclusion of other results, nor are they necessarily concerned with potential compensation tests. Rather, the end results to be pursued are those defined as important by individuals involved in the process. Hutchison comments that the majority of economists are not necessarily

> completely devoted to exclusively materialist goals but rather that they are inevitably tempted to focus on measurable, quantitative objectives rather than qualitative non-measurable ones, and measurable goals inevitably tend to be somewhat materialistically conceived. As is well known, qualitative elements . . . largely elude indices of production or consumption. (1964, p. 155)

But, in the terminology of Sugden and Williams, the economist engaged in policy science adopts the *decision-making approach* rather than the *Paretian approach*. The tradition in benefit–cost analysis is, for the most part, to favor the Paretian approach. Here the objectives to be pursued in an investment program are not the proper domain of either the decision maker or the analyst. Rather, the Paretian approach holds that the proper objectives are given by the conceptual foundation of benefit–cost analysis – welfare economics and the criterion of a potential Pareto improvement. In the Paretian approach the economist rejects the view that a decision maker has the right to determine what constitutes social welfare. The proponents of the Paretian approach admit the difficulty in determining universal ethical propositions that will guide investment programs, and they therefore settle for the one that permits economists to reach a decision on only one dimension – that of economic efficiency. Those effects that happen not to have the aura of scientific respectability are disregarded in a process that Tribe calls "rendering irrelevant extra-paradigmatic concepts." Or, to quote Viner:

> To reach final conclusions upon the basis of consideration of a single value, or of a very limited set of values, is liable to result in what has been called "the fallacy of the unexplored remainder." (1961, p. 230)

Changes in economic efficiency are identified by the potential Pareto improvement criterion which is the keystone of the Paretian approach. By way of contrast, the decision-making approach to policy science means that the policy objectives are under the discretion of the "decision maker."[6] Here the role of the economist as policy scientist is to assist the decision maker in making choices that are consistent with the latter's objectives. The decision maker, by providing the policy objective that will guide the analysis of a particular collective choice, also "provides the value judgements upon which a particular cost–benefit analysis is constructed." (Sugden and Williams 1978, p. 236) It is not the economist's place to challenge the objectives of the decision maker(s). The economist adopts the following position: "given that your objectives are this, here is the best thing to do." The decision maker(s) implicitly decides what course of action to follow when the objectives are stated, and it then becomes the economist's task to develop the implications of this particular path. As pointed out by Sugden and Williams, once the decision maker's objectives are paramount in the evaluation process, all other valuations are irrelevant. This means that notions of costs and benefits will have meaning only with respect to the objective function of the decision maker.

Consider these differences in more detail. Under the traditional (or Paretian) approach there is only one objective – and that is to increase net national income; in the literature this is regarded as the "efficiency" objective. A particular project – or portfolio of projects – is acceptable only if there is a surplus of benefits over costs when converted to a present-value basis. In the decision-making approach the objective(s) of the undertaking can be whatever the decision makers want it (them) to be. Then the benefits of the project derive their definition from the stated objective(s). While, under conventional views of economic methodology, the Paretian approach has the appearance of scientific objectivity and the decision-making approach appears to be subjective, it should now be obvious that these claims are ill-founded.

The value judgments in the Paretian approach are several, although now so much a part of the convention of economics that their ethical content is easily overlooked; only a few will be mentioned here.[7] The first ethical proposition is that the views of individuals currently living are sufficient to determine what ought to be done; those as yet unborn are not considered at all unless those alive at the moment happen to regard their interests as relevant. The second value judgment is that increments to personal income are a valid indicator of the welfare position of members of society. The third ethical proposition is that an improvement in the income of one individual while the incomes of all others remain unchanged represents an increase in social welfare for the group. The fourth ethical proposition, and one that was stressed earlier, is that the current distribution of income among members of society is optimal such that one can safely conclude that the marginal utility of an increment of income to each member of society is identical.[8]

There are ethical propositions in the decision-making approach as well. First it is assumed that the decision makers or those most closely involved in the choice problem speak for the interests of society or those affected by the situation at hand. Second, it is assumed that the impacts from investment activities can be valued (or weights assigned) in such a way that is true to the feelings of the individuals who must live with those impacts. Finally, it is necessary to assume that social well-being can increase in the absence of an increase in net national income – for collective decisions are really about increasing social well-being regardless of what may happen to net income.

Policy science is, therefore, an ethical undertaking regardless of which of the two approaches is adopted. The ethical tone is set either by the decision maker, or by the economist who appeals to the potential Pareto improvement criterion. But to suppose that policy science is more normative or value laden than theory science is to misunderstand the value judgments that enter in to the observation and interpretation of "facts" as the economist builds theory. More importantly, it is to confuse objectivity of the scientist with the presumed objectivity of the science.

II INSTITUTIONS AND A NEW RESEARCH PHILOSOPHY

I suggest that collective choice situations are most properly modeled as situations in which individuals and groups of individuals have interests in particular outcomes. Those interests can be manifest in a variety of ways, but the essence of collective action is that individuals will attempt to have their interests translated into claims on some new situation of advantage, and then ultimately transformed into recognized entitlements by the state. It is this process, whereby interests become transformed into entitlements, that is the essence of collective action and institutional change. By *interests* I mean that someone (or a group of individuals) has some strong feeling about a particular situation – they have a *stake* in the situation at hand. That interest could be about the plans of the government to store spent nuclear fuel in the vicinity, it could be about the polluted river that serves as a sewer for an unfettered paper manufacturing industry, or it could be about the inability to compete against Brazilian soybean producers. These interests are often dismissed as the selfish actions of a few "influential special interests."

Those who denounce such expressions of concern with the status quo are usually uninterested in the observation that bargained (that is, market) outcomes reflect the underlying wealth position of those able to make their interests effective with dollar "votes." This is particularly curious since the greater part of the wealth of today's citizens reflects collective actions taken "yesterday." The mention of this inconsistency is met with the reminder that political matters are outside of the "objective" domain of economic science. Yet economic analysis operates within a structure of resource endowments and wealth positions that define the choice domains over which individuals will (and can) maximize.

As seen in earlier chapters, there are two levels of transactions in a society. The first is concerned with negotiations and bargains over the structure of choice sets. It is here that transactions (*Ordnungspolitik*) take place over the "rules of the game." The second level of transactions, more familiar, concerns market transactions from within choice sets. Dahlman comments that:

> In the process of defining property rights, the economic system must make two interrelated decisions . . . The first is to decide on the distribution of wealth; who shall have the rights to ownership of the scarce economic resources even before, as it were, trading and contracting begin. The second refers to the allocative function of property rights; they confer incentives on the decision makers within the economic

system, for the attenuated rights determine what can be done and cannot be done with any specific economic asset. It is clear, therefore, that we must deal with costs of making the "transactions" that constitute the defining of a social contract that sets the preconditions for the ensuing economic trading game. We can separate them into two parts: one set of decisions must be treated as endogenous for the system, and constitute the exogenous conditions for each trading agent in the resulting set of trades; the second set of decisions is made in the context of the making of these trades. (1980, p. 85)

The essence of the first level of transactions is the determination of choice sets. Those who are successful in having their interests (or claims) transformed into entitlements are thus assured of an income stream into the future; they have acquired property out of a mere claim. The ability of independent agents to undertake transactions over the nature of choice sets, or transactions within choice sets, requires the prior acquiescence of the state. Recall that even in a democracy the citizens grant to the state – subject to procedural niceties – the power to control the process whereby choice sets will be defined, as well as to regulate behavior within those choice sets as individuals go about the business of daily living. These choice sets are defined by the institutional structure of the society under consideration. That is, entitlements (presumed or actual) derive from the institutional arrangements in place at any given moment. As individuals and firms go about their daily business, there are myriad ways in which the actions of one undertaking hold important implications for others. These situations occur rather more frequently than the classical economists imagined. The term "externalities" has come to signify the situation in which these extra-firm (or extra-individual) impacts are present.

Some would suggest that the state, except in the rarest of circumstances, ought merely to define the conditions (including property entitlements) that will allow volitional exchange among parties to joint costs[9]. This preference is based on familiar arguments that bargained exchange among wealth-maximizing agents will produce the largest social dividend. But the reliance on bargained exchange in joint-cost situations raises a number of concerns, particularly in those instances where uncertainty is present. Indeed the social legitimacy of volitional contracts is intimately bound up with some collective sense – with the state acting as agents for the future –of the relative benefits and costs of individual contracts as opposed to some command solution to joint costs. There is also an equity question; when, for example, victims of noxious wastes are attempting to pay some large chemical company to take its refuse elsewhere.

The existence of joint costs presents the state with a necessary choice of attempting to force a resolution, or of leaving it to the parties to work out. Part of the choice is dependent upon the nature of those joint costs. Is the situation one of mere nuisance or are health effects probable? Are the joint costs intermittent or constant? Are there significant third-party effects? Are transaction costs high and likely to remain so, or high and capable of being reduced? Is there a unique damage function? Are irreversibilities present (Bromley 1978)? But there is another dimension to this choice and that is the potential costs of making the wrong decision. When the state grants contracting rights to a variety of economic agents it does so on the assurance that the social dividend will be thus enhanced, and that there is a small risk of immoderate losses. Of course not all societies grant this franchise so willingly, but in the market-oriented countries this is quite prevalent. In such settings joint costs present a special dilemma; so much economic activity is organized through markets (or through market-like arrangements) that to do otherwise is seen as the exception. Good Coasians ask why it is that all joint-cost situations cannot be resolved through volitional bargains. Others offer good reasons why this will not be done (Okun 1975).

But having decided that volitional exchange is not the appropriate means for resolving persistent problems of homelessness, hunger, abortion, transportation, acid rain, groundwater contamination, soil erosion, wilderness preservation, hazardous wastes, and other prevalent joint-cost situations, the state is still faced with the problem of what to do. Recall the problem of acid rain. It is well understood that the large number of affected parties – and the very great distances that separate all of them – generally precludes a market-oriented solution from altering the status quo. The electric utilities would suggest that they have a "right" to burn coal as they wish, and those who claim damages from such action should therefore bear the burden of proof – and the transaction costs – to alter the status quo. But this is not a situation of "market failure" since there is no market present; nor is it possible for a market to exist. Some, opposed to government activity with respect to acid rain, would like to suggest that the absence of a market is itself optimal – that when the benefits of reducing acid deposition finally outweigh the costs of reducing coal emissions (including the transaction costs) then there will be a change. But the problem is precisely one of the legal right to dump potentially harmful matter into the atmosphere. This right has never been established and so the current emitters merely have a presumptive right (privilege) while the alleged victims have no rights. Those who are made to bear the possible damages from acid deposition would claim that they have a "right" to be free of such costs; that is, they presume an entitlement structure. Indeed, the current debate is over the very nature of the entitlement structure – the victims claiming that they have a "right" to be free from the real (or potential) damages, and the utilities claiming that they have a "right" to be free from the higher costs of controlling their pollutants.

This situation is familiar; it is encountered in the domain of industrial chemical use, in soil erosion debates, in concern for urban sprawl, and in other conflicts where the status quo structure of behaviors results in joint costs. The choice problem can be rather paralyzing; in the absence of better information about the long-run implications of prevailing behaviors it may be thought wasteful to insist that such behaviors be altered. And yet it is always those benefiting from the status quo who will seek delays in government action, arguing that more information is required before a correct decision can be taken. The proponents of change will base their case on the incidence of unwanted costs, while the proponents of the status quo will rest their defense on a benefit–cost analysis that shows the uncertain future benefits of emission reductions to be outweighed by the known and current costs of emission controls. The protagonists are making two quite different arguments. One party is saying joint costs – that is, incidence – matter, the other is saying that there is yet no "market failure" and hence nothing should be done. Economists will usually feel more comfortable with the "market failure" position taken by the utilities since arguments on the incidence of costs and benefits are thought to fall outside of the domain of objective science.

However, what exists is simply a particular configuration of resource use and outputs that carries with it a vector of costs and benefits – both their magnitude as well as their incidence. And it is the incidence of costs and benefits that motivates public action and so the expression of an interest that some hope to transform into an entitlement. This, by the way, is what the policy makers have been saying all along. The primacy of cost incidence places special emphasis on the way in which the decision problem is formulated. Indeed, unlike efficiency analysis where one assumes that the beneficiaries can compensate the losers from a particular policy choice and still retain a surplus – the Kaldor-Hicks condition – a broader analysis focuses immediately on potential winners and losers. And this, then, requires that one understand the nature of institutional arrangements that define individual and group choice sets.

III SUMMARY

Positivism in its many variations has been in decline within the philosophy of science for the last twenty years or so, and that knowledge is now filtering down into the special sciences . . . Few economists keep up with developments in the philosophy of science, and as such it is understandable that many may still labor under the illusion that economics is, or can be, a positivist discipline. (Caldwell 1982, p. 4)

Economists adopted a particular research philosophy – logical positivism – just as it was being abandoned by philosophers of science. The positivist's dream of a clear demarcation between the meaningful and the metaphysical was soon to be regarded as a false dichotomy. The idea of an objective scientist, as opposed to an objective science, however can still be regarded as pertinent to economics as both theory and policy. Economics should require no less than principled adherence to high standards of observation, interpretation, and synthesis. But the persistent belief that economists who advocate efficiency are being objective scientists is simply too much to accept. If one seriously believes in consumers' sovereignty then it follows that the analyst must become concerned with the goals and objectives of individuals and groups, even when those goals and objectives are expressed in terms of cost incidence rather than in terms of improving the net social dividend as measured in monetary terms.

This concern for objectivity in assessing the relationship between theory and reality will require that more attention be paid to the nature of cost and benefit incidence of the status quo; it is, after all, the bearing of unwanted costs, or the perceived opportunity for individual gain, that animates most individuals in their daily lives. Once freed from the unnecessary and false belief that to worry about cost incidence is to abandon the rigors and purity of the detached and objective analyst, economists are then liberated to address the pressing problems of collective action and public policy with renewed interest and with justified intellectual legitimacy. That inquiry into collective action, and the process of helping to decide what is best to do, will necessarily proceed from a clearer understanding of the way in which the status quo magnitude and incidence of costs and benefits is an artifact of the prevailing institutional arrangements. It is these rules and conventions that determine what is a cost, who must bear those costs, and who will gain from an alteration in the institutional arrangements that define individual and group choice sets.

The economist as policy scientist will continue to face a difficult task. There will be difficulty in maintaining the sharp distinction between policy objectives and policy instruments. To the extent that this distinction seems to offer a safe haven for the policy scientist to choose instruments while avoiding objectives, we are again misled.[10] This distinction presumes that decision makers first choose policy objectives, and only then begin to search for policy instruments to achieve those objectives. Blaug reminds us that decision makers often will start with existing activities and gradually define and formulate objectives in view of experience with policies. That is:

> Decision makers do not try to get what they want; rather they learn to want by appraising what they get. Means and ends are indissolubly related, and evaluation of past decisions, or technical advice about future decisions, searches in vain for a social preference function that is not there. (1980, p. 151)

The feasible thing for the policy scientists, it would seem, is to become involved in the policy process in a way that will facilitate the dialectic evolution of both policy objectives and policy instruments. In some instances productive efficiency will be the objective, while in other settings economic opportunity will be purposely reallocated. Yet other situations will see conscious efforts to redistribute income, or to redistribute economic advantage. An objective scientist can further the cause of economic rationality, given the evolved policy objectives of the polity and the decision makers therein. This neither suggests, nor requires, that false notions of scientific objectivity hamper or delude the economist.

NOTES

1 For a thorough reconsideration of efficiency, optimality, and Pareto improvements, see Coleman (1983).
2 His later position on methodology and the distinction between positive and normative analysis would seem to have moderated somewhat. See Hutchison (1964).
3 Hume's problem concerns the ability to justify inductive inferences: is there any justification for the belief that the future will be like the past? Or, "Can the claim that a universal theory is true be justified by assuming the truth of a certain number of tests or observation statements?" (Caldwell 1982, p. 40)
4 Blaug notes that, in instrumentalism, "theories are *only* instruments for making predictions . . . Thus, the as-if formulation of economic hypotheses

not only refuses to offer any causal mechanism linking business behavior to the maximization of returns; it positively rules out the possibility of such an explanation." (1980, pp. 105–6)

5   When Chevrolet decided to build a car for marketing in South America its clever marketing department hit upon the name Nova. That *no va* in Spanish means "doesn't or won't go" might have been of some significance in explaining the lackluster sales of the Nova

6   I put "decision maker" in quotations to remind the reader that there is never one decision maker; rather, a large number of individuals are usually involved in the choice process.

7   An example of a value judgment is: I believe that Alpha should be made better off at the expense of Beta. An example of an untestable proposition that is *not* a value judgment is: this program will make Alpha better off at the expense of Beta.

8   Blaug comments: "The three postulates of Paretian welfare economics (consumer sovereignty, individualism of social choice, and unanimity) are frequently described as innocuous because they command either universal or almost universal assent. The belief that almost everyone accepts the Paretian postulates is sometimes interpreted to mean that Paretian welfare economics is value free. This is still another nonsense definition of value judgments: value judgments are those ethical propositions that are controversial." (1980, p. 148)

9   See Anderson (1982), Buchanan (1972a), Coase (1960), and Demsetz (1967).

10   In commenting on this, Nelson has observed: "Economists tend to view their proper professional role in the governing process as that of experts separate from politics, value judgments, and other subjective and normative factors. However, this view has not held up well in the light of experience. Economists coming into direct contact with government decision making have found that they cannot limit their role to that of neutral technicians; to do so would be to make themselves irrelevant and ultimately excluded. Instead, the more effective economists serve as active proponents for a way of thinking derived from basic economic training and for the policy conclusions it yields." (Nelson 1987, pp. 49–50)

9
The Policy Problem

If the task of the economist is primarily to elucidate the choice of policies and to focus attention on the need to choose, and on the consequences and costs of different choices in terms of alternatives, the formulation of the objectives of policy in the manner of welfare analysis is liable to be seriously misleading, if it is not simply inhibiting.

Hutchison, *"Positive" Economics and Policy Objectives*

Public policy is essentially about the structure of institutional arrangements that define individual and group choice sets. The policy problem, therefore, is concerned with changes in those institutional arrangements. In chapter 2 I introduced the idea of a policy hierarchy illustrating that institutional arrangements arise from the policy level, and from the organizational level, to define choice sets for atomistic agents at the operational level. The hierarchy of figure 2.1 is reproduced here as figure 9.1. Collective action and the institutional transactions that result will modify existing institutional arrangements, or the collective action will be unsuccessful and the status quo institutional structure will be upheld for the moment. The status quo, to be regarded as socially efficient, must be characterized by concordance between marginal rates of transformation in production and marginal rates of substitution in consumption, where the full consumption set is determined by a Bergson-Samuelson social welfare function, and a related social utility function.

The view taken here is that policy analysis and institutional change must start with the concept of individual and group choice sets that

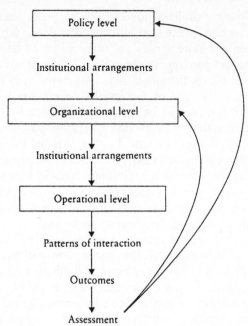

Figure 9.1   The Policy Process as a Hierarchy

are defined (that is, determined) by the structure of institutional arrangements. These institutional arrangements consist of both conventions and entitlements. The problem of collective choice arises when the existing institutional arrangements are found wanting in the face of new technical opportunities, or with the recognition of new tastes and preferences, or with the acquisition of new knowledge, or with the realization that one party is bearing unwanted costs.

The conventional wisdom of market, market failure, and government intervention places the emphasis on situations of conflict, on evidence of inefficiency in the status quo, and then on government action in the form of regulation. But to call the status quo the "market" is unduly to sanctify today's results of yesterday's institutional change. To talk of "market failure" is to reinforce that picture. And to talk of "government intervention" is to distort the reality of how the status quo ever appeared out of a Hobbesian war in the absence of a state, of property, of a common currency, of a commercial code, of a judicial system, and on and on and on. Just when government *intervened* is quite difficult to pin down. But it *is* clear to those well served by the status quo that any change can be more effectively opposed if it is labeled as "government intervention."

When the state mobilizes government to make society safe (and inexpensive) for commerce and industry it is doing what is expected of it. But when the state shows an interest in acid deposition, mine safety, child labor, poverty, the homeless, or the use of industrial and agricultural chemicals then *that* is government intervention. I have suggested that a way out of this market/market-failure circle is to understand that the essence of society (and especially is this true for modern societies) is that of conflicting *interests* in *patterns of interaction* and in *outcomes*. To see the world in the sense of the market and of government intervention is to miss the essence of society and of collective choice. If it is understood that individuals have interests that they will articulate as *claims* in the hope of acquiring *entitlements* then one can immediately see the essence of collective action. It is the struggle for legal sanctions to have one's interests protected.

The process by which this goes on is here called *institutional transactions* in contrast to the more conventional *commodity transactions*. A *decision unit* may be an individual, a family, a kinship, a firm, or the state. In some societies the relevant decision unit will change as the seasons change.[1] Decision units take actions that will sometimes transcend their nominal boundaries. The geographic extent of these extra-unit effects shows us the real boundaries of the decision unit. The problem of public policy (or of collective choice) is precisely one of efforts to deal with the institutional arrangements that define individual and group choice sets.

The obvious question becomes whether or not there exists an analytical process whereby this institutional change can be judged. I believe that the approach taken here offers hope for those who see the need to abandon the conventional dichotomy between those changes that are thought to be efficient and those that are merely redistributive. Consider the mine safety problem again. If the status quo did not include mine safety, if the willingness (really the ability) to pay of the laborers was insufficient to justify a change in the status quo, and yet if the change were somehow brought about politically, there would be a tendency among economists to consider this as inefficient "government intervention in the market" and as merely a redistribution of income away from mine owners and in the favor of laborers.

But such a view overlooks the fact that the political process is about the specification of the relevant social welfare function. The value judgments inherent in the social welfare function do not weaken the analytical stance of the economist, but rather provide the data against which economic analysis can be used to assess any particular institutional change. Those value judgments from the political

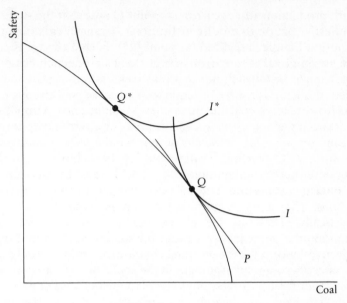

Figure 9.2   Disequilibrium and the New Social Efficiency

process – where interests are expressed, claims are made, and entitlements are sought – drive the process of institutional change. Analytically, the economist lets the political process suggest a particular social welfare function from which results a family of social utility functions.

Consider again the matter of mine safety. The process of institutional change could begin with a gradual change in attitudes and preferences relating to safety in coal mines; that is, it is decided that there should be an improved safety regime in coal mines, even if it is known that this will make coal marginally more expensive. The first manifestation of this will be a change in the marginal rate of substitution of coal for mine safety as depicted in social indifference curves. In figure 9.2 this would mean a shift from the social indifference curve I to, say, I^*. Changes in social attitudes do not manifest themselves in relative prices; rather relative prices are the result of changes in social attitudes which are initially manifest through modified consumption or production decisions, or through collective action that results in institutional transactions. So there arises a disequilibrium in which marginal rates of substitution in consumption are not equal to marginal rates of transformation in production, or to relative prices (P in figure 9.2).

With production still occurring at point Q note that the stage is set for collective action to modify institutional arrangements such that a new output bundle is realized (at point Q^*). Such a change is clearly not redistributional as such a movement along a production possibilities frontier might be labeled, nor is it rent seeking as that term has been applied. Rather, it is collective action to see that the new attitudes about the relative merits of coal and mine safety result in a new output bundle that is socially efficient; it is a reallocation of economic opportunity to attain a new socially efficient output bundle. Not all individuals, to be sure, will favor more safety and less coal. But then collective action never need be unanimous. The issue here is the aggregation of individual judgments into some collective judgment about desired social outcomes. That is what political economy is about.

Practically speaking, the above change implies a new social recognition that mine laborers count for something, and that there is a collective concern for the working conditions in mines. Analytically, mine safety becomes an argument in the social utility function and so in social indifference curves. No longer is a greater level of mine safety either "efficient" or "merely redistributive." Given the explicit recognition of mine safety as a social good – along with coal – a new mining regime is recognized as an example of reallocating *economic opportunity*. That is, an interest in greater mine safety does not imply an efficiency loss for society, nor does it mean a conscious decision to redistribute income to laborers.

This process, as reflected in the mine safety problem, serves to emphasize that the conventional dichotomy between institutional transactions that are in the interest of efficiency, or else merely redistribute income, is much too restrictive to reflect the full array of institutional transactions. Indeed, I have suggested that there are four types of institutional transactions. The first is when collective action gives rise to a new structure of institutional arrangements such that overall productive output is enhanced. Such changes improve the productive efficiency of the economy and this would be depicted as a movement to a higher production possibilities frontier in output space. The second type of institutional transaction is one whose explicit purpose is to redistribute income directly. The example used here is a new income tax law with different marginal rates for the rich and the poor. The third type of institutional transaction is one that reflects new politically articulated social preferences regarding patterns of interaction among members of society. Here institutional transactions will reallocate economic opportunity. Finally, there are institutional transactions that do not reflect shared values (and hence are not depicted by a new family of social indifference curves) but rather reflect the ability of an effective group to protect its interests to the overall detriment of society. I call this a redistribution of economic advantage. If the owners of coal mines were able, in spite of overwhelming public sentiment, to resist efforts to improve mine safety then this would be an example of their ability to maintain (as opposed to redistribute) economic advantage.

The obvious concern will be one of how the economist is to know one of these changes from the other. The answer lies in a greater effort to discern the nature of the relevant social welfare function and the associated social utility function. The difficult analytical problems come, unfortunately, not at the extremes but rather at the margin where choices must be made about conflicting instruments to achieve agreed-upon objectives, or where objectives are not unanimously accepted. Recognizing this simply means that one must fashion a model of institutional transactions that does not bias the analysis, and one that admits disparate expressions of economic and social interests. An approach that disparages objectives other than economic efficiency (often variously and vaguely defined), and that demands proof of market failure before institutional transactions are regarded as legitimate, is hardly suited to the critical task of guiding public policy.

The market of much appeal is, in fact, nothing more than the constellation of policy instruments and the derivative patterns of interaction mentioned above – the prevailing institutional structure, and the resulting behaviors, that lie between the policy objectives and the resulting outcomes. By not having to prove the existence of market failure, it may appear, especially to those who wish for less government "interference", that the flood gates are being lowered to justify all manner of tinkering by the state. I do not believe that this is the case, but there is a more important point here. If having to prove *market failure* is, by design or by default, the economist's protection against a meddling state then welfare economics and policy science is in more serious trouble than even the most prodigious critics could have hoped. Put another way, is volitional exchange through market processes venerated because it offers the best of all possible worlds, or because to waver in the faith will only encourage greater governmental involvement in the economy?

The central flaw in the market/market-failure approach is that it perpetuates the iron law of public policy: *leave it alone or resort to government action*. In fact, the choice is not between doing nothing and invoking the heavy hand of the state. The earlier example of mine safety is certainly not a choice between producing coal according to the status quo institutional structure as opposed to state-run coal mines on the Soviet or Chinese models. It is, rather, a choice of producing coal with the status quo institutional structure versus the same companies producing coal under a different institutional structure. It is nonsense to talk of this as a situation of government intervention in the business of coal mining. What this situation reflects is the articulation by coal miners of a concern for their working conditions, a broader reflection among the populace that existing mine safety is unacceptable, an effort to have that interest represented as a claim in the political arena, and eventually (if they are successful) given effective protection through a structure of entitlements that forces the owners of coal mines to recognize the miners' rights in their future income stream.

The issue here – and in most public policy problems – is not one of the market versus government but rather of a conflict of interests as between miners and the owners of mines. It is too easy to see volitional bargains, arising as they do out of a *constrained* mutuality of interests on the part of atomistic agents, as beneficent and thus to miss the more obvious fact that society and the economy are more properly characterized by conflicts of interests. Alpha imposes costs on Beta; mine owners are able to ignore the safety concerns of an abundant workforce; nascent capitalists are able to exploit child labor; Philippine rice farmers are able to impose a new wage bargain on abundant landless laborers; domestic shoe manufacturers are able to restrict cheaper Italian imports; my neighbor can destroy the economic value of my solar collector.

The economy and society are such that patterns of interaction produce outcomes that are either benign or offensive, and the social problem is to struggle with the ways and means to address the antisocial outcomes while maximizing the chances of preserving the desirable ones. The linkage between institutions, patterns of interaction, and outcomes provides a model of cause and effect. The linkage between outcomes and policy objectives provides a model of the feedback process out of which corrective action may or may not arise. The control mechanism is found in the institutional arrangements that link policy objectives to patterns of interaction.

If it is determined that excessive deaths are occurring in the nation's coal mines then the search begins to find ways and means to reduce those deaths; if it is decided that 14-hour days in the factory are inhumane treatment for eight-year-olds then collective action will focus on ways to alter working conditions in factories; if it is decided that cheap Italian shoes threaten the domestic shoe industry then there will be a search for ways to reconcile the natural desire to protect local jobs with the desire that consumers of shoes not be victimized by a slothful protected industry. Facile pronouncements about economic efficiency cast this problem in deceptively simple terms – and incomplete terms at that. For it is the status quo institutional structure that defines the efficient solution.

When faced with an incongruity between outcomes and policy objectives it is first necessary to determine the status quo structure of institutions – both conventions and entitlements – that give rise to those particular outcomes. Behaviors will need to be investigated to see whether the parties to an undesirable outcome are defined by the correlates of privilege and no right, or by those of right and duty. Which party is being made to bear unwanted costs as a result of the status quo institutional structure? Which party sees an opportunity for gain that is thwarted by the status quo institutional environment?

It is then necessary to determine the socially efficient outcome under the status quo institutional structure, and do likewise under the counterfactual institutional structure. As illustrated in chapter 6, what seems to be efficient under the status quo institutional setup is indeed different from the efficient solution under the counterfactual setup. Were it not for the seductive fiction of Coasian symmetry this point would require little comment.

This process of searching for social efficiency must be understood to require a careful determination of the relevant social objectives, the pertinent social welfare function, and the social utility function (and its derivative social indifference curves). The desire to appear as objective scientists, and the fear of engaging in interpersonal comparisons of utility, have caused, I suggest, a failure to devote the proper level of attention to these matters. But it is incontrovertible that judgments about social efficiency require the specification of a social indifference map, which can be specified only when there is explicit recognition of the relevant social welfare function. It is equally incontrovertible that pronouncements about productive efficiency are incomplete, and possibly false, guides to public policy.

The problem is, really, one of consistency of actions, from policy objectives down through the daily actions of economic actors: consistency in expressing the social welfare function correctly, consistency in translating that into a social utility function, consistency in deriving social indifference curves, and consistency in formulating institutional arrangements. When those institutional arrangements then give rise to certain patterns of interaction and outcomes, consistency is once again important in judging those outcomes *vis-à-vis* the policy objectives and modifying the policy instruments – the institutional arrangements. Institutional transactions that modify the prevailing institutional arrangements are the stuff of public policy.

The usual concern with the Arrow results about the social welfare function can, and possibly has, become paralyzing to the economist engaged in policy science. While it is fine to speculate, in seminars, about the legitimacy of concepts such as social welfare functions and social utility functions, life goes on. Most economists are engaged, rather frequently, in policy analysis. It is too easy to teach graduate students one brand of welfare theory, and then to practice quite another when called upon to assist in the problems of collective choice and institutional change. My intent here has been to expand the conventional welfare theoretic apparatus to incorporate a fuller range of motivations for – and results of – institutional change.

It demeans mine workers, the poor, those who care about environmental quality, and any others not well served by the status quo, if welfare economics will only consider as legitimate those institutional changes that increase productive efficiency. More seriously, it means that there are very few public policy issues in which economists might play an important role. Virtually all institutional change is driven by efforts to reallocate economic opportunity or to redistribute economic advantage. To fail to have analytical concepts for this process is a serious indictment of economics in general, and welfare economics in particular. I have here provided the conceptual case for these forms of institutional change. The job now, it would seem, is to devote greater attention to the difficult task of differentiating one from the other.

NOTE

1   This is particularly true in agricultural settings where animals may use individually (or family) controlled pastures during part of the year, and communally controlled pastures during the remainder of the year.

Bibliography

Ackerlof, George 1970: The market for "lemons": quality, uncertainty, and market mechanism. *Quarterly Journal of Economics*, 84, 489–500.

Alchian, Armen and Demsetz, Harold 1973: The property rights paradigm. *Journal of Economic History*, 13, 16–27.

Anderson, Terry L. 1982: The new resource economics: old ideas and new applications. *American Journal of Agricultural Economics*, 64, 928–34.

Arrow, Kenneth J. 1975: *Social Choice and Individual Values*. New Haven: Yale University Press.

Ault, David E. and Rutman, Gilbert L. 1979: The development of individual rights to property in tribal Africa. *Journal of Law and Economics*, 22, 163–82.

Axelrod, Robert 1984: *The Evolution of Cooperation*. New York: Norton.

Azzi, Corry F. and Cox, James C. 1973: Equity and efficiency in evaluation of public programs. *Quarterly Journal of Economics*, 87, 495–502.

Bator, Francis 1957: The simple analytics of welfare maximization. *American Economic Review*, 47, 22–59.

——1958: The anatomy of market failure. *Quarterly Journal of Economics*, 72, 351–79.

Baumol, William J. 1972: On taxation and the control of externalities. *American Economic Review*, 62, 307–22.

—— and Oates, Wallace E. 1975: *The Theory of Environmental Policy*. Englewood Cliffs, NJ: Prentice-Hall.

Becker, Lawrence C. 1977: Property Rights: philosophic foundations. Boston: Routledge and Kegan Paul.

Ben-Porath, Yoram 1980: The f-connection: families, friends, and firms and the organization of exchange. *Population and Development Review*, 6, 1–30.

Berck, Peter and Levy, Amnon 1986: The costs of equal land distribution: the case of the Israeli moshavim. *American Journal of Agricultural Economics*, 68, 605–14.

Bergson, Abram 1938: A reformulation of certain aspects of welfare economics. *Quarterly Journal of Economics*, 52, 310–34.

——1954: On the concept of social welfare. *Quarterly Journal of Economics*, 68, 233–52.

Bettelheim, Charles 1975: *Economic Calculation and Forms of Property*. New York: Monthly Review Press.

Bhagwati, Jagdish 1980: Lobbying and welfare. *Journal of Public Economics*, 14, 355–63.

——1982: Directly unproductive, profit-seeking (DUP) activities. *Journal of Political Economy*, 90, 988–1002.

——and Srinivasan, T. N. 1980: Revenue seeking: a generalization of the theory of tariffs. *Journal of Political Economy*, 88, 1069–87.

——, Brecher, Richard A. and Srinivasan, T. N. 1984: DUP activities and economic theory. In David C. Colander (ed.), *Neoclassical Political Economy*, Cambridge, Mass.: Ballinger.

Binswanger, Hans P. and Ruttan, Vernon W. 1978: *Induced Innovation: technology, institutions, and development*. Baltimore: Johns Hopkins University Press.

Bishop, Richard C. and Heberlein, T. A. 1979: Measuring values of extra-market goods: are indirect measures biased? *American Journal of Agricultural Economics*, 61, 926–30.

Blaug, Mark 1980: *The Method of Economics: or how economists explain*. Cambridge: Cambridge University Press.

Boadway, Robin 1974: The welfare foundations of cost–benefit analysis. *Economic Journal*, 84, 926–39.

——1975: Cost–benefit rules in general equilibrium. *Review of Economic Studies*, 42, 361–73.

——1979: *Public Sector Economics*. Cambridge, Mass.: Winthrop.

—— and Bruce, Neil 1984: *Welfare Economics*. Oxford: Basil Blackwell.

Brandl, John E. 1985: Distilling frenzy from academic scribbling: how economics influences politicians. *Journal of Policy Analysis and Management*, 4, 344–53.

Brennan, Geoffrey and Buchanan, James M. 1985: *The Reason of Rules*. Cambridge: Cambridge University Press.

Bromley, Daniel W. 1976: Economics and public decisions: roles of the state and issues in economic evaluation. *Journal of Economic Issues*, 10, 811–38.

——1977: Distributional implications of the extended economic zone: some policy and research issues in the fishery. *American Journal of Agricultural Economics*, 59, 887–92.

——1978: Property rules, liability rules, and environmental economics. *Journal of Economic Issues*, 12, 43–60.

——1982a: *Improving Irrigated Agriculture: institutional reform and the small farmer*. Washington, D.C.: World Bank Staff Working Paper 531.

——1982b: Land and water problems: an institutional perspective. *American Journal of Agricultural Economics*, 64, 834–44.

——1982c: The rights of society versus the rights of landowners and operators. In Harold G. Halcrow, Melvin Cotner, and Earl Heady (eds),

Soil Conservation Policies, Institutions, and Incentives, Ankeny, Ia: Soil Conservation Society, chapter 10.

——1985: Resources and economic development: an institutionalist perspective. *Journal of Economic Issues*, 19, 779–96.

——1986: Markets and externalities. In Daniel W. Bromley (ed.), *Natural Resource Economics: policy problems and contemporary analysis*, Boston: Kluwer–Nijhoff, chapter 3.

——1987: Irrigation institutions: the myth of management. In Wayne R. Jordan (ed.), *Water and Water Policy in World Food Supplies*, College Station, Tex.: Texas A & M Press, chapter 27.

——and Bishop, Richard C. 1977: From economic theory to fisheries policy: conceptual problems and management prescriptions. In Lee G. Anderson (ed.), *Economic Impacts of Extended Fisheries Jurisdiction*, Ann Arbor: Ann Arbor Science, chapter 15.

——Taylor, Donald C. and Parker, Donald E. 1980: Water reform and economic development: institutional aspects of water management in the developing countries. *Economic Development and Cultural Change*, 28, 365–87.

——and Verma, B. N. 1983: Natural resource problems in agricultural development. In A. Maunder and K. Ohkawa (eds), *Growth and Equity in Agricultural Development*, Oxford: Gower.

——and Chapagain, Devendra P. 1984: The village against the center: resource depletion in South Asia. *American Journal of Agricultural Economics*, 66, 868–73.

Buchanan, Allen 1985: *Ethics, Efficiency, and the Market*. Oxford: Oxford University Press.

Buchanan, James M. 1959: Positive economics, welfare economics, and political economy. *Journal of Law and Economics*, 2, 124–38.

——1972a: Politics, policy and Pigovian margins. In James M. Buchanan and Robert Tollison (eds), *Theory of Public Choice*, Ann Arbor: University of Michigan Press, 169–82.

——1972b: Politics, property and the law: an alternative interpretation of Miller et al. v. Schoene. *Journal of Law and Economics*, 15, 439–52.

——and Stubblebine, William C. 1962: Externality. *Economica*, 29, 371–84.

——and Tullock, Gordon 1975: Polluters' profits and political response: direct controls versus taxes. *American Economic Review*, 65, 139–47.

Burnett, John 1966: *Plenty and Want*. London: Thomas Nelson.

Calabresi, Guido and Melamed, A. Douglas 1972: Property rules, liability rules, and inalienability: one view of the cathedral. *Harvard Law Review*, 85, 1085–128.

Caldwell, Bruce J. 1982: *Beyond Positivism*. London: George Allen and Unwin.

Chavas, Jean–Paul, Bishop, Richard C. and Segerson, Kathleen 1986: Ex-ante consumer welfare evaluation in cost–benefit analysis. *Journal of Environmental Economics and Management*, 13, 255–68.

Cheung, Steven N. S. 1970: The structure of a contract and the theory of a non-exclusive resource. *Journal of Law and Economics*, 13, 49–70.
———1983: The contractual nature of the firm. *Journal of Law and Economics*, 26, 1–21.
Cheyney, Edward P. 1901: *An Introduction to the Industrial and Social History of England*. London: Macmillan.
Chipman, J. S. 1974: A welfare ranking of Pareto distributions. *Journal of Economic Theory*, 9, 275–82.
———and Moore, J. C. 1978: The new welfare economics, 1939–1974. *International Economic Review*, 19, 547–84.
Ciriacy-Wantrup, S. V. 1963: *Resource Conservation: economics and policies*. Berkeley: University of California Press.
———1969: Natural resources in economic growth: the role of institutions and policies. *American Journal of Agricultural Economics*, 51, 1314–24.
———1971: The economics of environmental policy. *Land Economics*, 47, 36–45.
———and Bishop, Richard C. 1975: Common property as a concept in natural resources policy. *Natural Resources Journal*, 15, 713–27.
Coase, Ronald 1937: The nature of the firm. *Economica* (new series), 9, 386–405.
———1960: The problem of social cost. *Journal of Law and Economics*, 3, 1–44.
Cohen, Morris 1978: Property and sovereignty. In C. B. Macpherson (ed.), *Property: mainstream and critical positions*, Toronto: University of Toronto Press, chapter 10.
Colander, David C. (ed.) 1984: *Neoclassical Political Economy: the analysis of rent seeking and DUP activities*. Cambridge, Mass.: Ballinger.
Coleman, Jules 1983: The economic analysis of law. In Mark Kuperberg and Charles Beitz (eds), *Law, Economics, and Philosophy*, London: Rowman and Allanheld.
Commons, John R. 1961: *Institutional Economics*. Madison: University of Wisconsin Press.
———1968: *Legal Foundations of Capitalism*. Madison: University of Wisconsin Press.
———1970: *The Economics of Collective Action*. Madison: University of Wisconsin Press.
Dahlman, Carl J. 1979: The problem of externality. *Journal of Law and Economics* 22, 141–62.
———1980: *The Open Field System and Beyond*. Cambridge: Cambridge University Press.
Dasgupta, P. S. and Heal, G. M. 1979: *Economic Theory and Exhaustible Resources*. Cambridge: Cambridge University Press.
Davis, Lance E. and North, Douglass C. 1970: Institutional change and American economic growth: a first step towards a theory of institutional innovation. *Journal of Economic History*, 30, 131–49.

——— ———1971: *Institutional Change and American Economic Growth*. Cambridge: Cambridge University Press.

Demsetz, Harold 1964: The exchange and enforcement of property rights. *Journal of Law and Economics*, 7, 11–26.

———1966: Some aspects of property rights. *Journal of Law and Economics*, 9, 61–70.

———1967: Toward a theory of property rights. *American Economic Review*, 57, 347–59.

Denman, D. R. 1958: *Origins of Ownership*. London: George Allen and Unwin.

———1978: *The Place of Property*. Berkhamsted, England: Geographical Publications.

Dobb, Maurice 1969: *Welfare Economics and the Economics of Socialism*. Cambridge: Cambridge University Press.

Einhorn, H.J. and Hogarth, Robin M. 1987: Decision making under ambiguity. In Robin M. Hogarth and Melvin W. Reder (eds), *Rational Choice*, Chicago: University of Chicago Press.

Ely, Richard T. 1914: *Property and Contract*. New York: Macmillan.

Farrell, M. J. 1957: The measurement of productive efficiency. *Journal of the Royal Statistical Society*, 120, 253–81.

Feyerabend, P. K. 1975: *Against Method: outline of an anarchistic theory of knowledge*. London: New Left Books.

Field, Alexander James 1979: On the explanation of rules using rational choice models, *Journal of Economic Issues*, 13, 49–72.

Firth, Raymond 1929: *Primitive Economics of the New Zealand Maori*. New York: Macmillan.

Freeman, A. M., III 1984: The sign and size of option value. *Land Economics*, 60, 1–13.

———1985: Supply uncertainty, option price, and option value: a note. *Land Economics*, 61, 176–81.

Friedman, James W. 1986: *Game Theory with Applications to Economics*. Oxford: Oxford University Press.

Friedman, Lawrence M. 1973: *A History of American Law*. New York: Simon and Schuster.

———1975: *The Legal System*. New York: Russell Sage.

Friedman, Milton 1953: *Essays in Positive Economics*. Chicago: University of Chicago Press.

———1962: *Capitalism and Freedom*. Chicago: University of Chicago Press.

Furubotn, Eirik and Pejovich, Svetozar 1972: Property rights and economic theory: a survey of recent literature. *Journal of Economic Literature*, 10, 1137–62.

Gordon, H. Scott 1954: The economic theory of a common property resource: the fishery. *Journal of Political Economy*. 62, 124–42.

Graaff, J. de V. 1967: *Theoretical Welfare Economics*. London: Cambridge University Press.

Guttman, Joel M. 1978: Understanding collective action: matching behavior. *American Economic Review*, 68, 251–5.

Hallowell, A. Irving 1943: The nature and function of property as a social institution. *Journal of Legal and Political Sociology*, 1, 115–38.

Hardin, Garrett 1968: The tragedy of the commons. *Science*, 162, 1243–8.

Harris, Marvin 1979: *Cultural Materialism*. New York: Random House.

Hayek, F. A. 1960: *The Constitution of Liberty*. Chicago: University of Chicago Press.

Hicks, J. R. 1939: The foundations of welfare economics. *Economic Journal*, 44, 696–712.

——1959: *Essays in World Economics*. Oxford: Clarendon Press.

Hirschman, Albert O. 1970: *Exit, Voice and Loyalty*. Cambridge: Cambridge University Press.

Hoebel, E. Adamson 1942: Fundamental legal concepts as applied in the study of primitive law. *Yale Law Journal*, 51, 951–66.

Hohfeld, W. N. 1913: Some fundamental legal conceptions as applied in judicial reasoning. *Yale Law Journal*, 23, 16–59.

——1917: Fundamental legal conceptions as applied in judicial reasoning. *Yale Law Journal*, 26, 710–70.

Honoré, A. M. 1961: Ownership. In A. G. Guest (ed.), *Oxford Essays in Jurisprudence*, Oxford: Oxford University Press, chapter 5.

Hurst, James Willard 1956: *Law and the Conditions of Freedom*. Madison: University of Wisconsin Press .

Hutchison, T. W. 1964: *"Positive" Economics and Policy Objectives*. London: George Allen and Unwin.

Johnson, Glenn L. 1986: *Research Methodology for Economists*. New York: Macmillan.

Just, Richard E., Hueth, Darrell L. and Schmitz, Andrew 1982: *Applied Welfare Economics and Public Policy*. Englewood Cliffs, NJ: Prentice-Hall.

Just v. Marinette County 1972: 56 Wis. 2d 7, 201 N.W. 2d 761.

Kahneman, Daniel and Tversky, Amos 1979: Prospect theory: an analysis of decision under risk. *Econometrica*, 47, 263–91.

Kaldor, Nicholas 1939: Welfare propositions of economics and interpersonal comparisons of utility. *Economic Journal*, 49, 549–52.

Knetsch, Jack L. and Sinden, J. A. 1984: Willingness to pay and compensation demanded: experimental evidence of an unexpected disparity in measures of value. *Quarterly Journal of Economics*, 99, 507–21.

Krueger, Ann 1974: The political economy of the rent–seeking society. *American Economic Review*, 64, 291–303.

Kuhn, Thomas 1975: *The Structure of Scientific Revolutions*. Chicago: University of Chicago Press.

Lang, Mahlon George 1980: Economic efficiency and policy comparisons. *American Journal of Agricultural Economics*, 62, 772–7.

Langlois, Richard N. (ed.) 1986: *Economics as a Process*. Cambridge: Cambridge University Press.

Lewis, David 1986: *Convention: a philosophical study*. Oxford: Basil Blackwell.
Libecap, Gary D. 1978: *Economic variables and the development of the law: the case of western mineral rights. Journal of Economic History*, 38, 338–62.
Little, I. M. D. 1949: A reformulation of the theory of consumer's behaviour. *Oxford Economic Papers*, 1, 90–102.
——1950: *A Critique of Welfare Economics*. London: Oxford University Press.
Macpherson, C. B. 1973: *Democratic Theory*. Oxford: Clarendon Press.
——(ed.) 1978: *Property: mainstream and critical positions*. Toronto: University of Toronto Press.
Marchand, James R. and Russell, Keith P. 1973: Externalities, liability, separability, and resource allocation. *American Economic Review*, 63, 611–20.
Marshall, Alfred 1926: *Official Papers* (ed. J. M. Keynes). London: Macmillan.
Matthews, R. C. O. 1986: The economics of institutions and the sources of growth. *Economic Journal*, 96, 903–18.
Messerschmidt, Donald A. 1976: Ecological change and adaptation among the Gurungs of the Nepal Himalayas. *Human Ecology*, 4, 176–85.
Miller, James C., III and Yandle, Bruce (eds) 1979: *Benefit–Cost Analysis of Social Regulation*. Washington, DC: American Enterprise Institute.
Mishan, E. J. 1960: A survey of welfare economics. *Economic Journal*, 70, 197–265.
——1964: *Welfare Economics*. New York: Random House.
——1969: *Welfare Economics: an assessment*. Atlantic Highlands, NJ: Humanities Press.
——1971: The postwar literature on externalities: an interpretative essay. *Journal of Economic Literature*, 9, 1–28.
——1974: The economics of disamenity. *Natural Resources Journal*, 14, 55–86.
——1975: The folklore of the market. *Journal of Economic Issues*, 9, 681-752.
——1976: *Cost–Benefit Analysis*. New York: Praeger.
Neale, Walter C. 1969: Land is to rule. In Robert Frykenberg (ed.), *Land Control and Social Structure in Indian History*, Madison: University of Wisconsin Press, chapter 1.
Nelson, Richard R. 1981: Assessing private enterprise: an exegesis of tangled doctrine. *Bell Journal of Economics*, 12, 93–110.
——and Winter, Sydney G. 1982: *An Evolutionary Theory of Economic Change*. Cambridge, Mass.: Belknap Press.
Nelson, Robert H. 1987: The economics profession and the making of public policy. *Journal of Economic Literature*, 35, 49–91.
Netting, Robert 1976: What alpine peasants have in common: observations on communal tenure in a Swiss village. *Human Ecology*, 4, 135–46.
——1977: *Cultural Ecology*. Menlo Park, Calif.: Cummings.

North, Douglass C. 1981: *Structure and Change in Economic History*. New York: Norton.
——1983: A theory of economic change. *Science*, 219, 163–4.
——and Thomas, Robert Paul 1970: An economic theory of the growth of the western world. *Economic History Review*, 23, 1–17.
—— ——1971: The rise and fall of the manorial system: a theoretical model. *Journal of Economic History*, 31, 777–803.
—— ——1973: *The Rise of the Western World*. Cambridge: Cambridge University Press.
—— ——1977: The first economic revolution. *Economic History Review*, 30, 229–41.
Nozick, Robert 1974: *Anarchy, State and Utopia*. New York: Basic Books.
Okun, Arthur M. 1975: *Equality and Efficiency: the big tradeoff*. Washington, DC: Brookings Institution.
Page, Talbot 1977: *Conservation and Economic Efficiency*. Baltimore: Johns Hopkins University Press.
Parfit, Derek 1984: *Reasons and Persons*. Oxford: Oxford University Press.
Parker, Rowland 1975: *The Common Stream*. London: Paladin Books.
Pearce, David W. (ed.) 1981: *The Dictionary of Modern Economics*. Cambridge, Mass.: MIT Press.
Pigou, A. C. 1962: *The Economics of Welfare*. London: Macmillan.
Posner, Richard A. 1977: *Economic Analysis of Law* (2nd edn). Boston: Little Brown.
Randall, Alan 1972: Market solutions to externality problems: theory and practice. *American Journal of Agricultural Economics*, 54, 175–83.
——1974: Coasian externality theory in a policy context. *Natural Resources Journal*, 14, 35–54.
——1983: The problem of market failure. *Natural Resources Journal*, 23, 131–48.
Rawls, John 1971: *A Theory of Justice*. Cambridge, Mass.: Harvard University Press.
Rhoades, Robert E. and Thompson, Stephen J. 1975: Adaptive strategies in alpine environments: beyond ecological particularism. *American Ethnologist*, 2, 535–51.
Ringrose, D. R. 1973: European economic growth: comments on the North–Thomas theory. *Economic History Review*, 26, 285–92.
Robbins, Lionel 1981: Economics and political economy. *American Economic Review*, 71, 1–10.
Rosenberg, Alexander 1985: Prospects for the elimination of tastes from economics and ethics. In Ellen F. Paul, Fred D. Miller, Jr., and Jeffrey Paul (eds), *Ethics and Economics*, Oxford: Basil Blackwell, 48–68.
Rousseau, J.-J. 1959: *The Social Contract*. New York: E. P. Dutton.
Runge, Carlisle F. 1981: Common property externalities: isolation, assurance, and resource depletion in a traditional grazing context. *American Journal of Agricultural Economics*, 63, 595–607.

——1984: Institutions and the free rider: the assurance problem in collective action. *Journal of Politics*, 46, 154–81.

——and Bromley, Daniel W. 1979: *Property Rights and the First Economic Revolution: the origins of agriculture reconsidered*. Madison: University of Wisconsin–Madison, Center for Resource Policy Studies, Working Paper 13.

Ruttan, Vernon W. 1978: Induced institutional change. In Hans P. Binswanger and Vernon W. Ruttan (eds), *Induced Innovation*, Baltimore: Johns Hopkins University Press, 327–57.

——and Hayami, Yujiro 1984: Toward a theory of induced institutional innovation. *Journal of Development Studies*, 20, 203–23.

Ryan, Alan 1984: *Property and Political Theory*. Oxford: Basil Blackwell.

——1987: *Property*. Milton Keynes: Open University Press.

Samuels, Warren 1971: The interrelations between legal and economic processes. *Journal of Law and Economics*, 14, 435–50.

——1972: In defense of government as an economic variable. *Journal of Law and Economics*, 15, 453–9.

——1981: Welfare economics, power, and property. In Warren J. Samuels and A. Allan Schmid (eds), *Law and Economics*, Boston: Martinus Nijhoff.

——1984: A critique of rent–seeking theory. In David C. Colander (ed.), *Neoclassical Political Economy*, Cambridge, Mass.: Ballinger.

Samuelson, Paul A. 1938: A note on the pure theory of consumers' behaviour. *Economica*, 5, 61–71.

Sax, Joseph 1971: Takings, private property and public rights. *Yale Law Journal*, 81, 149–86.

——1983: Some thoughts on the decline of private property. *Washington Law Review*, 58, 481–96.

Schelling, Thomas C. 1960: *The Strategy of Conflict*. Cambridge, Mass.: Harvard University Press.

——1978: *Micromotives and Macrobehavior*. New York: Norton.

Schlatter, Richard 1951: *Private Property: the history of an idea*. London: George Allen and Unwin.

Schmid, A. Allan 1972: Analytical institutional economics: challenging problems in the economics of resources for a new environment. *American Journal of Agricultural Economics*, 54, 893–901.

——1986: Neo–institutional economic theory: issues of landlord and tenant law. In Terence Daintith and Gunther Teubner (eds), *Contract and Organization: legal analysis in the light of economic and social theory*, New York: Walter deGruyter, 132–41.

——1987: *Property, Power, and Public Choice* (2nd edn). New York: Praeger.

Schotter, Andrew 1981: *The Economic Theory of Social Institutions*. Cambridge: Cambridge University Press.

Scott, Anthony 1955: The fishery: the objectives of sole ownership. *Journal of Political Economy*, 63, 116–24.

Sen, A. K. 1967: Isolation, assurance, and the social rate of discount. *Quarterly Journal of Economics*, 81, 112-24.

——1977: Rational fools: a critique of the behavioral foundations of economic theory. *Philosophy and Public Affairs*, 6, 317-44.

——1979: *Collective Choice and Social Welfare*. Amsterdam: North Holland.

——1982: *Choice, Welfare and Measurement*. Oxford: Basil Blackwell.

Shackle, G. L. S. 1961: *Decision, Order, and Time in Human Affairs*. Cambridge: Cambridge University Press.

Shubik, Martin 1982: *Game Theory in the Social Sciences*. Cambridge, Mass.: MIT Press.

Siegen, Bernard H. 1970: Non-zoning in Houston. *Journal of Law and Economics*, 13, 71-148.

Spur Industries, Inc. v. Del E. Webb Development Co. 1972: 108 Ariz. 178, 494 P. 2d 700.

Sugden, Robert 1984: Reciprocity: the supply of public goods through voluntary contributions. *Economic Journal*, 94, 772-87.

——1986: *The Economics of Rights, Cooperation, and Welfare*. Oxford: Basil Blackwell.

—— and Williams, Alan 1978: *The Principles of Practical Cost-Benefit Analysis*. Oxford: Oxford University Press.

Swift, Jeremy 1977: Pastoral development in Somalia: herding cooperatives as a strategy against desertification and famine. In Michael Glantz (ed.), *Desertification: environmental degradation in and around arid lands*, Boulder: Westview Press, chapter 11.

Tawney, R. H. 1978: Property and creative work. In C. B. Macpherson (ed.), *Property: mainstream and critical positions*, Toronto: University of Toronto Press, 135-51.

Thomson, James T. 1977: Ecological deterioration: local-level rule making and enforcement problems in Niger. In Michael Glantz (ed.), *Desertification: environmental degradation in and around arid lands*, Boulder: Westview Press, chapter 4.

Tigar, Michael E. and Levy, Madeleine R. 1977: *Law and the Rise of Capitalism*. New York: Monthly Review Press.

Tribe, Laurence H. 1972: Policy science: analysis or ideology? *Philosophy and Public Affairs*, 2, 66-110.

Tversky, Amos and Kahneman, Daniel 1981: The framing of decisions and the psychology of choice. *Science*, 211, 453-8.

—— ——1987: Rational choice and the framing of decisions. In Robin M. Hogarth and Melvin W. Reder (eds), *Rational Choice*, Chicago: University of Chicago Press, 67-94.

Ullmann-Margalit, Edna 1977: *The Emergence of Norms*. Oxford: Clarendon Press.

Varian, Hal R. 1978: *Microeconomic Analysis*. New York: Norton.

Verma, B. N. and Bromley, Daniel W. 1987: The political economy of farm size in India: the elusive quest. *Economic Development and Cultural Change*, 35, 791–808.

Viner, Jacob 1961: Hayek on freedom and coercion. *Southern Economic Journal*, 27, 230–6.

Williamson, Oliver E. 1975: *Markets and Hierarchies*. New York: Free Press.

——1981: The modern corporation: origins, evolution, attributes. *Journal of Economic Literature*, 19, 1537–68.

——1985: *The Economic Institutions of Capitalism*. New York: Free Press.

Willig, Robert D. 1976: Consumer's surplus without apology. *American Economic Review*, 66, 589–97.

Wolf, Charles, Jr. 1979: A theory of non-market failure: framework for implementation analysis. *Journal of Law and Economics*, 22, 107–40.

Index

Index by Jackie McDermott